PELICAN BOOKS

KEYNES AND AFTER

Michael Stewart was born in Leeds in 1933, but spent his childhood in Australia, He was at Magdalen College, Oxford, from 1952 to 1955, getting a First in Philosophy, Politics and Economics. After research at Oxford, and a year as Barnett Fellow at Cornell University in the United States, he spent five years at the Treasury, including a spell as Secretary to the Council on Prices, Productivity and Incomes. For much of this period he lived at Toynbee Hall in the East End of London, doing part-time social work. From 1962 to 1964 he was Assistant Editor of the *National Institute Economic Review*. He became Assistant to the Economic Adviser to the Cabinet in October 1964 and then worked at 10 Downing Street as a Senior Economic Adviser. He stood as Labour candidate at Folkestone and Hythe in 1964 and Croydon North West in 1966. He lives in Hampstead with his wife, who is also an economist, and two small daughters, but they are at present in Kenya, where Michael Stewart is on a two-year appointment as Economic Adviser to the Treasury.

MICHAEL STEWART

KEYNES AND AFTER

———

PENGUIN BOOKS

Penguin Books Ltd, Harmondsworth, Middlesex, England
Penguin Books Inc., 7110 Ambassador Road, Baltimore, Maryland 21207, U.S.A.
Penguin Books Australia Ltd, Ringwood, Victoria, Australia

—

First published 1967
Reprinted 1968
Reprinted with minor revisions 1969

—

Copyright © Michael Stewart, 1967

—

Made and printed in Great Britain by
Cox & Wyman Ltd, London, Reading and Fakenham
Set in Monotype Baskerville

CONTENTS

PREFACE   7

INTRODUCTION   9

Part One · Keynes

1 KEYNES THE MAN   13
2 ECONOMICS BEFORE KEYNES   21
3 UNEMPLOYMENT BETWEEN THE
   WARS   48
4 THE GENERAL THEORY   71
5 THE ISSUES BETWEEN KEYNES
   AND THE CLASSICS   106
6 THE TWENTIES AND THIRTIES IN
   THE LIGHT OF KEYNES   128

Part Two · After

7 UNEMPLOYMENT SINCE THE WAR   151
8 PRICES   171
9 GROWTH AND THE BALANCE OF
   PAYMENTS IN THE POST-WAR
   PERIOD   188
10 THE PROBLEM OF INTERNATIONAL
   LIQUIDITY   208
11 THE UNITED STATES:
   UNEMPLOYMENT AND AUTOMATION   237
12 CONCLUSION   251

EXPLANATORY NOTES   255
BIBLIOGRAPHICAL NOTES   263
INDEX   267

TO FRANCES

PREFACE

Two points need to be recorded.

First, this book was commissioned, planned and in part written before I re-entered the Civil Service in 1964. The views and interpretations it contains are my own, and not necessarily those of anyone else in Whitehall.

Secondly, a number of people, and in particular Joan Robinson (Chapter 1), Robin Major (Chapter 10) and Margaret Marsh were kind enough to read parts of the book when in draft, and I am grateful for their advice even though I have not always been sensible or energetic enough to take it. I am especially indebted to my wife, whose comments throughout nicely blended intellectual integrity with conjugal tact.

July 1967

... I believe myself to be writing a book on economic theory which will largely revolutionize — not, I suppose, at once but in the course of the next ten years — the way the world thinks about economic problems.

Letter from John Maynard Keynes to George Bernard Shaw, 1 January 1935.

INTRODUCTION

A COUPLE of years after the end of the First World War –
the war that was supposed to lay the foundations of a
better world – Britain plunged into a depression which
lasted for twenty years. Between 1921 and 1940 unemployment never fell below a rate of 10 per cent; in the early
1930s, when the whole world was experiencing the worst
slump in history, unemployment in Britain was over 20
per cent.

This represented a total failure of the economic system.
Desperate poverty lay cheek by jowl with idle men and un-
used resources. Governments were helpless. They did what
their advisers told them, and things got worse. Capitalists
shivered; the more cold-blooded Marxists rubbed their
hands. In some countries democracy foundered. In Britain,
as it happened, it survived. But could it survive for ever in
the face of paralysingly heavy unemployment?

Mass unemployment was brought to an end by the Second
World War. It has never returned. Despite dire predictions
in 1945, Britain has now enjoyed full employment* for a
quarter of a century. Such a tremendous transformation
might be expected to have many causes. But in this case one
can point to one cause above all others: the publication in
1936 of a book called *The General Theory of Employment,
Interest and Money* by John Maynard Keynes.

In Part One of the present book we discuss the historical
background to Keynes's work, what it was that he said, how
it differed from what other economists were saying, and
why it was that while their views were irrelevant and even

* For a brief account of what is meant by 'full employment' see
Explanatory Note 1, page 255.

9

harmful, Keynes's theory has become the foundation of modern economic policy.

But has full employment come to stay? What about the periodic recessions Britain has suffered since the war? What about the problem of regional unemployment? Is full employment threatened by a shortage of international liquidity? Is the high unemployment in the United States an indication that Keynesian theory cannot cope with automation? Is full employment incompatible with other economic objectives such as stable prices, and if so, which is to be sacrificed? How does growth fit into the picture? These are the themes dealt with in Part Two.

Part One · Keynes

CHAPTER I

KEYNES THE MAN

JOHN MAYNARD KEYNES is generally described as an economist of genius, ranking with such giants of the past as Adam Smith and Karl Marx. But this is a bloodless sort of way to characterize the man. He certainly possessed superlative intellectual powers: more than one good judge said that he was the cleverest man they had ever met. But he was not simply a very high-powered academic: he had a great practical grasp of the economic and political problems of the real world. So fertile, moreover, was he in suggesting solutions to them that for more than thirty years top politicians and civil servants in both Britain and America, though they might not always take his advice, nevertheless listened to it very carefully. His pragmatism was always the servant of his principles: he had a passionate desire to make the world a better place. He felt particularly strongly about the misery of the 1930s, and was fiercely critical of governments for doing far too little about it; he was convinced that this problem – indeed most problems – could be solved by thinking clearly and acting firmly. He had many interests outside economics and politics: he loved philosophy and farming, paintings and the ballet, old books and modern poetry. Some people found him distant and arrogant, yet with his friends he was an easy and kindly person, a high-spirited iconoclast with a warmth and a wit that lit up a room when he entered. Many worlds mourned him when he died.

He was born in Cambridge in 1883 (the year Marx died), the son of a don who was himself a lecturer in economics and logic. From a local preparatory school he won a scholarship to Eton, where he soon started to blossom out. He won prizes for classics, mathematics, history and English essays, wrote papers on contemporary problems, rowed, played the notorious Wall Game with conspicuous success, debated, acted, and still managed to read omnivorously and become something of an expert on medieval Latin poetry. By the time he went up to King's College, Cambridge, in 1902 he was already gaining a reputation as an exceedingly clever and sophisticated young man.

At Cambridge the range of his activities widened even further. He did just enough mathematics to end up with a First, but his main interests lay elsewhere. He studied philosophy for his own pleasure (Alfred Whitehead was later to bracket Keynes and Bertrand Russell as his best pupils); he became President of the Union and President of the University Liberal Club; he was a leading light in a variety of discussion societies; he became intimate with people such as Lytton Strachey and Leonard Woolf, who were later to form the nucleus of the 'Bloomsbury Group'; he read and argued endlessly; yet found plenty of time to row and play bridge, to look at pictures, collect rare books, go to the theatre, and keep up a weighty correspondence with family and friends. In fact, he was a fairly formidable character.

A year after taking his degree Keynes sat the Civil Service examination. He had spent much of the intervening period studying economics, devouring the existing literature, attending Marshall's lectures and being coached by Pigou; but this did not prevent him getting a relatively low mark in the economics paper. Keynes himself was quite clear about what had happened: 'I evidently knew more about economics than my examiners.' He probably did. Nevertheless he passed second into the Civil Service and was assigned to the India Office. This he found distinctly irksome, and after two years of office hours spent mainly on private work of his own (a dissertation on Probability) he resigned, claiming that his only official achievement had been to get one pedigree bull shipped to Bombay. He returned to Cambridge, first as a lecturer in economics and later as a Fellow of King's, a post he retained for the rest of his life. He continued his work on Probability and eventually, in 1921, published it as *A Treatise on Probability* – a book described by Bertrand Russell as 'one which it is impossible to praise too highly'. He also continued to pursue a multitude of other interests, ranging from breakfasting with Henry James and having interminable discussions with Wittgenstein to reorganizing the college finances and speaking at Liberal meetings in General Elections.

In spite of all this, his energies came increasingly to be directed towards economics – learning it, teaching it, beginning to make original contributions to it, and above all, perhaps, emphasizing the bearing of economic theory on the practical problems facing governments and firms. In 1911 he became Editor of the *Economic Journal* – certainly at that time, and perhaps even now, the most important economic periodical in the world. In 1913 he showed that his time at the India Office had not been completely wasted by publishing *Indian Currency and Finance*, an important book of which at least one chapter is still regarded as a classic. As a result of this he was appointed a member of a Royal Commission set up to examine the Indian currency problem. In this capacity he made a marked impression on the Chairman (Austen Chamberlain) and the other leading politicians and civil servants involved, not only with his mastery of the complex questions of whether the emergence of the gold exchange standard in India had been a good thing, and how the central banking system ought to develop, but also with his feeling for the political and human problems involved. In fact, he started to establish a reputation as that rare creature – a top-flight economic theorist who really understands how the world works.

It was during the First World War that Keynes really came into his own. Drafted into the Treasury at the beginning of 1915, initially in a fairly junior capacity, he rose rapidly and was soon in charge of one of the most vital aspects of the war economy, the problem of coordinating the foreign exchange expenditure of Britain and her allies on essential imports from abroad. He came to know and be relied on by Lloyd George and other war leaders, though even at this relatively early stage in his career he was no respecter of persons. On one occasion when Lloyd George had been pontificating at length on the situation in France, and asked for comments, Keynes replied politely: 'With the utmost respect, I must, if asked for my opinion, tell you that I regard your account as rubbish.' It is not unknown for civil servants to feel like speaking thus to ministers; but few go to the lengths of actually doing so. Keynes tended to make rather a habit of it.

Towards the end of the war the question of how much the Germans should pay in reparations began to loom large. Keynes was asked to consider this problem, and estimated that a reasonable figure would be £2,000 million, paid over a period of years. Another estimate, arrived at largely under the influence of the Bank of England, was £24,000 million – the full cost of the war to the Allies. Keynes had always had a healthy disrespect for the economic wisdom of bankers; this incident did nothing to relieve it. Reparation payments, he argued, could not be made by simply signing a cheque; they must consist in goods produced in Germany and shipped abroad without payment. In relation to the size and condition of the post-war German economy a figure of £2,000 million, to be paid over a period of years, made some sense; a figure of £24,000 million made no sense whatever.

After a great deal of to-ing and fro-ing between the Allies (in the course of which Keynes proposed – unsuccessfully – that initially German reparations should be financed by American loans – rather along the lines of the Marshall Plan of the 1940s) the Versailles Peace Treaty was signed. It contained no detailed figures, but the whole structure and tone of the Treaty made it clear that heavy reparation payments would be exacted from Germany. Keynes was convinced that the attempt to exact such payments would not only be unsuccessful, but would have disastrous political consequences. He resigned his post at the Treasury and set out his views in *The Economic Consequences of the Peace*. 'If we aim deliberately at the impoverishment of Central Europe,' he said, 'vengeance, I dare predict, will not limp.' There would before long be a war 'which will destroy, whoever is victor, the civilization and progress of our generation'.

To this day there are two views on whether Keynes was right. Some think that his intervention played a major part in preventing a permanent crushing of the power of Germany, and in encouraging the disastrous American withdrawal from Europe. Others think that the reparation demands were, as Keynes said, impossible (in the end the Germans paid far less even than Keynes's estimate of £2,000 million) and that the attempt to exact them created a social revolution, and laid a foundation of bitterness, that were major factors behind the success of Hitler. The weight of the evidence is, perhaps, on Keynes's side.

Right or wrong, *The Economic Consequences of the Peace* was an immediate best-seller. It caused considerable annoyance in the Westminster–Whitehall Establishment, but brought Keynes's name before a large – indeed international – audience as someone with immensely well informed and cogently argued views on some of the main economic and political problems of the day. The mantle of formidable and controversial public figure now descended on him, and his views on many aspects of economic policy became well known to readers of the *Manchester Guardian* and *The Nation* (later absorbed by the *New Statesman*; Keynes was Chairman of both). But he continued to pursue many other interests: he lectured in Cambridge; talked in Bloomsbury; became Chairman of a life insurance company; started to speculate in the foreign exchange and commodity markets (using his economic judgement to such purpose that he eventually made a fortune of £500,000); became Bursar of King's (for which he also made a fortune on the Stock Exchange); and married a leading ballerina from the Diaghilev Ballet.

In 1923 he published *A Tract on Monetary Reform*, in which he argued that Britain should not (as the government and everyone else obviously intended) go back to the pre-war gold standard system. This pamphlet constituted an attack on one of the main pillars of the British economic system, and Keynes found himself virtually alone. When it became apparent that the government was quite determined to go back to the gold standard, Keynes argued that at least it should not return at the pre-war parity; but here again he failed. In *The Economic Consequences of Mr Churchill* (the Chancellor who took the final decision to return) Keynes demolished the arguments behind the decision, insisting that the result would be an over-valued currency and a persistence of heavy unemployment. As so often, he was right. He called for large-scale government expenditure on public works to cope with unemployment, even though this would mean a large Budget deficit, but he could not provide a theoretical justification of this 'patently unsound' idea, and was largely ignored. However he had enough influence with Lloyd George to ensure that the Liberal party programme in the 1929 election consisted chiefly of promises of higher public expenditure to counter unemployment.

In 1930 Keynes published *A Treatise on Money*, a massive work which distilled all his accumulated knowledge of the subject and developed many of the concepts and relationships that were to be finally pulled into shape with such dramatic effect in the *General Theory*. He was appointed a member of the Macmillan Committee on Finance and Industry (set up by Snowden in 1929) and had a marked influence on its recommendations, though not succeeding in persuading it of the efficacy of public works.

In 1930 he was appointed by the Prime Minister as Chairman of a committee of economists to advise the government on what it should do about mounting unemployment. (Keynes's answer, given that public works were ruled out, was Protection.) In 1935 he set on foot the building of the Arts Theatre in Cambridge. 1936 saw the publication of the *General Theory*. In 1937 he suffered a serious heart attack. He had always been dogged by ill-health, and was now to be a semi-invalid for the rest of his days – though a semi-invalid of such determination that many who met him never realized it.

With the outbreak of the Second World War he was again brought into the Treasury, this time not as an administrator but as a free-ranging adviser of great reputation and influence. His *How to pay for the War*, published in 1940, made radical new proposals on the problem of internal war finance; and he had more than a finger in many other famous pies – such as the Beveridge Report on social security and the 1944 White Paper on employment policy. He was given a peerage in 1942, and in the same year – as evidence that his versatility had not diminished – he was appointed Chairman of a new 'Council for the Encouragement of Music and the Arts', which a few years later became the Arts Council. But his main contribution during the Second World War was as negotiator – in effect, chief British negotiator – with the Americans, first over Lend-Lease, then in the discussions which led up to the establishment at Bretton Woods of the World Bank and the International Monetary Fund, and finally on the post-war U.S. loan. All these negotiations were extremely complex and difficult, and in all of them Keynes was the acknowledged master of proceedings, displaying a quickness of grasp, a fertility of imagination, an understanding of large panorama and tiny detail, a wit and tact that brought him the unqualified admiration of all involved in them, and an outcome, some would say, considerably better than any other man could have achieved. But even Keynes could not always win. The U.S. only granted the post-war loan (essential to Britain's survival once Lend-Lease had stopped) on terms which jeopardized Britain's economic recovery – a fact of which Keynes was bitterly aware. He strained every nerve in his efforts to get the Americans to understand the nature of the new economic problems the war had left, but he failed. Perhaps this failure literally broke his heart.

He died of another heart attack in April 1946, at the age of 62. His death removed from the scene a man whose wisdom might have been of immeasurable value to the battered and limping post-war British economy. But he left behind him an explanation of how the economic system works which has transformed the world.

CHAPTER 2

ECONOMICS BEFORE KEYNES

THERE was one particularly alarming feature of the heavy unemployment between the wars. This was that although practical men tackled it in a common-sense sort of way, they not merely failed to cure it, but actually made it worse. Keynes had an explanation of this. 'The ideas of economists and political philosophers,' he wrote in the *General Theory* 'are more powerful than is commonly understood. Indeed the world is ruled by little else. Practical men, who believe themselves to be quite exempt from any intellectual influences, are usually the slaves of some defunct economist.' It was precisely because the practical men of the 1920s and 1930s were the slaves of defunct economists – defunct in the sense that since their time the world had changed, invalidating as it did so some of the assumptions on which their theories were based – that things went so badly wrong. In order to understand the inter-war years, and the significance of Keynes's theory, we must begin by taking a look at what pre-Keynesian economists had said on the subject of employment.

SMITH, RICARDO AND MALTHUS

Economics goes back a long way – economic pronouncements can be found in the writings of Hesiod and the Hebrew prophets – but for practical purposes one can take the founder of modern economics to be Adam Smith, who published *The Wealth of Nations* in 1776. Smith, possibly the original eccentric, absent-minded professor, dictated this book standing with his back to the fire, and perhaps in consequence it rambles over the whole field of human knowledge: in the vast index (not compiled by Smith) the As begin with *Abassides, during reigns of, Saracens opulent* and the Zs with *Zama, battle of, and armies engaged in.* Yet, despite its great sweep, the book contains no discussion of why the level of employment is what it is. Clearly, this was not a question which interested the author; indeed it probably never occurred to him to ask it. In Smith's day agriculture was still by far the most important economic activity, and in an agricultural society the line between being employed and being unemployed tends to be blurred: the whole family works, but may be underemployed. Moreover wages were so low that the distinction between employed and unemployed, when it could be made, seemed much less significant than other divisions within society – for example those between landowners, businessmen and workers. In effect, Smith simply assumed that there was always full employment.

The next economist of major importance was David Ricardo, a wealthy stockbroker, and later an M.P., who published the first edition of his *Principles of Political Economy and Taxation* in 1817. Like Adam Smith before him, and many nineteenth-century economists who came after him, his main interest lay in the factors which governed the distribution of a nation's income between the main social classes – landowners, capitalists and workers (in other words rent, profits and wages). We cannot get involved in Ricardo's main contributions to economics here; the relevant point for our purposes is that he regarded businessmen's investment in machinery and equipment as one of the most important activities in the economy. Businessmen must make large profits, he said, because they would invest them in new machinery; and this new machinery would enable more to be produced, and thus make the country richer.

In his view that investment in more and more machinery was a good thing, Ricardo found himself opposed by a clergyman called Thomas Malthus. Malthus is best known today for his theory of population, according to which there is a tendency for the population to increase much faster than the supply of food – a tendency which results in periodic famines. With this part of Malthus's work Ricardo did not disagree. But there was another side to Malthus's work which proved far more controversial, and in the lengthy dialogue which developed between Ricardo and Malthus we come across – perhaps for the first time – an explicit discussion of what it is that determines the level of employment.

Perhaps because he identified himself with the landed classes (as opposed to Ricardo, the spokesman of the up-and-coming manufacturers) Malthus took a dim view of the process of accumulating capital and investing it in industrial machinery. There was a danger, he argued, that this invest-ment would raise society's ability to produce at a faster rate than its ability to consume. The wages received by the work-ers, after all, represent only a part of the value of what they produce – so that only a part of all the goods produced can be bought by the workers. What is going to happen to the rest? Is there not a danger, as more machinery is installed in industry, and total production rises, that the country will find itself with a 'general glut of commodities' which cannot be sold? Will this not lead to unemployment? And is it not fortunate, he went on (overdoing it a bit, perhaps) that there is a large class of landowners who up till now, by producing nothing but consuming a lot, have managed to stave off the evil day when this general glut of commodities will appear?

Ricardo's reply was remarkable for both its plausibility and its durability: what Ricardo said in the 1820s was being solemnly repeated by orthodox economists in the 1920s. He agreed with Malthus that it was possible to have a glut of commodities – but only a temporary glut of a particular kind of commodity. Some sudden shock (a war, a change in fashion or taxation) could result in a fall in the demand for a particular commodity. There would, for a time, be a glut of this commodity on the market, and some of the machinery and men who produced it would find themselves idle. But meanwhile the demand for some other commodity would have risen, for if people spend less on one thing they will spend more on another, and there would be a shortage of this other commodity. High wages and profits could be earned by producing this new commodity, and so extra labour and capital would start moving into this industry; at the same time, of course, it would be moving out of the old industry whose products were no longer in demand. Before long, equilibrium would have been re-established with a new pattern of production. So the only kind of unemployment – of either men or machinery – that was possible was temporary unemployment, during the transitional phase of a shift in the pattern of demand.

As for Malthus's argument that there might be a *general* glut of commodities (and, by implication, widespread unemployment) because workers could only afford to buy a part of what they produced, this was absurd. Here Ricardo invoked the writings of a French economist called J. B. Say. What has come to be known as 'Say's Law' was first propounded in 1803, and has been a rich source of confusion ever since. It is usually summarized by saying 'supply creates its own demand'. This means that the very processes which result in a commodity being placed on the market also result in the creation of the income with which it can be bought. For the final price of a commodity is simply the cost of the materials and labour used to make it, plus the profit that accrues to the manufacturer. In other words the supplier of materials, the worker and the capitalist have between them made exactly enough money, by producing the article, to enable them to buy it. They do not, of course, buy the article they themselves have produced, but what is true of one firm is true of all firms taken together: exactly enough income is created to enable the population to buy everything that is produced. A glut of commodities – goods which get produced but for which no buyer can be found – is therefore an absurdity.

But Malthus was not satisfied. What happens, he asked, if the capitalists do not *spend* their profits, but *save* them instead? Surely, in that case, one would get a glut of commodities? For some of the money which has to be spent, if the market is to be cleared, is not being spent; it is staying in the capitalist's pocket.

Again, Ricardo had an answer. The money that the capitalist saves, he explained, does *not* simply stay in his pocket; it is invested – that is to say, it is spent on machinery, equipment, buildings and so on. In other words, the fact that the capitalist does not spend all his profits on consumer goods does not mean that the profits do not get spent. On the contrary, they are spent on machinery and other capital goods, and it is for this reason that firms which manufacture machinery are able, like other firms, to sell everything they produce.

What Ricardo said was more or less right, *at the time he said it*. During the early nineteenth century the only way most manufacturers could finance the new buildings and machinery needed to expand their business was out of their own profits. There was no organized Stock Exchange through which money could be raised, and bank lending was relatively undeveloped. There was rarely a problem of a manufacturer having more profits than he knew what to do with; on the contrary, after he had paid his household's living expenses, they were generally smaller than he could usefully employ. Indeed, the businessman who made himself and his family go short in order to plough every available penny back into the business was a favourite character of Victorian fiction.

Nevertheless, Ricardo's argument that wages and profits would all get spent, and that general unemployment was therefore an impossibility, had an analytical weakness, which Malthus sensed but was never quite able to identify. A number of other economists, particularly in the early years of the twentieth century, were to worry over the same problem, but it was left to Keynes – who was quick to spot the importance of the questions Malthus had been asking – to put his finger on the truth.

MARX

After Ricardo and Malthus the main stream of economic thought turned away from macroeconomic problems – the questions of what determines the size of the national income, or its division between the main social classes, or the overall level of employment.* For the best part of a century the fashion was for microeconomics – the question of what determines the output of an individual firm, or the price of a particular commodity or factor of production.† But to this general rule there were exceptions, and the most notable of them was Karl Marx.

As an economist Marx was very clearly in the debt of Adam Smith and Ricardo. He took over much of their framework of thought, and gave it a new twist. At the same time his work contained brilliantly original insights. He was the first major economist, for example, to build the trade cycle into his analysis: at the time he was writing (the 1850s and 1860s) the trade cycle had become a well known phenomenon, and any theory of economic development clearly had to take account of it.‡ Marx not merely took account of it – he

---

*For a fuller discussion of the difference between macroeconomics and microeconomics, see Explanatory Note 2, page 256.

† A *factor of production* is something which contributes to the production of a commodity. In the simplest case three factors of production are distinguished – land, labour and capital.

‡ We discuss the trade cycle more fully a little later on (see page 35).

saw it as an expression of the inner contradictions of the capitalist system; he expected trade cycles to get progressively worse, and to lead eventually to the collapse of the system.

There is an eel-like quality about Marx's analysis of the economic development of the capitalist system: one no sooner thinks one has grasped it than it slithers out of one's hands. But one interpretation of the kernel of his argument would go as follows.

Competition forces capitalist firms to invest their profits in labour-saving machinery, for if they do not do this their efficiency will drop, and they will be forced out of business. But if labour-saving machinery is installed, there will be a fall in employment and hence a rise in the number of unemployed. As unemployment rises, wages (if not already at subsistence level) will tend to fall – for those who still have jobs will be forced by the capitalists to accept lower wages under threat of being replaced by some of the 'reserve army' of the unemployed. But according to Marx, a fall in employment also meant a fall in profits, because the value of what is produced depends on the number of man-hours involved in producing it. This fall in profits leads before long to a crisis: profits fall so low that many businesses go bankrupt; investment in plant and machinery more or less ceases; more workers lose their jobs, and the reserve army of the unemployed grows. In fact, the economy is in the depths of a depression. Eventually the crisis comes to an end, as big firms swallow up small firms, buying their plant and equipment at knock-down prices, and thus getting back into a position where they can make profits. But in spite of these periodic recoveries, there is a long-term trend at work which makes each crisis worse than the previous one. The main factor in this is the growing monopolization of business – the result of bigger firms taking over smaller ones at times of crisis. As firms become bigger and the economy more monopolized, the competition which originally impelled firms to invest their profits in machinery weakens, and with it the incentive to continue this sort of investment. In the long run, therefore, firms will have little incentive to invest their profits (as Ricardo had assumed they would) and, since only a small part of the capitalists' profits can be spent on consumption, the general glut of commodities that Malthus had been afraid of will become a reality. As a result, unemployment will get heavier and heavier.

To many people in the 1930s Marx's work came as a blinding revelation. He had, it seemed, not merely predicted the slump and explained its underlying causes but even in a sense put forward a solution to it. (And, since it happened to be in Tsarist Russia that the revolution that Marx had predicted and called for actually took place, it was therefore towards Soviet communism that many of the most intelligent and sensitive people in Western Europe were drawn in their search for a solution to the mass unemployment of the 1930s.)

But although there are great nuggets of truth in Marx's analysis, as an explanation of what happened in the 1920s and 1930s it will not really do. There were many similarities between what happened and what Marx said would happen, but the ineluctable fact remained that Marx's whole analysis depended on the standard of living of the average worker remaining in the long run at subsistence level, whereas experience had been quite different: in Britain real income per head in 1920 (and even in the worst year of the slump, 1932) was more than double what it had been in 1860.

Nevertheless, in spite of the fact that his theory of economic development cannot be swallowed whole, Marx did represent a very significant landmark in the evolution of economic theory. He was the first major economist to notice that heavy unemployment was quite a frequent occurrence in the developing industrial countries of Western Europe, and needed to be explained; and his analysis contained a most important new thought, which suggested that Ricardo might have been wrong in supposing that profits were automatically invested in more machinery. It is possible, Marx was saying, that society's capacity to produce *will* outstrip its capacity to consume: in the capitalist economy the workers cannot consume much because they are on subsistence wages; the capitalists cannot consume much because there are so few of them; and there is no point in them putting their profits to their other possible use (investment), because there will not be enough demand for the goods that new machinery could turn out to make it worthwhile.

THE THEORY OF PRICE

Marx, as we have said, was an exception. Most economists during the century or so after about 1820 concerned themselves mainly with microeconomic problems. Much of this lies outside our field, but we must spotlight a few strands of this microeconomic theory because of their importance to an understanding of what economists thought in the 1920s.

The main concern of nineteenth-century economics was with what determined the *price* or *value* of an article, or a factor of production. (The price of something was not thought to be necessarily the same as its value – this distinction was itself the source of endless discussion.) Quite soon after the death of Ricardo the price of an article came to be explained less in terms of what it had cost to produce, and more in terms of what people were willing to pay for it. Adam Smith and Ricardo had said, in effect, that an article cost £1 because four hours' work, at a rate of pay of 5s. an hour, had been needed to make it; the new 'theory of utility' said that it cost £1 because that was what someone was willing to pay for it. The new approach was summed up by an economist (later an Archbishop) called Whately who said, 'It is not that pearls fetch a high price *because* men have dived for them; but on the contrary, men dive for them because they fetch a high price.' As the century wore on more sophisticated theories came to be advanced, both of what determined how much it cost to produce an article, and of what determined how much people were willing to pay for it. The whole thing was summarized by the Cambridge economist Alfred Marshall, who said that supply and demand should be regarded as the two blades of a pair of scissors – both of them being necessary to explain the price of an article. For any article one could (if one had perfect knowledge) construct a 'demand curve', which would tell you how many of these articles would be demanded (i.e. bought) at different prices. In general, one would expect that the higher the price, the smaller the number of this particular article that would be bought. The exact number bought at any particular price would depend on such factors as people's income and tastes, the prices of other articles (particularly those which were close substitutes) and so on.

In the same way, said Marshall, one could, at any rate in theory, construct a 'supply curve', which would tell you how many of these articles would be supplied (i.e. produced) at different prices. In this case, there is a presumption that the higher the price, the greater the number that would be produced, but the exact number produced at any particular price would depend on the price the manufacturer had to pay for his labour, materials and equipment – and the profit he required for himself in order to keep him in business. The price actually established would of course be the price at which the number of articles demanded was exactly equal to the number supplied; in other words the price at which the number that customers wanted to buy was the same as the number that manufacturers wanted to produce.

Refinement and synthesis of supply and demand theory did not stop with Marshall. It continued to form the main preoccupation of economists until the 1930s – and indeed was given a new lease of life in the early 1930s by a revolutionary change in the theory's framework of reference – a change which resulted from new thinking (with which Keynes himself was to some extent associated) in Cambridge and at Harvard.*

DIMINISHING RETURNS
AND MARGINAL PRODUCTIVITY

Now the important point about this supply and demand analysis for our present purpose is that it was supposed to be of general application, explaining the price of anything which had a price. Thus it was supposed to explain not only the price of goods, but also the price of *money* (i.e. the rate of interest) and the price of *labour* (i.e. wages). It is convenient to hold over until later (page 37 and pages 109–11) a discussion of what nineteenth-century economists thought about interest rates; here we concentrate on what they thought about wages.

The average wage, they said, was simply the price of labour, and it was determined, like the price of anything

* Nineteenth-century theory had assumed (reasonably enough, given the structure of agriculture and industry at the time the theory was evolved) that firms in the same industry were in 'perfect' competition with each other – meaning that they were relatively small, and all produced exactly the same product. Consequently the individual firm had no control over the price of its goods – it had to accept the price established 'in the market' by supply and demand. For if it raised its price above the market price it would immediately lose all its business; while if it lowered its price below the market price it would make a smaller profit. The new theory, of 'imperfect' or 'monopolistic' competition, recognized that a modern firm's products are not in fact considered by its customers to be exactly the same as its rivals'. Consequently it does have some control over its price – it can raise its price without losing all its business, and in some cases make bigger profits by lowering prices because it can then expand its sales.

else, by the interaction of supply and demand. In the short run the supply of labour was fixed – it was simply the total population, or at any rate those parts of it which were accustomed to work. (In the longer run, of course, the size of population changed, but we can ignore this for the purposes of the present analysis.) How, then, did elements on the demand side interact with this fixed supply of labour in order to determine its price – i.e. the average wage? In order to understand this we must take a brief look at two essentially simple bits of economic folklore, one rather confidently called the *Law of Diminishing Returns*, the other, more modestly, the *Theory of Marginal Productivity*.

The Law of Diminishing Returns was what Malthus had had in mind when predicting that world population would grow faster than world food supplies, leading to periodic famines. The Law said that beyond a certain point, the more of one factor of production you apply to a fixed amount of another factor of production, the smaller is the additional output. To take a concrete example, suppose that 10 men work on 1 acre of land and produce a total of 100 beetroot a year – 10 per man. Now assume an increase in the labour force (on the same 1 acre of land) to 11. Production of beetroot will rise, says the Law, but only to 109. The extra man only produces 9 beetroot, whereas each of the previous men produced, on average, 10. Add a twelfth man; production will rise again, but only to 117. The twelfth man has only produced 8 beetroot. Diminishing returns have set in. One result of this, of course, is that average production per man employed has dropped – from 10 beetroot per man when there were only 10 men to $9\frac{3}{4}$ when there were 12 men. (It was precisely this effect, on a much larger scale, that Malthus was afraid of.) But it is the fact that each additional man has the effect of raising production *less than the previous additional man* that is important in the present context.

Now let us look at the Theory of Marginal Productivity.

This states that each factor of production will be paid the value of its marginal product. In other words the pay of labour (the average wage) will be equal to the value of what is produced by the marginal man – the man that the farmer or manufacturer thinks it is just worth his while to employ. Let us go back to the beetroot example in order to make the argument clear.

Suppose, for the sake of simplicity, that the demand for beetroot is such that each beetroot can be sold for £1, regardless of how many are produced. In our example, in which the Law of Diminishing Returns was operating, when the labour force increased from 10 to 11, the addition to output was 9 beetroot, which would be worth £9. If, therefore, the wages of this eleventh man were £8, it was obviously in the farmer's interest to take him on: his sales have risen by £9, his costs by only £8, and therefore his profits by £1. If, on the other hand, the eleventh man's wages had been £10 it would not have been worth taking him on – taking him on would have involved the farmer in a £1 loss. In fact, it will benefit the farmer to take the man on provided that his wage is £8 19s. 11d. or less. Since it will also benefit other farmers to do the same, competition will ensure that the man *is* taken on at a wage of £8 19s. 11d. (which let us call £9) – i.e. *at a wage equal to the value of what he produces.* But if this man is paid £9, then all other men (of similar skill etc.) will also be paid £9, for 'perfect' competition makes it impossible for different prices to be paid for identical articles or factors of production.

In our example, then, if the labour force consists of eleven men, the wage that each of them receives will be £9, since this is the value of the extra output that accrues as a result of taking the eleventh man on. But suppose, as in our previous example, that the labour force is increased to 12, and that the addition of this twelfth man to the same 1 acre of land only results in the production of 8 more beetroot, worth £8. In that case, of course, the wage of each of the 12 men will be only £8. In other words, *the larger the number of men employed, the lower the average wage.*

Nineteenth-century theory did not claim that this principle operated at all times and in all places. It was obviously not true that (as in our simplified example) an ever-growing labour force was being continuously added to a fixed amount of land. Land was not in practice a fixed factor of production – new land could be brought into cultivation in this or other countries (during the nineteenth century emigration from Britain to much more sparsely populated countries was, in fact, at its height). And the quantity of man-made capital (machinery and equipment) was of course being continuously increased. Moreover, even in the extreme case in which an increasing labour force was working with the same amount of land or capital, there was a range over which there were *increasing* returns to each additional man.

Nevertheless it was broadly accepted that in most cases, and particularly in the short run (roughly defined as a period within which there would not be much change in the size of population or amount of land and capital) the Law of Diminishing Returns and the Theory of Marginal Productivity would both operate.

The implications of this are worth stressing. The Law of Diminishing Returns said that the more men were employed, the less would the last man produce. The Theory of Marginal Productivity said that the last man would be paid the value of what he produced. Therefore the more men were employed, the less would the last man be paid. But since competition will ensure that the last man is paid much the same as other men, this means that the more men are employed, the less will each man in the labour force be paid – in other words the less will be the average wage. This apparently inexorable connexion between employment and wages lay deep in the subconscious minds of the practical men of the 1920s and 1930s, as we shall see.

THE TRADE CYCLE

As we have indicated, during the late eighteenth and early nineteenth centuries economists were not particularly interested in what determined the level of employment, or in the distinction between employment and unemployment. In a semi-agricultural society it is broadly true that everyone old enough to work does work, and widespread *underemployment* is a much more characteristic feature than a clear-cut division between those who have jobs and those who have not.

But as the nineteenth century wore on Britain became increasingly industrialized, and the distinction between being employed and being unemployed began to assume some substance. The phenomenon which drew attention to this distinction had probably been operating in a subdued way since some time in the eighteenth century, but it was only now that people really became aware of it. This was the 'trade cycle'.*

The trade cycle was, as the term implies, a pattern of events which was repeated in similar form at fairly regular intervals. From beginning to end it would last some eight or ten years. On the up-swing everything would expand: production, employment, wages, profits and prices would all rise, and unemployment would fall to a low level – perhaps 1 or 2 per cent of the labour force. This phase would last for perhaps four or five years. Then everything would level off and, sometimes immediately, sometimes after a year or two, would start to fall again. The down-swing would last, in a typical instance, for three or four years, with production, employment, incomes and prices all falling, and unemployment rising to a rate of 8 or 10 per cent. Then it would level off, and the stage would be set for another burst of expansion. The cycle was superimposed, however, on a rising trend: at each peak, production and employment tended to be higher

* The Victorians said 'trade' where we would tend to say 'production'. To avoid ambiguity the Americans use the term 'business cycle'.

than at the previous peak, and would not fall as low in each trough as in the previous trough. A graph of production or employment during the nineteenth century would look rather like a staircase tilted slightly forward.

As we have seen, Marx was one of the first people to give serious attention to the trade cycle. His account was soon to be followed by many others. One of the most engaging was provided in 1878 by W. S. Jevons, Professor of Political Economy in the University of Manchester. According to Jevons, the cycle was caused by sun-spots: sun-spot cycles caused weather cycles, which caused harvest cycles, which in turn resulted in trade cycles. In support of his theory Jevons argued that during the previous 150 years each trade cycle had lasted, on average, for some 10·44 years; the average length of the sun-spot cycle was 10·45 years. These figures were too close to each other to be a coincidence.

This pleasingly direct link between celestial and terrestrial events was soon abandoned. Later calculations suggested different figures for the average length of the trade cycle, and in any case those who supported the theory could never agree among themselves on the vital point of whether good harvests had good or bad effects on the rest of the economy. But the main reason for the abandonment of the kind of harvest theory originated by Jevons was simply that as the economy became more industrialized (and this applied to the United States and Germany as well as Britain) a theory of the trade cycle which relied so heavily on agricultural developments became less and less satisfactory. Instead, people began increasingly to look – as Marx had done – for sources of instability within the industrial system itself.

During the first twenty or thirty years of this century a great deal of thought was devoted to the trade cycle, not only in Britain, but in many of the other most advanced industrial countries as well – economists in the U.S., Germany, Sweden, Russia, France, Austria and several other countries contributed to the pool of ideas. At the same time a great deal of statistical information began to be collected and analysed, particularly in the United States, and it became easier to examine a theory in the light of the facts. By around 1930, when the first real impact of the Slump was being felt by the U.S. and Western Europe, there was a fair amount of agreement about the main features of the cycle.

The most convenient place to start is at the lower turning-point of the cycle, when unemployment is at its heaviest. What starts off the recovery? There was pretty general agreement that the recovery begins with a rise in investment; in other words, with businessmen starting to build new factories, install new machinery and so on. Different economists emphasized different reasons for this rise in investment. One school of thought, for example, stressed the role of interest rates. During the down-swing, as more and more factories became idle, there became less and less reason for new investment – if existing machinery was unemployed what was the point of installing more? This meant that there was a fall in the demand for loans to finance the new investment. At the same time, it was argued, as the down-swing went on, and production fell and unemployment rose, the uncertain outlook caused people to cut their spending and save as much as they could; thus they accumulated more and more idle cash. This combination of a fall in the demand for what have been called *loanable funds*, and a rise in the supply of these funds, resulted in a fall in the rate of interest (for the same reason that a fall in the demand for, or a rise in the supply of, any other commodity tends to reduce its price). Well then, this school of thought argued, there comes a time when the rate of interest is pushed so low by the operation of these forces that it becomes profitable to borrow money, and invest it in new factories or equipment. The rate of return to be made on this new investment may not be very high, but money can be borrowed so cheaply that even a low rate of return makes the operation worthwhile.

Other economists thought it was not only the lower cost of borrowing money that stimulated new investment, but the lower cost of everything else as well. During the down-swing wages and prices always fell. This meant that at the bottom of the depression businessmen could buy or hire factors of production more cheaply than before: the price of raw materials and capital equipment would have fallen, and – more important still – wages would be a good deal lower than they had been a few years before. Other economists, again, took a more positive view about the reasons for the turn-up, arguing that new investment was stimulated not only by the lower costs of doing it, but also by the greater profitability of doing it. During the down-swing and the depression, they said, new products and processes are invented, new markets appear, and sooner or later businessmen will start investing in order to exploit these new developments.

Whatever the differences in emphasis, there was wide agreement about the basic point: the thing that started off the recovery from a slump was a rise in investment, and one of the main factors behind the rise in investment was the fall in wages and interest rates that occurred during the down-swing.

There was also wide agreement about what happened after the recovery got under way, though again the emphasis varied. As some new investments started paying off, other businesses would be encouraged to start investing as well. These new investments would create more employment – some people would be needed to build the new factories and machinery, other people would be needed to operate them. As more people were brought into employment (i.e. as the demand for labour rose) wages and salaries would rise and so, in consequence, would the amount spent by wage- and salary-earners on consumer goods. This in turn would create an incentive to businessmen to increase their investment even more in order to meet the new demand. During the early and middle stages of the up-swing there would be no difficulty in financing this new investment. It would be financed out of the idle hoards of cash that people had accumulated during the down-swing and the slump; or out of the profits being made by the newly erected factories; or (and some economists attached particular importance to this) out of credit advanced by the banks. For the banks make their living, after all, by earning a commission on the money they lend out; little satisfactory business comes their way during a slump and they, like individuals, accumulate idle hoards. When the recovery brings a rise in the demand for loans, they are only too glad to make large amounts of credit available at low rates of interest.

And so the up-swing gathers pace. As more money is spent on new investment, this creates more jobs and more incomes. This in turn results in more money being spent by consumers. In order to meet this higher demand for consumer goods, more raw materials are needed, more factories and equipment and components, more transport facilities, more warehouses and shops. And rising demand for labour and goods leads to rising wages and rising prices. Thus a cumulative process is set up. Sooner or later, however, this expansionary process comes to an end. The up-swing flattens out. Perhaps immediately, perhaps only after several years of stability, the economy starts to contract. Why?

The basic reason for the down-turn was thought to be that during the up-swing of the cycle the industries making *capital* goods expanded faster than the industries making *consumer* goods.* The result of this was that when full employment was reached the distribution of the nation's resources between

---

* Consumer goods, as the term implies, are the final goods bought in shops by consumers – everything from hi-fi sets to hairpins. Capital goods, on the other hand, consist of the machinery and equipment bought by firms, and used in the process of production.

capital goods production and consumer goods production was distorted: too much labour and capital was engaged in making steel and heavy machinery and cement, and too little in making cutlery and furniture and clothing. Production of capital goods fell, and men and machinery in these industries (unable to be quickly or easily transferred to the production of consumer goods) became idle. As men were thrown out of work, consumption fell, and as consumption fell, so did the incentive to invest. The down-turn had begun.

THE ACCELERATOR

There was a particular, and not immediately obvious, reason why the up-swing saw too big an expansion of the capital goods industries. This was called the *accelerator* principle. In essence, the principle states that a small change in the output of the kind of goods bought in the shops by consumers tends to result in a much bigger – or accelerated – change in the output of goods needed to make these consumer goods. The principle is easiest to grasp in the form of a simple example.

Suppose that a firm produces 100 £1 Easter eggs each year. And suppose that to produce these 100 Easter eggs it needs £500 worth of machinery. And suppose, finally, that each year 10 per cent of its machinery wears out, so that it buys £50 worth of new machinery. This is an equilibrium situation which can go on for ever, with the firm selling £100 worth of Easter eggs each year, and buying £50 worth of equipment. Now suppose that for some reason there is a 5 per cent rise in the demand for Easter eggs, and the firm finds that it can sell 105 Easter eggs each year. Since it takes £5 worth of machinery to produce one Easter egg, it will have to install another £25 worth of machinery in order to produce these 5 extra eggs. Consequently this year it will buy not its usual £50 worth of machinery, but £75 worth. In other words, a 5 per cent rise in the demand for Easter eggs has led to a 50 per cent rise in the demand for Easter egg-making machinery. In order to raise its output by 50 per cent, the firm that makes the machinery may have to increase its own capacity by 50 per cent – and this might mean, according to the accelerator principle, that its own purchases of machinery and equipment were suddenly trebled or quadrupled. Obviously this is the extreme case – in practice the capital goods industries will have a lot of spare capacity at the beginning of the up-swing, and may in any case respond to a big rise in the demand for their products by lengthening their order books rather than increasing their capacity. Nevertheless one can see from the accelerator principle how fairly small and cautious decisions to expand output in the consumer goods industries can lead to a big expansion of the capital goods industries.

But the influence of the accelerator does not stop there. Precisely because it is responsible for the undue expansion of the capital goods industries, it is also a major factor in the down-turn. For after a while it goes into reverse: just as a small rise in the output of consumer goods may result in a much larger rise in the output of capital goods, so a small fall in the output of consumer goods may result in a much larger fall in the output of capital goods. This can be seen if we go back to our example. We saw that a 5 per cent increase in the output of Easter eggs (from 100 to 105) resulted in a 50 per cent rise in the output of Easter egg-making machinery. But if in the following year the output of the firm making Easter eggs falls by about 5 per cent (back to 100) its demand for machinery will fall from £75 to £25. For it will have £525 worth of machinery, but will only need £500 worth. Assuming that as usual £50 worth wears out, it will only need to buy £25 worth. So in this case a 5 per cent fall in the output of consumer goods has led to a fall of no less than two thirds in the output of capital goods.

So far, for the sake of simplicity, we have been talking of

the accelerated effect on the capital goods industries as being the result of an actual rise or fall in the output of consumer goods. But in fact nothing so dramatic is needed to bring the accelerator into play; it can be brought into play by a slight variation in the *rate of change* of output of consumer goods (e.g. a slight slowing down in the rate of increase). Without going through all the arithmetic, if in our example the output of Easter eggs in the second year had continued to rise, but only by 4 per cent instead of 5 per cent, then the firm's purchases of machinery (assuming it kept its capacity in line with its output) would still have been lower than in the first year. In other words a mere slowing-down in the rate of increase of consumer goods production can result in an actual fall in the output of capital goods. As the economy rapidly approaches the full employment ceiling during the up-swing of the trade cycle the rate of increase of consumer goods production is bound to be slowed down by an increasing shortage of labour, if by nothing else. The accelerator principle shows how this slowing-down will result in an actual fall in output and employment in the capital goods industries, and thus topple the economy over into a down-swing.

This, very briefly, is how economists in the 1920s and 1930s thought the trade cycle operated. Even today most economists would not dissent from many of the basic elements of the argument. But there are two features of it which do need emphasizing.

First, in spite of the existence of the trade cycle itself, and of a wide measure of agreement about the factors responsible for it, full employment was still assumed to be the natural condition of the economy. The unemployment that developed during the down-swing of the cycle was thought of as a temporary aberration from normality, which in no way cast doubt on the arguments Say and Ricardo had advanced for supposing that full employment was the state of affairs that God had ordained.

The second interesting feature of the theory was the *inevitability* with which the cycle was assumed to operate. Given that during the up-swing the capital goods industries expanded too fast, it was taken for granted that before long the boom would come to an end and the economy would topple over into recession. It is true that some economists wanted to moderate the expansion of the capital goods industries at an early stage in the up-swing, by deliberately raising interest rates and restricting bank credit, and thus making it more difficult for businessmen to finance new investment projects. But this was regarded as a rather visionary approach; most people took a curiously fatalistic view. Indeed one can almost detect a faint Puritan satisfaction in the acceptance that a penalty must be paid for the years of frenzied expansion – a penalty that could not be avoided (though it might sometimes be postponed) by doing clever things during the later stages of the boom. Some economists, indeed, appear to have seen the economy as a somewhat dissipated human being, and to have thought of the trade cycle in terms of getting drunk and suffering the after-effects – as is suggested by the frequent use of words like 'excesses' and 'hangover'. The more boisterously one drank, the more acute and prolonged would be the eventual hangover. And human nature being what it is, there was little hope of avoiding hangovers in the future by drinking more slowly and stopping drinking sooner.

There was, however, a compensation for the inevitability of the down-turn: the up-turn was inevitable too. During the down-swing wages, prices and interest rates would fall, and new inventions would be made and developed. Before long investment would once again become profitable, and the stage would be set for recovery. It was inconceivable that the economy could get stuck at the bottom of the cycle as long as events were allowed to take their natural course. If by any chance it did get stuck, this could only be because some artificial restraint had been introduced which was impeding the smooth working of the system.

STATE OF THEORY IN THE 1920S

Let us now pull together the main threads we have been following in this chapter, and summarize the theory of employment as it stood in the 1920s and early 1930s.

First, and most basically, full employment was assumed to be part of the natural order of things. This assumption derived from Say's Law. Say's Law stated that supply created its own demand – that the process of creating an article also resulted in the creation of just enough purchasing power to buy that article. Therefore there could be no general surplus of articles, or of the labour employed in making the articles. This Law had been qualified as long ago as the early nineteenth century as far as surpluses in *particular industries* were concerned. Ricardo had argued that some shift in fashion could result in a sudden fall in the demand for the products of a particular industry, thus creating unemployment and spare capacity within that industry. But by definition the shift in fashion would have resulted in a rise in the demand for the products of some other industry. Capital and labour would move from the first industry to the second, so that the unemployment originally created would disappear.

The emergence during the nineteenth century of the trade cycle, and the attempts made to account for it, can be regarded as resulting in a further qualification to Say's Law. In addition to a process (perhaps fairly continuous) of unemployment appearing in one or two industries, and then being absorbed by the expansion of other industries, one now had the periodic and simultaneous appearance of unemployment in a large number of industries, particularly those making capital goods. So one had to agree not only (as Ricardo had done) that at any given time one or two industries might be suffering from unemployment; one also had to admit that every now and then the whole economy might suffer from it.

Nevertheless, Say's Law was still held to be valid. In principle, the economy would always absorb all the commodities it was capable of producing. The periodic unemployment associated with the trade cycle was an aberration, a consequence of the unbalanced structure of production caused by too rapid an expansion of the capital goods industries. Once this too-rapid expansion had occurred, a downswing was inevitable. Many economists thought that all one could do was to stand back and let events take their course: as the existing (and excessive) stock of machinery and capital equipment which had been left over at the top of the boom wore out or rusted away; as falling employment led (as it always had done) to falling wages and prices; as the falling demand for loanable funds, and the rising supply of them, led to lower interest rates; and as time passed and new products and processes were invented – so, gradually, the conditions necessary for a recovery would come into being. Other economists were rather less passive than this – they felt that the down-swing phase of the cycle could be hurried up, for example by taking deliberate steps to reduce interest rates, instead of merely waiting for them to fall. But by and large there was agreement on the kind of things that had to happen before the up-swing could get under way again and full employment be restored.

Full employment, then, was accepted as the normal state of affairs. From time to time quite heavy unemployment would develop and, insofar as it could not be cured, must be endured. But such unemployment was a temporary phenomenon which always cured itself after a year or two.

This was all very well. But what if, in fact, after the downswing, the economy did not start to recover again; what if it simply got stuck at the bottom of the cycle, with heavy unemployment persisting year after year? How could this be accounted for?

To most economists in the 1920s and early 1930s the answer seemed obvious. Something must be happening to obstruct the adjustments which normally accompanied the down-swing of the trade cycle. These adjustments consisted, on the one side, of reductions in costs: wages, interest rates and the price of capital equipment were all supposed to fall, so that after a while it became cheaper (and therefore more profitable) to hire labour, borrow money and buy capital equipment. The other set of adjustments consisted of the emergence of new products or techniques of production which it was profitable to exploit. If, therefore, the economy refused to revive and heavy unemployment persisted, this must either be because one of the cost elements had not fallen as it should have done, or because no new products or processes were being developed which looked profitable enough to exploit. The problem was to identify the guilty factor, and then do something about it.

Identification was made, with the devastating certainty of a fingerprint test, by the Law of Diminishing Returns and the Theory of Marginal Productivity. Together, these two bits of economic theory showed that the more of a factor of production that was employed, the less it would be paid. Therefore if the total available quantity of a factor of production is to be employed, each unit of the factor of production must be paid less than if only 90 per cent of it is to be employed. To be more specific, if there is to be full employment of the labour force, the average wage will have to be lower than if there is only 90 per cent employment (i.e. 10 per cent unemployment). Therefore if there is a persistent unemployment rate of 10 per cent, average wages must be too high. The only way to get back to full employment is to have some reduction in wages.

But could this account explain the persistent unemployment of the 1920s and the refusal of the economy to budge from the bottom of the trade cycle? Had something happened to make wages too high in the first place? Or had something happened to prevent them falling in the way they had always fallen in previous down-swings?

The answer to both questions seemed clear. On the first point, the tremendous demand for labour during and immediately after the First World War had resulted in an enormous rise in wages: in the seven years between 1913 and 1920 wage rates nearly trebled. Past up-swings of the trade cycle had, of course, seen quite substantial increases in wages, but a rise on this scale was quite unprecedented.

On the second point, too, the evidence seemed conclusive. During the War there was a great increase in the size and power of the trade unions – the same seven years that saw a near-trebling of wage rates also saw a near-trebling of the number of trade unionists affiliated to the Trades Union Congress. By the early 1920s millions of workers who twenty or thirty years before would have had to bargain with their employers as individuals or small isolated groups were now spoken for by large and powerful unions.

To the economists of the 1920s the case was now made out. Wages were too high, and as a result part of the available labour force could not find employment. Full employment could only be restored if wages fell. During the nineteenth and early twentieth centuries this would have happened automatically during the down-swing of the trade cycle, and before long this would have enabled a revival to get under way. But now the unions were strong enough to resist wage reductions. Until they were persuaded, or forced, to see the error of their ways heavy unemployment would continue.

This is what the majority of economists in the 1920s and early 1930s thought. Let us now take a brief look at the period in the light of the views they held and the advice they gave.

CHAPTER 3

UNEMPLOYMENT BETWEEN
THE WARS

FOR the first couple of years after the end of the First World War the British economy boomed. There was pent-up demand for the consumer goods which had been unobtainable during the war; and heavy expenditure to replace buildings and capital equipment. Although the boom was more short-lived than most, it was in the classical trade cycle tradition, with a great burst of capital investment. But before the end of 1920 the usual down-swing started: production, employment, wages and prices all began to fall. As usual, after a couple of years or so the down-swing flattened out, and people began to look forward to the usual recovery.

But the recovery never came. Year after year went by, and every day more than a million men – often more than two million – were out of work. Not until nearly a generation later – in 1940, when the army had been pulled out of Dunkirk, and London was being pounded by the *Luftwaffe* – did unemployment fall convincingly below 10 per cent.

EXPORT PRICES

Looking at the problem in the early 1920s from a practical rather than theoretical standpoint, it was clear that much of the trouble lay in the export field: it was the traditional export industries – coal, cotton and shipbuilding – that were worst hit. During the war many of Britain's overseas markets had been lost to other countries, and attempts to recapture them after the war was over were hampered by the fact that our prices were now too high. During the war and immediate post-war period, wages and profits had nearly trebled, and the general level of prices, including export prices, had risen at much the same rate. Wages and prices had risen in other countries as well, but not so much as in Britain, and our competitiveness had been substantially reduced. The result was that in the early 1920s the volume of British exports was only about two thirds of what it had been in 1913, with corresponding effects on production and employment.

Now if one's exports are too expensive, there are two things one can do. One can reduce wages, profits and other costs, so that, for example, a pair of boots which previously cost £1 to make now only costs 15s. Or one can lower the exchange rate between sterling and other currencies, for example making £1 equal to $4 instead of $5, so that a pair of British boots which costs £1 to make will now sell in America for $4 instead of $5. A good many of Britain's economic problems in the 1920s stemmed from the fact that successive governments preferred the first of these alternatives to the second.

One of the reasons for this preference we have already encountered, though in the context of general unemployment rather than unemployment created by lack of competitiveness in export markets. Experience of the trade cycle had convinced economists that wages and other costs must fall during the down-swing as one of the preconditions of eventual recovery. This conviction was reinforced, on a theoretical level, by the marginal productivity doctrine, which said that if there was unemployed labour it could only be re-employed at a lower level of average wages. So the moral pointed by both theory and experience was clear: if full employment was to be restored in Britain's export industries, wages must be reduced.

The other reason was more subtle than this, more elusive, and more difficult to pin down. To explain it, we must say a little about the gold standard.

THE GOLD STANDARD

During the nineteenth century a country was said to be on the gold standard if the paper currency was backed by gold – in other words if a unit of its paper currency could be freely exchanged for a certain amount of gold. Britain was on the gold standard before the First World War because you could take a pound note along to the Bank of England and be given (in the form of a sovereign) a certain amount of gold in exchange. Obviously, any two countries that were on the gold standard must have a fixed rate of exchange between their currencies: in 1913 the same amount of gold that could be bought for £1 in London could be bought for approximately $4·85 in New York, and therefore £1 had to exchange for about $4·85 if someone was not to make a fortune by shipping all the gold in one country across the Atlantic to the other.

Now if a country is on the gold standard it is supposed to preserve a pretty fixed relationship between the amount of gold in the Central Bank and the amount of money (in the form of bank notes and bank deposits) in the country. If there is too little gold in relation to the total amount of money there is a danger that the Bank will not be able to sell gold to all those who arrive flourishing £1 notes and asking for it. But if there is too much gold in relation to the total amount of money the Bank will be passing up a profitable opportunity – by simply sitting on the gold instead of using it as the basis of loans which bring in interest payments. Therefore the Central Bank will manipulate the total amount of money in the country in order to keep it in a fairly fixed relationship to the amount of gold it has in its vaults. It does this by what are called 'open-market operations'. If there is too little gold in its vaults, it will sell government securities to the ordinary commercial banks in return for cash. This loss of cash will make the commercial banks reduce their customers' deposits, because they have to keep a minimum ratio of cash to deposits for the same reason as the Central Bank – they would be in trouble if they could no longer cash their customers' cheques. The commercial banks reduce their customers' deposits by reducing individuals' overdrafts, and the advances they have made to business firms – in fact all the measures which have now come to be known as a 'credit squeeze'. This is supposed to lead to a fall in consumption and investment, and hence in production and employment and hence (according to trade cycle theory) in wages and prices as well.

By acting in this way, therefore, the Central Bank reduces the amount of money in the country, hoping that the reduction will be just big enough to bring the total amount of money back into the desired relationship with its own stock of gold. In the opposite case – when the Central Bank has too much gold in relation to the amount of money in the economy – the reverse happens. The Central Bank buys government securities from the commercial banks in return for cash; this rise in their cash holdings leads them to increase their customers' deposits by lending more, and consumption and investment start to rise. This leads in turn to rising production and employment, and rising wages and prices.

Now the crucial aspect of the gold standard system stemmed from the fact that countries settled their international debts in terms of gold. If Britain imported more from America than she exported to her, thus incurring a trade deficit, she would pay the difference in gold. This had a double effect. The Bank of England would lose gold, and would therefore contract the amount of money in Britain. This would lead to some fall in wages and prices, and British exports to America would become cheaper, and rise. Simultaneously, the Federal Reserve banks in America would gain gold, and therefore expand credit, with the eventual result that wages and prices would rise. American exports would become more expensive

51

and therefore fall. In this way Britain's trade deficit with America would be eliminated.

This was the real trick about the gold standard. It provided, at any rate in theory, a beautiful, self-equilibrating mechanism which ensured that maladjustments in international trade would be automatically eliminated. In practice, according to recent historical research, the gold standard never worked quite like this. It is true that during the nineteenth century balance of payments maladjustments were fairly quickly and easily eliminated. But this was not in the main due to the workings of the gold standard – for on the whole Central Banks did not maintain the strict relationship between the amount of gold and the amount of money that the theory required, nor were prices so closely related to the amount of money as the theory implied. It was due rather to other factors – partly to the effect of interest rates on short-term capital movements, and partly to the fact that there really was some tendency for an imbalance in trade to cure itself: a rapid rise in exports may lead in the short run to a trade surplus, but it also creates incomes which will be partly spent on imports; in the same way the emergence of a trade deficit has effects on incomes which will tend to depress imports.

But these finer distinctions were not apparent to economists and politicians in the 1920s. As they saw it, in the nineteenth century the gold standard had been in operation, and the international payments mechanism had worked smoothly. If it was to work smoothly again, the gold standard must be restored. And this could only be done if Britain herself went back on to the gold standard.

RETURN TO PRE-WAR PARITY

Britain had formally abandoned the gold standard in 1919, but this was regarded as a strictly temporary measure designed to give the country time to get back to normal after the upheavals caused by the war. It was generally accepted that before long the country would return to the gold standard: without it there could be no order in international economic life, and no guarantee against limitless expansion of the currency and hence uncontrollable inflation (a point later driven forcibly home by the German hyper-inflation of 1922–3). Above all, perhaps, it was necessary to return to the gold standard in order to preserve sterling as the world's major trading currency, and to restore the City of London to the lucrative position it had held before 1913 as the capital of the world's financial system.

It was these last considerations which were probably decisive, not merely in causing Britain to go back on to the gold standard, but to go back *at the pre-war parity*. For to go back at a lower parity (i.e. with £1 being equal to a smaller amount of gold or dollars than before the war) would mean that foreigners who held sterling, or assets in Britain, would find the value of their holdings, in terms of gold or dollars, reduced. Everyone in the City, and indeed most economists and politicians, were convinced that this would constitute a default by Britain that would make it impossible to restore sterling and the City of London to their former status.*

Since 1919 the exchange rate between sterling and the dollar had been well below the pre-war level of $4·85. If the pre-war parity between gold and sterling (and therefore, since the U.S. had remained on the gold standard, between the dollar and sterling) was to be restored, it was clear that wages and prices in Britain would have to come down sharply from their inflated post-war levels. The attempt to bring this about became one of the main features of economic

---

*A typical comment came from Montagu Norman, Governor of the Bank of England, who said, 'I think that the disadvantages to the internal position [of going back at the pre-war parity] are relatively small compared with the advantage to the external position.' (Macmillan Committee, Minutes of Evidence, Question 3332.)

policy in the first half of the 1920s. Eventually it resulted in the General Strike.

The severe recession which began late in 1920 was in fact accompanied, as both theory and experience suggested it would be, by big reductions in wages and prices: over the next three years they both fell by about a third. This augured well for a return to the gold standard at the pre-war parity, and the government finally took this step in April 1925. But it was clear that despite this big fall in wages and prices, British exports were still not fully competitive at the pre-war exchange rate, and that there would have to be some further cuts in wage rates. A small number of people thought that this would not happen automatically or easily. Keynes himself was the leading exponent of this view. He noted that the fall in wages had come to a halt in 1923, and believed that any further fall could only be brought about by a deliberate deflationary policy on the part of the government. With unemployment already at a rate of more than 10 per cent, he thought this was too high a price to pay for going back on the gold standard at the pre-war parity, and opposed the decision to do so. But in this he was pretty well a lone voice in the wilderness. Most economists, politicians and businessmen thought that the necessary wage cuts could be brought about fairly easily.

Not least among this group were the mine-owners. Faced with the additional difficulties in exporting created by the return to the pre-war, and less favourable, exchange rate, they decided that wages must be cut, and proposed reductions of 10–25 per cent. The miners refused, and in self-defence revived the Triple Alliance – originally a pre-war association between themselves, the railwaymen and the transport workers. For a while the clash was postponed by the government agreeing to give the industry a subsidy until 1 May 1926, so reducing the mine-owners' costs without reducing wages. At the same time it set up a Royal Commission to inquire into the industry. This Commission reported in March 1926, saying among other things that the subsidy must end on the appointed day and never be renewed. The government accepted this, and at the end of April many mine-owners announced reductions in wages. This led immediately to the General Strike.

The strike failed, in the sense that the miners eventually went back to work at substantially reduced wages. But it provided Britain with a taste of dissension and chaos that nobody much liked, and after it was over the unions and the Conservative government treated each other with considerable circumspection. Few attempts were made to force through wage cuts in other industries, and wage rates remained at about the 1925 level for the rest of the decade. As a result British exports remained uncompetitive and unemployment in the export industries (though not only in these industries) remained high. Indeed the export problem grew worse later in the 1920s when other countries, such as France, also returned to the gold standard, but at a much lower parity than pre-war, thus ensuring that their exports were considerably cheaper than ours.* And so our balance of *trade* remained highly unfavourable (in the sense that imports were much higher than exports). However our balance of payments as a whole was in reasonable equilibrium. The trade deficit was offset by the 'invisible' earnings which derived from the profits received from British investments overseas, and from the banking, insurance and shipping services provided through the City of London. Less satisfactorily, the long-term investments overseas that Britain continued to build up over this period were financed by short-term borrowing from abroad. This caused trouble later, as we shall see.

*The French were much more intelligent about this than we were. Their new parity was deliberately chosen as one which would make their exports competitive *without* requiring any reduction in wages.

But although for these reasons the uncompetitiveness of exports did not have the drastic consequences for the *balance of payments* that it has had in more recent years, it was nevertheless an obvious source of *unemployment*. And, according to the economic theory of the day, which still relied heavily on the Law of Diminishing Returns and the Theory of Marginal Productivity, the same factor which caused exports to be uncompetitive – the excessive level of wages and prices – was itself responsible for unemployment quite apart from the effect on exports. So throughout the later 1920s economists continued to bewail the inflexibility of wages and prices, caused, as they saw it, by the strength of the trade unions on the one hand and restrictive business practices on the other, and to argue that only if this inflexibility could be overcome, and wages and prices made to fall, would full employment be restored.

THE WALL STREET CRASH

During the 1920s unemployment had been mainly a British problem. By and large, other countries prospered. But in 1929 came the Wall Street Crash and the beginning of the Great Slump. All over the world unemployment came to seem less the exception than the rule.

During the years 1922 to 1929 the U.S. appeared not only to have recovered from such effects of the war as she had suffered, but to have found the secret of permanent economic expansion. Unemployment was very low; employment, production, wages and profits all rose steadily year after year. On the other hand prices remained roughly stable, and this persuaded many economists and politicians that the economy was not just experiencing the usual up-swing of the trade cycle (for this should have been characterized by rising prices), but had found some more permanent stability. (In fact many prices did rise during this period, but this was masked by a steady fall in food prices caused by a steep rise in agricultural productivity.) The general optimistic, not to say euphoric, atmosphere engendered by the belief that employment, wages and profits (particularly profits) would not be hit by the usual down-swing, but would go on rising for ever, went to many people's heads. They decided that if profits were going to go on rising for ever they had better get their hands on some of the shares which entitled their holders to a portion of those profits. Even if the shares seemed unduly expensive, even if you had to borrow money in order to pay for them, or indeed merely promised to pay for them in the future, the only way to get rich was to buy as many as you could. As a result share prices shot up during the few years before October 1929 to ridiculous levels – levels which no conceivable future rise in profits could possibly justify. 'The present level of stock prices,' one observer commented in 1929, 'discounts not just the future but the hereafter.' Sooner or later, the market was bound to collapse.

The Crash actually came in October 1929, though there was no particular reason why it should have come in that month rather than in any other month. A wave of selling hit the New York Stock Exchange, and once a wave of selling gets under way in a situation where share prices are much too high, it tends to gather pace. Those who have bought shares on borrowed money decide they must sell before prices fall so far that the value of what they possess is less than the amount they owe. The more they sell, the more prices fall, and the more prices fall, the more they sell. Within a month of the beginning of the Crash industrial shares on the New York Stock Exchange had lost more than a third of their value. For more than two and a half years share prices continued to fall. By the middle of 1932 the average industrial share was worth less than a sixth of what it had been worth in October 1929.

THE GREAT SLUMP

The Wall Street Crash can be said to have ushered in the Slump and even, by its dramatic effects on business and consumer confidence, to have played a major role in aggravating it. But it was not the real cause. The factors which underlay the Stock Exchange boom and collapse were basically the same factors which had always caused the up-swing and down-swing of the trade cycle. There was a rapid rise in investment in the U.S. during the later 1920s – not only in productive industry, but in the form of house-building as well. The output of capital goods rose by nearly a quarter between 1927 and 1929, and the great house-building boom which had begun in 1921 continued happily upwards. This investment boom broke in the middle of 1929 – several months before the Stock Exchange collapsed. Industrial production began to fall, and unemployment to rise. As usual, it was the capital goods industries which were worst hit. By 1932 the output of capital goods was only about a quarter of what it had been in 1929. The fall in the output of consumer goods, though much less sharp than this, was still fairly severe, and the net result was that in 1932 industrial production was no more than half what it had been three years before. Because of falling output in other sectors of the economy the National Income* as a whole, by 1932, was only two thirds what it had been in 1929. This fall in production was accompanied by a violent fall in employment. Unemployment rose from about $1\frac{1}{2}$ million in 1929 to more than 12 million in 1932.

This tremendous contraction of economic activity in the United States had repercussions all over the world. We shall be looking more closely at some of the reasons for this – the fall in American imports and the catastrophic decline in

* For a brief discussion of the meaning of the term 'National Income' see Explanatory Note 3, page 256.

primary product prices – in Chapter 6. Here we concentrate on one particular reason – though an extremely important reason – for the devastating speed and intensity with which the Slump spread. This was the precarious structure of international debt which had grown up during the 1920s.

America had invested a great deal of money abroad during the 1920s, particularly in Germany. Much of this money was used to finance German industry, but a good deal of it was used to finance German reparation payments to France, Britain and a number of other countries. For although German reparation payments had been successively scaled down from the enormous figures fixed at the end of the war (and bitterly criticized by Keynes) she had proved unable to raise her exports or reduce her imports enough to finance even this reduced level of payments out of her own trade balance. What happened, in effect, was that money flowed from the United States to Germany; some of it went from Germany to France (and to a lesser extent to Britain); and some of the money that came to France went back again to America, in repayment for money that France had borrowed from America. In 1928 the American outflow of capital to Germany fell off, principally because Americans decided it was much more profitable to invest in their own booming Stock Exchange than in Germany. After the 1929 Crash, this fall became even more pronounced. As a result German industry found itself without adequate funds; investment fell, and the whole economy started to contract. Moreover Germany now found that she could no longer meet her reparation and other debt payments to France, Britain and other countries. This led to exactly the same kind of scramble for cash in the international field as the New York crash had led to within the United States. When people start defaulting on debt everyone who is owed money starts calling it in before their creditors go bankrupt as well. This leads to more defaulting, and the spiral worsens. Countries started withdrawing from other countries the money they had lent to them. Since gold was the accepted medium for settling international debts, people in effect started arriving at the Central Banks of Britain, France and Germany waving IOUs and demanding gold in return.

Britain was particularly hard hit by this. Her gold reserves were relatively low, because her return to the gold standard in 1925 at the pre-war parity had made exports too expensive and imports too cheap. Consequently there were large deficits on the balance of trade, and although, as we have seen, invisible earnings from banking, insurance, shipping and similar services turned this into a surplus for current transactions as a whole, this surplus was too small to pay for the large outflow of capital into investments overseas. These investments were quite inappropriate to Britain's new and much weaker economic position, but nevertheless they continued to be made.* Since they could not be financed by a current account surplus, they had to be financed by short-term borrowing from abroad, and this made Britain's position more vulnerable than ever. For of their very nature, Britain's long-term investments overseas, which represented factories in Australia or tea plantations in Ceylon, could not be quickly or easily liquidated; but the money Britain had

---

*They continued to be made on the sound British principle that what was good enough for the past is good enough for the present. When justification seemed to be needed, however, it was argued that a high level of British exports depended on a high level of British investment overseas. Exactly the same argument was used 40 years later to attack the Corporation Tax and other measures to restrict overseas investment introduced in 1965. This argument was largely disposed of by the publication in 1967 of an Interim Report on some recent research commissioned, ironically enough, by the Confederation of British Industry. This showed that the extra exports arising from investment overseas were extremely small. (W. B. Reddaway: *Effects of U.K. Direct Investment Overseas*, Cambridge University Press, 1967.) It is noticeable that neither Germany nor Japan – the two countries whose exports expanded fastest in the 1950s and 1960s – have ever done much overseas investment.

borrowed to finance them, representing 3-month Treasury Bills, or even ordinary deposit accounts in banks, could be called back virtually overnight. The situation was made worse by the fall in Britain's exports after 1929, the steep decline in invisible earnings which attended the falling-off of world trade, and the reduction in profits and dividends from investments overseas as production slumped in one country after another. Gold flowed out of Britain, and unemployment grew.

As if all this were not bad enough, this rise in unemployment in itself created a new crisis. For as unemployment rose, from 10 per cent in 1929 to 16 per cent in 1930 and 21 per cent in 1931, the unemployment benefits paid out by the National Insurance Fund rose, and the contributions paid into it fell. The result was that by 1931 the Fund was heavily in debt to the Exchequer. The Exchequer itself had already been running a small deficit for some years, and this development made things much worse.

A BALANCED BUDGET

Ever since, in the nineteenth century, the government had become an important spending agency it had been a cardinal principle of financial and economic orthodoxy – indeed of ordinary common sense – that the government must cover its expenditure out of its income. Exceptions were sometimes permitted in wartime; if the government could not raise enough money by taxation to cover the cost of fighting a war, it was accepted that it would have to borrow to make up the difference. But in normal peacetime conditions it was self-evident that the Budget must be balanced, with the government's income equalling or exceeding its expenditure. After all, it is important for any individual to keep his expenditure within his income; it was obviously infinitely more important for a government to balance its books – particularly the government of a country like Britain, in which large amounts of foreign money were invested, and in whose currency more than half the world's trade was conducted.

During the First World War government expenditure had, inevitably, risen enormously. Taxation had risen as well but not nearly enough to fill the gap, the rest of which was financed by borrowing. After the war government expenditure fell sharply but (even after allowing for the change in price levels) not nearly back to the pre-war figure. This was partly due to the effects of the war itself – the cost of paying pensions to disabled ex-servicemen and war widows, and the cost of paying interest on the money borrowed to finance the war (i.e. on the now much increased National Debt); and partly to the cost of implementing wartime and post-war pledges to build 'homes for heroes' and to pay increased scales of unemployment benefits.

This high level of public expenditure required high taxes to pay for it. Indeed, taxes had to be rather more than enough to pay for current government expenditure, for the government accepted the orthodox view that it was not enough merely to pay the *interest* on the sums it had borrowed during the war; it must start repaying the *principal* as well. In other words each year it must achieve a Budget surplus with which to pay off a little bit of the National Debt. During the first half of the 1920s this was in fact done. But the taxes needed to achieve this surplus were bitterly criticized, particularly by businessmen, who argued, predictably, that high taxation was throttling enterprise and was thus responsible for stagnation and unemployment. These arguments impressed the government, and taxes were reduced. With a fall in the yield of taxation, it was obvious to all that there must be a corresponding fall in government expenditure. But as countless politicians have discovered before and since, this was easier said than done. The government's expenditure was indeed cut, but not as much as its income. Consequently the small

Budget surpluses achieved in the first half of the 1920s gave way to small deficits in the second half. These deficits were greeted with much lip-pursing and head-shaking, but it seemed impossible either to raise taxes or reduce expenditure, and nothing much was done.

But when it became apparent, in 1930, that the Exchequer deficit was rapidly increasing, considerable alarm began to be expressed both at home and abroad. A Treasury memorandum presented to the Royal Commission on Unemployment Insurance in January 1931 said that 'continued State borrowing on the present vast scale, without adequate provision for repayment by the [National Insurance] Fund, would quickly call in question the stability of the British financial system'. In February the Labour government set up a Committee on National Expenditure, under Sir George May, to advise on what should be done; at the same time the Chancellor of the Exchequer (Mr Snowden) said that 'the national position is grave; drastic and disagreeable measures will have to be taken if the Budget equilibrium is to be maintained and industrial recovery is to be made'. (Note the assumed connexion between a balanced Budget and industrial recovery.)

By the time the May Committee reported, at the end of July 1931, the international payments position had grown very much worse. The Credit Anstalt, the largest bank in Austria, had got into difficulties, and had partially suspended payments. Mistrust of European banks and financial institutions spread rapidly, and there was an intensification of the process by which countries called in their own money from abroad while doing their best to freeze their own liabilities to other countries. Inevitably Britain, unable to recall much of the money she had lent abroad, but committed by her adherence to the gold standard to giving gold to all those who wanted to remove their money from London, suffered particularly severely. By the second half of July gold was flowing out of the country at a rate of £12–15 million a week, and by the end of the month the gold reserves were down to £133 million.

BRITAIN GOES OFF THE GOLD STANDARD

The May Report forecast that at the end of the current financial year (1931–2) there would be a Budget deficit of £120 million, and recommended some increase in taxation and drastic cuts in expenditure, particularly on unemployment benefits, in order to close the gap. This report (which Keynes described as 'the most foolish document I have ever had the misfortune to read'), coupled with the obvious reluctance of the Labour government to cut unemployment pay and the wages of public servants, increased alarm both at home and abroad. The outflow of gold accelerated, though the reserves were temporarily boosted by a £50 million loan from the French and American Central Banks at the beginning of August. Late in August the government fell, and was replaced by a National government (with Ramsay Macdonald still Prime Minister) pledged to preserve the value of the pound at any price. But although a further £80 million was borrowed from France and the U.S. towards the end of August, and the new government announced increases in taxation and cuts in expenditure early in September, the situation was out of control. By 19 September the remaining gold reserves were rapidly disappearing. The government had no choice. On 21 September it suspended gold payments. After six years of struggle Britain had been finally forced off the gold standard.

The effects of this on the whole system of international trade and payments were far-reaching and long-lasting, but for present purposes the point to notice is the effect on employment in Britain. The immediate effect was favourable. The price of sterling was now free to fluctuate according to supply and demand, and since more people were trying to sell it than buy it, its price fell. By the middle of 1932 the price in relation to the dollar had fallen from the $4·85 implied by being on the gold standard to $3·58. This meant that Britain's exports were now cheaper and her imports more expensive, and there was some corresponding improvement in the trade balance. But the effects of this were small and short-lived. The countries which had not devalued in relation to gold took other steps to relieve their balance of payments and to protect their home markets from the foreign competition which threatened to further reduce their employment. Tariffs were raised, import quotas extended, and exchange controls imposed. Britain and other countries which had left the gold standard retaliated in the same way. By 1932 the value of world trade had fallen to a third of the 1929 level, and everywhere production continued to fall and unemployment to rise. In Britain, in 1932, unemployment was worse than ever before, at a rate of 22 per cent. In Germany and the U.S. it was even higher.

VIEWS OF THE EXPERTS

And what, meanwhile, did the experts have to say about all this? Much the same as ever (though it is fair to add that some of them said it with rather less conviction than before). One must sit it out. One must wait for the down-swing of the trade cycle to flatten out and eventually turn into an up-swing. To assist this process one must cut wages and prices, and reduce interest rates. And above all one must ensure that government expenditure is cut so as not to exceed government income, for how can the economy recover if the state itself is heading for bankruptcy?

Such views were widely held by economists, and near-universally by those in politics, the civil service and the City who were concerned with economic policy.

But some economists did dissent from such views. By the mid-1920s Keynes and another Cambridge economist, D. H. Robertson, were calling for *more* government expenditure, not less. They argued that it was unnecessary simply to wait passively until private investment recovered and set in motion a general expansion. Instead, the government itself should step in and spend money on public investment, by building houses, harbours, roads and so on. In this way some of the unemployed men and equipment in the capital goods industries would immediately become employed again.

This argument was so simple that it was clear to most experts that it must be wrong. It was, in fact, attacked on two counts. First, there was the obvious point that it would run the Exchequer into deficit – the government would be spending a lot more money but getting little or nothing back by way of extra tax revenue. Deliberately running the state into the red like this was patently unsound. At best, it would shake business confidence and delay recovery; at worst, the consequences could be catastrophic.

Secondly, and even more formidably, the Treasury and many economists argued that quite apart from the effect on the Exchequer of the kind of public investment advocated by Keynes and Robertson, it would do more harm than good even in terms of its own objectives. There was only a certain amount of savings in the economy available for investment, it was said. If these savings were invested in largely unproductive projects such as houses and roads, they would not be available for investment in productive industry, for example factories. And by building factories one was obviously going before long to raise output and employment a lot more than by building houses. Therefore investment in public works would probably make unemployment worse, and would certainly delay the beginning of a proper and soundly based recovery.

Keynes could not really answer this theoretical case, and

although, supported by some others, he continued to advocate public works in the early 1930s, he was like a man calling on emotional grounds for a course of action that the intellect showed was wrong. The subordination of emotion to reason represented by government policy in the early 1930s is a sufficiently rare phenomenon in politics to call for encouragement and praise; it must have been particularly galling to an arch-intellectual like Keynes that it should happen in a case where he was stubbornly convinced that reason had got it wrong.* It was clear that until somebody could answer reason with reason, theory with theory, the voice of those who advocated more government expenditure as a solution to unemployment would go unheeded.

However, Keynes did not pin his entire faith on public works. He also advocated lower interest rates, and here, being in line with economic orthodoxy, he saw his wishes more fully realized. Bank rate, which had moved between 5 and 6½ per cent in 1929, had been brought down to 3 per cent in 1930, and although it rose to 6 per cent during the 1931 crisis, was brought down to 2 per cent by the middle of 1932. There it stayed, apart from a short period in 1939, until the return of the Conservative government in 1951. But during the rest of the 1930s these unprecedentedly low interest rates seemed to do little good. Unemployment fell a little from the 1932 rate of 22 per cent, but only to 20 per cent in 1933, 17 per cent in 1934, and 16 per cent in 1935. Even in 1939 it was still 12 per cent.

This failure of low interest rates to cure the situation led orthodox opinion to argue even more insistently that wages and prices must be reduced. Under the stimulus of falling world commodity prices, prices did indeed fall – between 1929 and 1933 retail prices in Britain fell by 15 per cent and wholesale prices by 25 per cent. But throughout

* In the United States emotion won: the non-intellectual Roosevelt inaugurated the New Deal in the teeth of expert advice (see page 142).

this period wages hardly fell at all. This, said the orthodox observers, was the heart of the trouble. The normal adjustment processes that were supposed to operate during the down-swing of the trade cycle were being thwarted by the refusal of the trade unions to agree to wage reductions. Until wages were reduced, unemployment would persist.

It is true that the logic of this view was pressed less far by some economists than others: economists are often circumspect, if sometimes catty, creatures. Professor Pigou, for example, one of the most distinguished economists of the day, could never be persuaded to advocate anything as definite as wage reductions; indeed he sometimes called for more public spending *à la* Keynes. But – as Keynes justly observed – the conclusion of his *Theory of Unemployment*, published in 1933, was that unemployment is primarily due to a wage policy which fails to adjust itself sufficiently to changes in the real demand function for labour.

The same argument was advanced more forcefully by Professor Lionel (now Lord) Robbins in his book *The Great Depression*, published in 1935.

But in general it is true to say that a greater flexibility of wage rates would considerably reduce unemployment. . . . If it had not been for the prevalence of the view that wage rates must at all costs be maintained in order to maintain the purchasing power of the consumer, the violence of the present depression and the magnitude of the unemployment that accompanied it would have been considerably less.

Robbins was aware of the sheer indecency of calling for wage cuts at a time when many of even those in employment were finding it a struggle to make ends meet, and went on to remark:

This is a hard saying, and there can be little wonder that men of humanity, especially those who are not themselves of the wage-earning classes and who therefore feel a natural reluctance to say anything which may seem to imply a desire that the position of others should be even temporarily worsened, should be loath to accept it.

But he concluded that 'the true humanitarian', when instructed in the truths of economic theory,

will realize that a policy which holds wage rates rigid when the equilibrium rate has altered, is a policy which creates unemployment.

On the subject of Roosevelt's attempt to pull the American economy out of the Slump by massive government expenditure on public works, Professor Robbins's view was also typical of the conventional wisdom of the time.

It is yet too early to say whether the American emergency legislation will prevent the coming of some degree of recovery. . . . The unbalancing of the Budget and the vast expenditures on public works have an inflationary tendency which may well override the various impediments to enterprise created in other directions and engender an inflationary boom – a boom which, if the analysis of earlier chapters is correct, would be likely to be followed by a deflationary collapse.

Here Robbins was stressing what we have seen was a constant theme of trade cycle theory – that the only way to prevent the down-swing of the trade cycle was to prevent any but the most moderate up-swing. It was better, the moral seemed to be, to have unemployment than employment that was created artificially.

The official attitude to unemployment can perhaps be rounded off by a quotation from the then Chancellor of the Exchequer. Speaking in the House of Commons in February 1935, Mr Neville Chamberlain said:

There may be circumstances when it is right and sound to follow a policy of that kind [i.e. a large expenditure of public money, including public works], but not for the purpose of providing employment, because the whole experience of the past shows that, for the purpose of providing employment, this policy of public works is always disappointing. . . . The conclusion I draw . . . is that the quickest and most effective contribution which any government can make towards an increase of employment is to create conditions which will encourage and facilitate improvement in ordinary trade.*

This negative approach did not go unanswered for very long. A year later saw the publication of the *General Theory*. For since his failure in the early 1930s to provide a theoretical justification of his views Keynes, in addition to pursuing his multitudinous official and private activities, had been working away. There seems to be no record of how he made one of history's major intellectual discoveries – whether it came in a flash or was pieced together bit by bit; whether he climbed a hill and suddenly saw the Pacific, or deduced its presence from the smell of the wind and the cries of the gulls. All we know is that on 1 January 1935, he wrote in a letter to Bernard Shaw '. . . I believe myself to be writing a book on economic theory which will largely revolutionize – not, I suppose, at once but in the course of the next ten years – the way the world thinks about economic problems.' Never was such apparent arrogance so amply justified.

* Hansard, 14 February 1935, Cols 2208–9.

CHAPTER 4

THE GENERAL THEORY

THE book is called *The General Theory of Employment, Interest and Money*, but we shall not go far wrong if we forget about the money, deal briefly with the interest, and concentrate on the employment. For the book is really about what determines the level of employment. However, the level of employment is significant not only on its own account, as a measure of whether or not people who want work can find it. It is also, because in the short run employment and output tend to move fairly closely in line with each other, a kind of shorthand way of describing the whole level of activity in the economy. Therefore although in this chapter we shall be discussing Keynes's theory mainly in terms of employment and unemployment – legitimately so, in view of the level of unemployment in the 1930s – we must remember that the subject matter might equally well be described as the level of output in the country, or the standard of living of its citizens. To this day there are those who refuse to accept that Keynes's analysis was right; but no one has ever questioned the importance of the subject he was dealing with.

Keynes was not interested in every kind of unemployment that had ever existed. He was not concerned, for example, with the question of why unemployment should appear from time to time in particular industries; this question had been satisfactorily answered by Ricardo, if not before. Nor was he mainly interested in explaining the bouts of unemployment which would appear from time to time in a wide range of industries, grow worse for a year or two, level off, and then disappear again. Although he included some illuminating *Notes on the trade cycle* in the *General Theory*, he thought that much of the trade cycle mechanism was already quite well understood. The thing that was not understood was how the economy could get stuck at the bottom of the trade cycle. According to the orthodox theory, this could not happen; yet, as we have seen, it did happen – in Britain heavy unemployment persisted year after year throughout virtually the whole of the 1920s and 1930s. How was this possible? What was wrong with the prevailing theory? These were the questions that Keynes set out to answer.

However, although he was concerned with the persistence of unemployment year after year, and not with the kind of temporary unemployment associated with fashion changes or the trade cycle, Keynes's theory was essentially a short-term theory. He was not concerned with the factors which determine what the volume of employment will be in twenty or fifty years' time; in the long run, as he put it, we are all dead. He wanted to know what determines employment now and next year. In short, he was concerned with a sufficiently brief space of time for it to be reasonable to assume that such factors as the number of people of working age, consumer spending patterns, industrial techniques and so on do not change enough to have much effect on employment.

EFFECTIVE DEMAND

Keynes began* by rejecting the idea that one can rely on full employment being maintained (or, after the down-swing of the trade cycle, restored) by the operation of some self-adjusting mechanism. Wages, prices and interest rates do not, he said, move by themselves in such a way as to ensure full employment. And even if they were *made to move* in the

---

*This does not mean that he actually began the *General Theory* in this way. I have tried in this chapter to expound the essence of Keynes's argument rather than to follow at all closely the order or terminology of the *General Theory* itself.

way required by orthodox theory, this would not necessarily
do the trick either. In fact, one must not simply assume that
full employment is the normal state of affairs, kept in being
by the flexibility of wages or interest rates in the same sort of
way that the temperature of a room is kept at a constant level
by the automatic operation of a thermostat. Instead one
must regard the level of employment, like any other variable
in economics (or life itself) as something determined by certain causal factors. One must think out what these factors
are, and consider whether they might work in such a way as
to result in a level of employment persistently lower than the
numbers seeking work.

In the short run, he went on, the level of employment is
determined by the level of output: if output is running at a
high level, firms will employ more men than if it is running at
a low level, and men will be engaged or laid off according to
whether output is rising or falling. Output, in turn, depends
on *effective demand*. Effective demand simply means demand
backed by money – in other words actual expenditure. Total
expenditure and total sales are the same thing from different
viewpoints, and sales (apart from changes in stocks) are
the same thing as output.* So one can see why output is
determined by effective demand. The real question is, what
determines effective demand?

To answer this question Keynes argued that one must
break down effective demand into two components, consumption and investment, and study each in turn. The
distinction between consumption and investment is concep-
tually fairly clear, though there are a number of technical
snags involved which we must not spend too much time on.
If an individual spends money on ice cream or a seat in a

---

* Total output, total expenditure and total incomes are all equal: they
are three different ways of measuring the same concept, which we shall
call the 'National Income'. For a fuller explanation, see Explanatory
Note 3, page 256.

theatre, this is obviously expenditure on consumption. Equally obviously, if a firm spends money on a new factory and new plant and machinery to put in it, this is investment. Some other cases are much less clear-cut. Money spent on a car, for example, counts as consumption if it is spent by a private individual, but investment if spent by a firm. Houses are bought by individuals, but count as investment. But the best rough-and-ready distinction for the purposes of our analysis is that money spent by individuals on goods and services in order to satisfy their own wants is consumption; money spent by firms on buildings and machinery in order to produce goods and services in the future is investment.

Of the total annual income of a modern country, something like a fifth will be spent on investment, and the other four fifths on consumption. Or, to look at it from the side of output rather than income, a fifth of the annual output of the country will consist of what are called *investment* or *capital* goods such as buildings and machinery, and the other four fifths of consumer goods and services such as clothes and haircuts.* If, therefore, one wants to know what determines the total output of a country (and hence the level of employment) one must examine what determines the level of consumption and what determines the level of investment. Let us take consumption first.

CONSUMPTION

An individual's consumption is determined mainly by his income; and his consumption will normally be rather *less*

* This breakdown of the National Income into only two categories – consumption and investment – is of course a simplification of reality which takes no account of such real-world complications as government current expenditure, stock-building and foreign trade. But throughout this chapter we shall inevitably be drastically simplifying reality – as Keynes himself did in the *General Theory* – in order to make the gist of the argument as clear as possible.

than his income. There are of course cases in which the opposite is true, and a rich or optimistic individual manages to spend more on consumption than he receives in income, by borrowing or dipping into past savings. There are probably a good many cases where income and consumption are exactly equal, with each week's pay packet being spent down to the last penny. But the majority of individuals or households probably save a little bit of their income, even if the saving only takes the form of paying premiums on a life insurance policy, or contributions towards a pension. They therefore spend rather less on consumption than they earn (savings being defined simply as the difference between income and expenditure on consumption). The factors that impel people to save are various: some save to provide for their children, or their own old age; some as an insurance against future illness or unemployment; some to build up a small business of their own; some out of sheer miserliness; and some, no doubt, because they cannot think of anything interesting enough to spend their money on.

Whatever the relative strength of these various motives, it seems fairly safe to say that if you take all the individuals or households in Britain together you will find that their total consumption is less than their total income – in other words that some proportion of their total income is saved. Just what this proportion will be – whether it will be a tenth or a fifth or a third – will depend on the way a whole host of factors affect a particular society at a particular time, such as the attitude to thrift, the generosity of state old age pensions, the extent to which the state provides free education or medical treatment, and so on. We must accept most of these factors as determined by historical or sociological processes outside our terms of reference, but two particular ones may be worth a brief mention.

First, the proportion of a country's income that is spent on consumption depends quite a lot on how the National Income is distributed. Not surprisingly, rich people save a larger proportion of their income than poor people. If income is distributed fairly equally no one may be rich enough to do much saving, and consumption may be relatively high. If on the other hand the distribution of income is very unequal, the rich will save a good deal, and the poor will not be able to offset this by dis-saving.* Another relevant point is the distribution of the National Income between wages (including salaries) on the one hand, and profits on the other. The proportion of profits that is saved is usually a good deal higher than the proportion of wages that is saved. Therefore the larger the share of wages in the National Income the higher will be the proportion of the National Income spent on consumption.

Secondly, the proportion of income spent on consumption may change as income changes. One might expect, for example, that in the long run, as a society grew richer and people's real incomes rose, the proportion of income saved would tend to rise as well. As it happens, there is very little evidence that this does in fact occur – perhaps, in some cases, because the effect of rising incomes is offset by the effect of a reduction in inequality (not to mention an increase in advertising). But that is in the long run. In the *short run* there is a good deal of evidence to suggest that the *proportion* of income spent on consumption does change as income changes – because the *amount* spent on consumption changes rather slowly. During the up-swing of the trade cycle, for example, when incomes are rising quite rapidly, it takes people a little time to adjust their expenditure patterns to their higher level of income, and while they are making up their minds how to spend the extra money, they save more. Consequently the proportion of their incomes that they spend temporarily

---

*i.e. spending more on consumption than they earn. You have to have assets to be allowed to run up a decent overdraft. In recent years the picture has, of course, been somewhat changed by hire purchase.

falls, and the same goes for the proportion of the National Income that is spent on consumption. Conversely, during the down-swing of the trade cycle, as people are put on to short time or lose their jobs altogether, and the household's income contracts, people find it difficult to cut their expenditure immediately in line with their reduced income; the tendency is to keep on with previous consumption patterns as long as possible, usually by dipping into *past* savings. As a result many people are, for the time being, spending more on consumption than they are earning, and so the proportion of the National Income as a whole which is spent on consumption during the down-swing is generally quite high.

THE MARGINAL PROPENSITY TO CONSUME

Before we leave consumption it may be as well to say a word about a concept which we shall need later on, which Keynes christened the *marginal propensity to consume*. Despite the slightly technical language, this is a fairly straightforward concept. It is the proportion of any *increase* in income that is spent on consumption. Suppose that 90 per cent of income is spent on consumption. In this case one would say that the *average* propensity to consume was 90 per cent, or 0·9. Now suppose that income rises, and of this *extra* income only 80 per cent is spent on consumption. In that case the *marginal* propensity to consume will be 80 per cent, or 0·8. As we have seen, the marginal propensity to consume may be relatively low during the up-swing of the trade cycle. But the simplest case to have in mind is where the marginal propensity is *equal* to the average propensity – where, say, 90 per cent of existing income is spent on consumption, and 90 per cent of any increase in income would also be spent on consumption. In that case both the average and the marginal propensity to consume would be 0·9. According to Keynes, the size of the marginal propensity to consume – whether it was 0·8 or o·85 or o·9 – was very important; but the really crucial thing about it was that it was almost certainly less than 1 – in other words that *some* part of any increase in income would be saved. As we shall see, this assumption – which is clearly a fairly safe one – played an important part in his analysis.

The main factor which determines a country's consumption, then, is its income, just as the main factor which determines a family's consumption is its income. The exact proportion of its income that a country will spend on consumption will depend on institutional arrangements, traditional attitudes to saving, the distribution of income, and so on. But we shall not go very far wrong, as far as getting to grips with Keynes's analysis is concerned, if we think of a country's expenditure on consumption as being a fairly high, and fairly stable, proportion of its income.

INVESTMENT

Now let us turn to the factors which, according to Keynes, determine the second element of effective demand, investment. Although at this point the story becomes a little more complicated (particularly in the way in which Keynes actually presented it) the essence of what he was saying is relatively simple.

The amount of money spent on investment, said Keynes, is determined by two things: on the one hand, by the amount the investment will yield, and on the other by the cost of borrowing the money needed to finance the investment. This seems fairly clear. Obviously, no one is going to borrow money in order to build a factory if the profits eventually made by the factory are smaller than the interest payments he has to make on the money he has borrowed. On the other hand, if the profits to be made out of a new factory are much larger than the interest payments, one would expect all sorts of businessmen to start borrowing money and building factories all over the place. The exact amount of new factory-building, or other kinds of investment, that takes place will therefore depend in some way on the relationship between the yield of investment on the one hand and the cost of borrowing money on the other.

But in saying this one has merely driven the crucial questions further back. One now wants to know what determines the yield of an investment? And what determines the rate of interest that a borrower has to pay? Let us take these two questions in turn.

THE YIELD OF INVESTMENT

In order to assess the yield of an investment, said Keynes, one must assess the probable returns from it over the whole of its life, and not just in the first year or two.* The future yield depends on the future volume of sales, and the price at which these sales will be effected. The businessman's assessment of this will in turn depend on the outlook for the economy as a whole, and in particular for the goods that the new investment is designed to produce. We have already seen, in our discussion of the trade cycle, the kind of factors which are relevant. Immediately after the trade cycle has gone into the down-swing phase, for example, the prospects for new investment will not look very exciting: with a large amount of fairly new capital equipment already standing idle there will not be much profit to be made by installing more. But a few

* The originality of the *General Theory* lay almost as much in the way it developed new tools of analysis as in the novel way it made use of old ones. Keynes's insistence that one must look at the whole series of returns expected throughout the entire anticipated life of a new piece of investment (and then seek a way of reducing this series of future yields to a common denominator) is a case in point. Until the *General Theory* economists had tended to look only at the immediate rate of return on an investment – i.e. the rate of return during the first year or two of its life.

years later, when some of this equipment has worn out, or rusted away, or been made out-of-date by the development of new products or techniques, it may again become profitable to build new factories and install modern machinery. This will apply particularly, of course, to the up-swing stage of the business cycle, when incomes have started rising and the demand for goods and services is beginning to expand again. During this stage the accelerator, which has a depressing effect on investment during the down-swing, acts as a stimulant.

It would probably not be too much of an over-simplification, therefore, to say that the main factors affecting the future yield of a new factory or piece of machinery are the *amount* of capital equipment already in existence, and the *extent* to which it is being used. If there is a lot of equipment about (as at the end of the boom) the profitability of new investment will tend to be less than when there is a relatively smaller amount (as at the beginning of the boom). And if what equipment already exists is under-utilized, the incentive to invest will be smaller than if all existing equipment is being used to capacity. This is fairly easy to see, and was indeed an element in the theory of the trade cycle. Keynes accepted this analysis, but significantly strengthened it by the emphasis he placed on *expectations*. It was not simply the present state of the economy which affected investment decisions, he insisted, but the expectations different businessmen had about the way things would develop in the future. The prospect of large immediate profits would not necessarily tempt them to invest in new projects if they thought that these profits would disappear in a year or two's time with the onset of a recession.

So far we have been looking only at one side of the investment decision, namely the yield to be expected from the investment if the businessman decides to go ahead with it. But before he can make his decision he will also need to know about the other side of the balance sheet, namely how much it will cost to borrow the money needed to pay for the investment; in other words, what is the rate of interest he will have to pay.* Our second question, then, is what determines the rate of interest?

THE RATE OF INTEREST

Keynes's theory of what determines the rate of interest, though highly ingenious, is not always easy to follow, and indeed was never quite pulled together in the *General Theory*. But the gist of it is roughly as follows.

The rate of interest is essentially a price – the price of borrowing money – and one would expect it to be determined, like any other price, by supply and demand. This, said Keynes, is correct. It is determined by the supply and demand for *money* – money, in this context, being cash, and bank deposits which can immediately be converted into cash. What, then, determines the supply of money, and the demand for money?

As far as the supply side is concerned the position is fairly straightforward. The quantity of money in the economy is decided by the Central Bank (or the government); we have seen (page 50) how the Central Bank uses 'open-market operations' (i.e. buys or sells securities) in order to affect the

---

*I am assuming, for the sake of simplicity, that the businessman raises money by borrowing at a fixed rate of interest from his bank. In fact he might raise money by issuing shares, or he might already have the money himself. But in both these cases the rate of interest is still relevant to his calculations; in the first case it will affect the terms on which he can raise money by a share issue, and in the second it will determine the return he can get by lending his money to somebody else instead of investing it himself. So even in these slightly more complicated cases the rate of interest is still a determinant of investment decisions. In practice, of course, there are many different rates of interest; when one talks of *the* rate of interest one is inevitably simplifying reality.

liquid reserves of the commercial banks, and hence the willingness of these banks to grant overdrafts or make advances, and hence the cash or bank deposits at the disposal of ordinary citizens. Thus the supply of money is determined, to all intents and purposes, by decisions of the government or Central Bank (subject only to whether or how far the gold standard rules are operating).

The demand side is more complicated. Let us be clear about the question we are asking. We are not asking the somewhat naïve question 'Why do people want money?' We are asking 'Why do people want to hold their wealth in the form of *money* (i.e. cash or bank deposits, which yield no interest) rather than in the form of industrial shares, government securities or other assets which yield some return?' In other words, what determines the amount of *money* that people want to hold, as compared with shares or other assets?

Keynes broke down the answer to this question into three parts, distinguishing three different reasons why people should want to hold some of their wealth in the form of money rather than interest-bearing assets. First, there is the *transactions* motive: people need ready cash for their everyday purchases. Secondly, there is the *precautionary* motive: they want money in their pocket, or at any rate immediately available in the form of a bank deposit, in case some unforeseen contingency arises – a sudden illness, a burglary, or a heavy fine for an alleged traffic offence. Finally, there is the *speculative* motive: people (or some people) want to have money in hand to take advantage of any profitable situation that may suddenly arise – for example the expectation of a fall in the price of shares or government bonds; or, to put it the other way round, they do not want to be caught holding bonds if they expect the price to fall, and so they sell out and hold money instead.

According to Keynes, the transactions and precautionary motives for holding money, though quite closely related to the money level of the National Income, are not affected very much by the rate of interest; the amount of money people require for these purposes is much the same whether interest rates are high or low. But the speculative motive is very closely affected by the existing, and expected, level of interest rates. If interest rates are already high, and people think that they are going to fall (which is another way of saying that the price of government bonds is going to rise)* then they will lend as much money at the present high level of interest rates (i.e. buy as much government stock at the present low level of prices) as they possibly can. In these circumstances the desire to make a speculative profit will prompt men to put their money into government securities, and they will hold very little cash; or, to use Keynes's own term, their *liquidity preference* will be very low. But in the opposite case, in which interest rates are low and there is a general belief that they will rise, the desire for cash to satisfy the speculative motive will be very high (i.e. liquidity preference will be very high). People will be anxious to have money immediately available to take advantage of the higher level of interest rates (lower level of government security prices) that they are expecting, and will not want to risk a capital loss by holding securities.

What all this adds up to, then, is that the demand for money to satisfy the speculative motive will be high at low rates of interest, and low at high rates of interest. Taking into account the transactions and precautionary motives for holding money, which are not much affected by interest rates, it will still remain true that the total demand for money will be higher the lower the rate of interest: as the rate of interest falls, the demand for money will rise. And the actual rate of interest that is established, said Keynes, will be that rate of interest at which the demand for money, as determined by these various motives, is equal to the supply of money, as

* See Explanatory Note 4, page 258.

determined by the Central Bank. In other words the rate of interest is determined by the amount of money created by the Central Bank on the one hand, and people's demand for money (or, as Keynes put it, their liquidity preference) on the other.

But Keynes was not content to leave the analysis there; he added an extra twist, which became an important part of his attack on orthodox theory. Consider what happens to the rate of interest, he said, when the Central Bank changes the quantity of money. As in the case of any other commodity, one would expect an increase in the supply to reduce the price (in this case the rate of interest), and a reduction in the supply to increase it. This, he agreed, would indeed be the tendency; but he qualified his agreement in one significant particular. He accepted that a reduction in the quantity of money would lead to a rise in interest rates if liquidity preference (i.e. the demand for money) remained unchanged. For if the supply of money was reduced (in effect, if people found their overdrafts being cut), while the demand for money remained unchanged, equilibrium could only be re-established by a rise in interest rates. Lenders would require higher interest rates if they were to part with ready cash; and borrowers would be willing to pay higher interest rates now that there was less money to be borrowed.

In theory, exactly the opposite should happen when the quantity of money is increased. With an unchanged demand for money, and a larger supply, one would expect interest rates to fall. But although this was true up to a point, said Keynes, it was not true all along the line. If, say, interest rates are around 6 per cent, a relatively small increase in the quantity of money may succeed in bringing them down to 5 per cent: with more money about, people will have more to lend, or less need to borrow, and interest rates will be driven downwards. But if interest rates are around 2 per cent to start with, even a large increase in the quantity of money may not succeed in forcing them down to 1 per cent. This, said Keynes, is because there is some level of interest rates below which people become very reluctant to lend money at all. Even if there is lots of money about, people will prefer to keep it in the form of cash or bank deposits, rather than lend it out, if the rate of interest is very low (below, say, 2 or $2\frac{1}{2}$ per cent). This is not simply because such a low rate of return is not worth the bother of lending money out, but also because of the effect of expectations. Past experience suggests to people that very low rates of interest will probably not last very long. Therefore anyone who ties his money up by lending it out at a very low rate of interest (i.e. buys government securities at a very high price) may get a nasty shock; any rise in interest rates (fall in government security prices) will leave him with a loss. Therefore, concluded Keynes, although in normal circumstances an increase in the supply of money will result in a fall in interest rates, it will not do so if interest rates are already unusually low. There is some level below which interest rates cannot be forced however much one increases the quantity of money. This is because there is some rate of interest (perhaps around 2 or $2\frac{1}{2}$ per cent) below which no one will be willing to lend.

Let us briefly recapitulate the determinants of investment, as Keynes saw them.* The amount of investment undertaken in a country in any particular period, he said, depends on the yield businessmen expect to see from individual investment projects on the one hand, and the rate of interest on the other. We have looked at the factors which determine investment yields and interest rates, and have seen that they include, in the one case, such things as the amount of capital equipment already in existence, the extent to which it is

*Nowadays, most economists would give rather less weight than Keynes to fluctuations in the rate of interest as a determinant of investment decisions, and rather more to the degree of uncertainty of the expected yield. But this is a difference of emphasis rather than of substance.

utilized, the number of newly developed products or techniques and the general outlook for the economy; and in the other case the preferences people have for holding money rather than interest-bearing assets, and the quantity of money that the Central Bank decides to create. The amount of investment that is actually done will be determined by the interaction of all these forces. Obviously, if the outlook for the economy is good, if existing capital equipment is being used to capacity, and if the rate of interest is relatively low, a good deal of investment will be done. If, on the other hand, the outlook is gloomy and existing equipment is under-used, the amount of investment done will tend to be relatively small, particularly if at the same time interest rates are high.

THE LEVEL OF OUTPUT AND EMPLOYMENT

We have seen, then, the factors which, in Keynes's view, determine what the level of consumption will be in a particular country at a particular time, and the factors which determine what the level of investment will be. Since he began the exercise by breaking down the National Income into the two components consumption and investment, it is clear that if one knows what determines each of them, one knows what determines the National Income. For consumption plus investment equals National Income. Or, to use Keynes's own notation, in which consumption is C, investment is I and National Income is Y, $C + I = Y$. And since, as we have also seen, output (= National Income) and employment move closely together in the short run, it is clear that consumption and investment together determine the level of employment.

Now, at last, Keynes was ready to explode his bombshell. I have shown, he said, that a certain level of employment results from the amount of consumption and investment that takes place in a country. *Now why*, he asked, *should this level of employment be full employment*? What is there in the economic system which ensures that the amount spent by businessmen on investment, and the amount spent by households on consumption, should together call forth a level of output which can only be achieved by employing everyone who is seeking work? What prevents consumption and investment from imposing demands on the economy which it cannot meet even by drawing into employment every able-bodied person in the country? At the other extreme, what prevents consumption and investment from being so low that they call forth only a relatively small output of goods and services, which can be produced by only 80 or 90 per cent of the labour force? In short, what reason is there to suppose that the millions of individual decisions to consume or not to consume, to invest or not to invest, will just happen to add up to a level of effective demand which will imply full employment?

To these questions Keynes returned clear and uncompromising answers. The level of employment which results from the amount of consumption and investment a country undertakes will *not* necessarily be full employment. There is *nothing* in the economic system to ensure that consumption and investment will call forth just enough output to entail full employment. There is *nothing* to prevent consumption and investment from imposing too many demands on the economy (thus leading to inflation) or too few demands on the economy (thus leading to unemployment). In short, there is *no* reason to suppose that the sum total of millions of individual decisions to consume or invest will just happen to add up to a level of demand that will result in full employment.

These answers came as a terrific shock to orthodox opinion. As we have seen (Chapter 2) full employment had always been thought of as the normal and natural state of affairs: unemployment represented an exceptional and temporary departure from normality. Now here was Keynes rejecting the idea that there was something normal about full employment, and asserting that full employment was merely one possible level of employment out of a large number of possible levels. If one had full employment, he was in effect saying, this was not because it was inevitable; it was simply good luck.

This, then, was the dramatic and imperative part of what Keynes was saying: dramatic because it stood existing economic theory on its head, imperative because it implied the need for government action of a kind, and on a scale, never before contemplated. If the government wants full employment, the message ran, it cannot simply sit back and hope that full employment will just happen: it must take steps to see that there is enough investment or consumption to ensure it. If this results in a Budget deficit – as it may well do – this does not matter. What is important is not that the government should balance its own accounts, but that it should ensure that there is enough demand in the economy to maintain full employment.

THE CONCEPT OF EQUILIBRIUM

But so far we have not penetrated to the heart of Keynes's theory. This becomes clear if one considers the incompleteness of the story so far. We said that the level of consumption is determined by the level, and distribution, of income. We then went on to say that the level of consumption, plus the level of investment, determines the total output of the country – which is the same thing as the total income of the country. In other words one is saying *both* that income determines consumption *and* that consumption (with investment) determines income. Surely this is a circular argument?

Not exactly. It is, rather, an example of the fact that in the subject matter of economics, everything is determined by everything else. One is dealing here with a set of *mutually dependent* variables. This means that if one changes one variable, this will result in changes in other variables, and these changes in the other variables will eventually result in a further change in the first variable. In this case, we are saying that total income and total consumption are mutually dependent variables. Consumption is determined by income, and income is determined, at any rate in part, by consumption. If one changes income, consumption will change – as we have seen. But this change in consumption will itself lead to further changes in income – as we shall see a little later on.

Now when one is dealing with two mutually dependent variables like this one can only explain why each of them is at the level it is by bringing in the concept of *equilibrium*. A situation is an equilibrium one if there is no tendency for any of the variables to depart from their existing levels. It is not a sufficient explanation of the level of consumption to say 'consumption is £80 a year because income is £100', if in fact it is also true that income is only £100 because consumption is £80. Instead, one must explain the level of consumption by saying 'consumption is £80 because the mutual relationships between income and consumption are such that this is the only level of consumption compatible, over a period of time, with an income of £100'. In other words, given that income is £100, one will only have an equilibrium situation if consumption is £80. If consumption was *not* £80, but £70 or £90, then income would not have settled down at £100.

The *General Theory* is a theory of equilibrium. It analyses the process by which four inter-related variables – consumption, investment, savings and the National Income – are brought into equilibrium with each other; and shows that the equilibrium established may, or may not, result in full employment. Indeed the essence of the *General Theory* can be expressed even more simply than this, as an account of the way in which *savings* and *investment* are brought into equilibrium with each other. And it is this that we shall now examine.

INVESTMENT AND SAVINGS IN EQUILIBRIUM

Let us begin our examination by looking at a simple but immensely significant piece of arithmetic. We have seen that expenditure on consumption plus expenditure on investment is equal to the National Income. Therefore investment is equal to National Income *minus* consumption. But if one looks at the National Income from the other angle, as the sum total not of all *expenditure* but of all *incomes* one can see that the National Income *minus* consumption is also equal to savings, because savings are defined as the difference between income and consumption. Therefore investment and savings must be equal to each other.

All this can be expressed much less clumsily in Keynes's own notation. Writing S for total savings, we have

$$Y = C + I$$
$$\therefore \quad I = Y - C$$
$$\text{But} \quad S = Y - C$$
$$\therefore \quad I = S$$

In other words, what one is saying is this: a nation's production is the same thing as its income; what it produces but does not consume is its investment; what it receives in income but does not spend on consumption is its savings. Therefore its investment must be equal to its savings.

The arithmetic is foolproof. But when one turns to apply it to the real world one cannot immediately see how it can be true. For, as we have seen, investment and savings are activities carried out by different groups of people for different reasons. Investment is decided on by businessmen in the light of the rate of interest and the return they expect from particular types of capital equipment. Savings, on the other hand, are decided on by millions of individual families, according to how much they think they should set aside out of current income for their own or their children's future.

How is it possible, except by a fantastic fluke, for the total amount that tens of thousands of businessmen decide to invest to be exactly the same as the total amount that millions of families decide to save?*

This is where the concept of equilibrium comes in. The level of National Income that is finally established, said Keynes, will be a level at which savings and investment are in equilibrium with each other – i.e. at which the amount that households *want* to save is exactly equal to the amount that businessmen *want* to invest. Any level of National Income at which savings and investment are not in equilibrium cannot persist; it will change until it reaches a level at which the amount that families want to save *is* equal to what businessmen want to invest. At this level the whole economic system will be in equilibrium – i.e. there will be no tendency for any further changes in any of the variables to occur. (But, to stress the main message again, this equilibrium level of National Income may involve substantial unemployment.)

Now before we go on to look at all this in more detail, we had better get absolutely clear a point that baffled even the experts when the *General Theory* appeared, and was responsible for many of the eminent economists of the 1930s never really understanding what Keynes was getting at. This is the difference between saying that savings and investment are *equal* to each other, and saying that they are *in equilibrium* with each other.

We have seen that savings and investment are the same thing, looked at from different angles: they are both the difference between the income or output of a country on the one hand, and the level of consumption on the other. That being so, they must always be equal to each other, however

---

*The distinction between 'businessmen' who invest and 'families' which save is a drastic simplification of reality used to aid the exposition. What actually happens is much more complicated, and is briefly discussed in the footnote on pages 108–9.

short a period of time one is considering. 2 is always equal to 2, however quickly one looks at it; not even for a millionth of a second is it equal to $1\frac{3}{4}$. Therefore what businessmen *actually* invest will always be equal to what families *actually* save.

But what businessmen *want* to invest, and what families *want* to save, is a quite different matter. These two quantities may be far from equal. But in that case, as a matter of logic, there will be a difference between what people want to do, and what they succeed in doing. If, for example, businessmen want to invest *more* than families want to save, then either the businessmen will find they cannot spend as much on investment as they want to (because, for example, the investment goods are simply not there to be bought); or families will find that they cannot consume as much as (i.e. are saving more than) they want to, perhaps because there is a diversion of output to investment goods, thus reducing the quantities of consumer goods available in the shops. Similarly, if businessmen want to invest *less* than families want to save either they will find they are investing more than they want to or, more probably, families will find they are saving less than they want to.

But although actual savings and investment will always be equal to each other, one will not have an equilibrium situation unless *desired* savings and investment are equal to each other, with the amount that businessmen want to invest being equal to the amount that families want to save. If one starts off in a situation in which businessmen want to invest more, or less, than families want to save, then, according to Keynes, the National Income will change, and go on changing, until it reaches a level at which what businessmen want to invest *is* equal to what families want to save.

THE MULTIPLIER

In order to see the process by which this happens, we must first of all look a little more closely at the marginal propensity to consume. We have already seen (page 77) that the marginal propensity to consume is that fraction of an increase in income that is spent on consumption. If, for example, a family (or a country) has an *increase* in income of £100, and spends £80 of this increase on consumption, then its marginal propensity to consume is $\frac{80}{100}$ or 0·8. Since by definition it must save the £20 that it does not consume, its *marginal propensity to save* must be $\frac{20}{100}$ or 0·2. (Just as any increase in income must be either spent on consumption or saved, so the marginal propensity to consume and the marginal propensity to save must together add up to 1·0, or unity.)

Now according to Keynes, the *size* of the marginal propensity to consume was the key to the size of the change in the National Income that would be needed to bring a disequilibrium situation, in which businessmen wanted to invest more or less than families wanted to save, into equilibrium. The higher the marginal propensity to consume, the bigger will be the change in National Income that results from a given change in investment, or savings. Let us look at a simple numerical example in order to make the position clear.

Suppose that a country with a marginal propensity to consume of 0·8 for some reason or other receives an increase in income of £100. Of this £100 it (or rather the actual individuals who receive it) will spend £80 on consumption. But the people who receive this £80 in the form of income (the retailers who sell the £80 worth of consumption goods, the manufacturers and workers who make them etc.), assuming they also have a marginal propensity to consume of 0·8, will themselves spend 80 per cent of this increased income of £80 (i.e. £64) on consumption goods. And the people who receive this extra £64 will spend 80 per cent of this (i.e. £51 4s.) on consumption – and so on. In other words the increase in the total income of the country (i.e. in the National Income) will not, at the end of the day, be £100; it will be £100 + £80 + £64 + £51 4s. + ... If one works this series out one will find that it adds up to £500 – in other words one has to multiply the original increase in income by 5 in order to find out the eventual increase in total income. Or, as Keynes put it, the *Multiplier* is 5.* Numerically, the Multiplier is in fact the reciprocal of the marginal propensity to save: it is 5 in this case because the marginal propensity to save is 0·2, or $\frac{1}{5}$. If people had consumed only two thirds of their increased income, so that the marginal propensity to save was $\frac{1}{3}$, then the Multiplier would have been 3, and the final increase in total income only £300. Similarly, if they had consumed 90 per cent of their increased income, so that the marginal propensity to save was only $\frac{1}{10}$, the Multiplier would have been 10, and the final increase in total income therefore £1,000. This obviously accords with common sense. The smaller the fraction of any increase in income that people save, the larger will be their extra expenditure on consumption, and thus the larger their contribution to increasing the incomes of others, and thus the larger the eventual increase in the income of the community as a whole. In the limiting case, in which people consume *all* of any increase in their income, so that the marginal propensity to consume is 1·0 and the marginal propensity to save is 0, incomes will go on rising for ever, because the Multiplier will be infinity. In fact, Keynes argued, the marginal propensity to consume is less than 1, so that the Multiplier is of manageable size and the

* The concept of the Multiplier had first been evolved by R. F. Kahn in 1931; Keynes modified it slightly and used it as one of the corner-stones of the *General Theory*.

eventual rise in the income of the community not tremendously large.*

Now, armed with this concept of the Multiplier, let us return to the question of how savings and investment are brought into equilibrium with each other (in the sense that *desired* savings and *desired* investment are made equal to each other) by changes in the National Income. Let us start off by assuming an equilibrium situation, in which the level of the National Income is such that the amount that businessmen want to spend on investment is just equal to the amount that families want to save, so that savings and investment are not only equal to each other, but are also in equilibrium with each other. The situation is in equilibrium, in the sense that there is no tendency for either savings or investment to change.

Now suppose that for some reason, such as the development of a new product, or a fall in the cost of borrowing money, businessmen suddenly decide to increase their spending on investment. The equilibrium between investment and savings will be broken. Instead of wanting to invest exactly the same amount as households are saving, businessmen are now trying to invest more. What happens? According to Keynes, the rise in investment results in a rise in the National Income bigger than the initial rise in investment – just how much bigger depends on the size of the Multiplier. If the people whose incomes rise as a result of the businessmen's increased expenditure on investment – the men who build the new factories or make the new machinery to put

* In practice, in the Britain of the 1960s, the Multiplier is probably pretty low – perhaps not much more than 2. This is because in present-day conditions something like a quarter or a third of any increase in income goes on direct and indirect taxes, and another fifth or so on imports. So even if only £10 of a £100 increase in income is saved, the first-round increase in the incomes of those who make consumer goods in Britain may not be £90, but only £40 or £50.

in them – spend a large proportion of their increased incomes on consumption the Multiplier will be high, i.e. the National Income will have to rise by a large amount to yield the extra quantity of savings needed to finance the higher level of investment. If, on the other hand, people *save* a large proportion of their extra income – i.e. if the Multiplier is low – the National Income will not have to rise very much before it is yielding enough extra savings to finance the new level of investment. In short, as the National Income rises, so will the total incomes of families and so, correspondingly, will *both* total consumption *and* total savings. National Income will rise to the point at which the total savings that families want to make out of their higher incomes are large enough to equal the new, higher level of investment that businessmen are undertaking. The smaller the fraction of any increase in income people save (i.e. the larger the Multiplier) the bigger will be the rise in the National Income before desired savings are again equal to desired investment, and equilibrium is restored.

It may be easier to see exactly what happens if we take a simple numerical example. As before, we denote the National Income by Y, consumption by C, investment by I, and saving by S.*

* For the sake of simplicity, we ignore real-world complications as far as possible. As before, we assume only two kinds of expenditure (consumption and investment), thus taking no account of the complications introduced by government transactions and foreign trade, changes in both of which can in practice affect the level of demand and employment in exactly the same way as changes in consumption and investment. Similarly, we ignore as far as possible the problem of time lags in the adjustment process, e.g. the fact that investment expenditures do not change immediately businessmen take decisions, but only after a series of time lags which differ for different types of investment. All these complications can be (and have been) built into systems of equations; and they must of course be taken explicit account of in the process of forecasting or attempting to influence economic developments (see Part Two of the present book). Here, however, they are better ignored.

Suppose that to start off with

$$
\begin{aligned}
\text{Actual Y} &= \pounds 100 \\
\text{Actual C} &= \pounds\ 80 \\
\text{Actual I} &= \pounds\ 20 \\
\text{Actual S} &= \pounds\ 20
\end{aligned}
$$

and that this is an equilibrium situation, in which business-men *want* to invest exactly the £20 that they are investing, and families have an average propensity to consume of 0·8, and therefore *want* to save the £20 that they are saving. Now suppose that businessmen start taking a more optimistic view of things, and decide to raise their investment from £20 to £25. In the first stage, this extra £5 of expenditure will raise the incomes of those who manufacture investment goods by £5, so that Y will become £105. Assuming that the marginal propensity to consume (like the average propensity to consume) is 0·8, people will want to spend £4 of this extra £5 income on consumption, and save £1 of it. So one will have, as a picture of what people are *trying* or *wanting* to do,

$$
\begin{aligned}
\text{Actual Y} &= \pounds 105 \\
\text{Desired C} &= \pounds\ 84 \\
\text{Desired (and} \\
\quad \text{actual) I} &= \pounds\ 25 \\
\text{Desired S} &= \pounds\ 21
\end{aligned}
$$

But some of these desires cannot be fulfilled. If actual investment is £25, then actual saving must, as a matter of arithmetic, be £25 too, and families will in practice be saving £25 and spending only £80 on consumption. What will have happened will be that the workers in the investment goods industries will, during this first stage of the adjustment process, have saved their extra income and not spent it – either because they have not yet made up their minds what to buy, or because there has not yet been time for the extra consumer goods to be manufactured or distributed to the shops. The actual position, in fact, will be this:

$$\text{Actual } Y = \pounds 105$$
$$\text{Actual } C = \pounds \ \ 80$$
$$\text{Actual } I = \pounds \ \ 25$$
$$\text{Actual } S = \pounds \ \ 25$$

As the gap between *desired* consumption and saving and *actual* consumption and saving indicates, this is not an equilibrium situation: there are further adjustments to come.

What happens in the second stage is that the workers in the investment goods industries succeed in spending the extra £4, because they have made up their minds what to spend their money on, or because the increased demand for consumer goods has resulted in an increase in the production of these goods. But by this time the Multiplier has come into operation: the very fact of an increase of £4 in consumers' expenditure has resulted in a rise of £4 in the income of those who manufacture the new consumer goods. So at this second stage the picture looks like this:

$$\text{Actual } Y = \pounds 109$$
$$\text{Actual } C = \pounds \ \ 84$$
$$\text{Actual } I = \pounds \ \ 25$$
$$\text{Actual } S = \pounds \ \ 25$$

But now that income has risen again, to £109, households are still spending less on consumption than they want to; they are actually spending £84, whereas out of a total income of £109 they *want* to spend (still assuming a propensity to consume of 0·8) £87 4s. Similarly, they *want* to save only £21 16s., whereas they are actually saving £25. So the situation is still out of equilibrium (though less so than it was before) and the still unsatisfied demand for consumer goods will result in a further rise in their production, and hence a further rise in the incomes of those engaged in making them.

And so the process goes on, via successive increases in

incomes and expenditure, until eventually households are once again actually consuming the same amount as they want to consume. The final picture will look like this:

$$\text{Actual Y} = £125$$
$$\text{Actual C} = £100$$
$$\text{Actual I} = £\ 25$$
$$\text{Actual S} = £\ 25$$

Out of the new level of income of £125 families are once again consuming the 80 per cent (£100) that they want to consume, and saving the 20 per cent (£25) that they want to save. Now that what they want to save is once again equal to what businessmen want to invest, savings and investment, and hence the whole economic system, are back in equilibrium. There is no tendency for any further changes to take place in any of the variables.

But why is the new equilibrium level of income £125, and not some other figure? Briefly, because we assumed a marginal propensity to consume of 0·8 (and therefore a marginal propensity to save of 0·2 or $\frac{1}{5}$). This means that the Multiplier was 5, and therefore that the eventual increase in total income would be 5 times the initial increase in investment expenditure, which was £5. Less technically, if businessmen want to invest £25 (and succeed in doing so) then equilibrium can only exist if families want to save £25 – and given a propensity to consume of 0·8, the only level of total incomes at which they will want to save £25 is £125.

So far we have been discussing what happens when the initial equilibrium is broken by an *increase* in investment, so that businessmen are investing *more* than households want to save. The same process operates in reverse when the equilibrium is broken by a *decrease* in investment, so that businessmen are investing *less* than households want to save. Suppose that in this case businessmen suddenly start taking a less optimistic view of the world, and reduce their expenditure on investment by £5. The first thing that happens is that those who build factories and make machinery find that their income has fallen by £5. The initial equilibrium situation, where

Actual Y   = £100
Actual C   = £ 80
Actual I   = £ 20
Actual S   = £ 20

therefore becomes

Actual Y   = £ 95
Actual C   = £ 80
Actual I   = £ 15
Actual S   = £ 15

whereas what individuals *want* to do in this situation can be represented as

Actual Y   = £ 95
Desired C   = £ 76
Desired (and
   actual) I = £ 15
Desired S   = £ 19

The actual situation, in fact, is now out of equilibrium, because households are actually spending £80 on consumption and saving only £15, whereas what they want to do out of a total income of £95 (still assuming a propensity to consume of 0·8) is spend £76 on consumption and save £19.

In the next stage consumption will fall to £76, because the workers in the investment goods industries, whose incomes have fallen by £5, will reduce their consumption by £4. But this £4 reduction in their consumption will lead to a £4 reduction in other people's income – and so the process will continue until a new equilibrium is established in which

Actual Y = £ 75
Actual C = £ 60
Actual I = £ 15
Actual S = £ 15

Total income has now fallen to a level at which the amount that households want to save is equal to what businessmen want to invest. As before, the extent of the change in total income is determined by the size of the Multiplier and the size of the initial change in investment expenditure – only this time the changes are downwards.

Following Keynes, we have been assuming throughout this analysis that it is changes – either increases or decreases – in *investment* which cause an existing equilibrium to be disturbed. This is in line with experience, which suggests that savings and consumption do not change very much of their own accord, and that it is changes in investment which represent the most unstable element in the economy. But if it was a change in savings – or, looked at the other way, in consumption – rather than in investment which upset the equilibrium the analysis would proceed in exactly the same way.

EMPLOYMENT

It only remains now to relate the changes in National Income we have been discussing to changes in employment. In our two examples we have seen how an initial relatively small increase (or decrease) in investment eventually resulted in a 25 per cent increase (or decrease) in National Income. A 25 per cent change in National Income does not necessarily involve a 25 per cent change in employment. The number of manual workers in a factory may change in fairly direct proportion to the level of output, but the number of administrative, clerical and technical staff may not vary nearly so much – many of them have much the same amount of work to do whether the factory is running flat out or only at half-cock. Therefore total employment tends to vary rather less than total output. But these are complications which do not substantially affect the analysis. The point is that the level of employment is determined by the level of National

Income, which is determined in turn by the levels of consumption and investment. One may start off with an equilibrium situation in which there is full employment – that is, in which consumption and investment are at such a level, and therefore National Income is at such a level, that everyone who wants to work is able to do so. But if there is then a fall in investment the National Income, and the volume of employment, will fall to a level at which savings are brought back into equilibrium with this lower level of investment. This may be an equilibrium at which there is a substantial amount of unemployment.*

Such an equilibrium, Keynes was saying, could persist for years – or indeed for ever. Unless investment (or consumption) rose and so, via the Multiplier, raised the National Income and the level of employment, heavy unemployment would just go on and on. Therefore if the government wanted full employment it should either persuade businessmen to increase their investment, or it should encourage a rise in consumption (for example by tax cuts) or – and here at last he justified his earlier advocacy of public works – it should itself undertake large-scale public investment expenditure. If it did, and judged the size of the Multiplier correctly, full employment would before long be restored. If it did not, unemployment would persist until investment or consumption eventually rose of their own accord – if they ever did.

In fact, if the government wanted full employment, it must itself accept responsibility for manipulating the level

* It is of course possible that one may start with a full-employment equilibrium and that investment may then *rise* rather than *fall*. In this case National Income will also rise (as in our example) but since there are no unemployed men to be drawn into employment the total amount of *output* cannot rise, and the rise in National Income will reflect a rise in prices – i.e. inflation. This was obviously not a situation with which Keynes was concerned in the 1930s, but it was relevant to what happened during and after the Second World War, and we shall be discussing it in Chapter 8.

of demand in a way that would ensure it. The fact that this might involve Budget deficits was not important.

SUMMARY

The *General Theory* is not an easy book to read, for although the basic message which emerges is clear, the underlying equilibrium analysis which forms the guts of the theory and the basis of the policy conclusions is not altogether easy to grasp; certainly many economists in the 1930s, brought up on classical ideas of how the economy worked, seemed to find it almost impossible to grasp. It may be helpful, therefore, to recapitulate briefly what this chapter has been saying.

First of all, said Keynes, it is a mistake to imagine that full employment is part of the natural order of things, and that departures from it are abnormal and temporary aberrations. On the contrary, full employment is only one of a number of possible situations. It is, in fact, a special case.

The level of employment in a particular country at a particular time depends on the level of output in that country, and this in turn depends on the amount of goods and services that individuals and institutions in that country purchase. All these purchases can be classified as either *consumption* (mainly done by individuals) or *investment* (mainly done by business firms). The level of employment, therefore, will depend on the level of consumption and the level of investment.

The level of consumption is the sum total of all the consumption expenditures of individuals or families, and families' consumption is determined mainly by their income. The level of investment is the sum total of all the investment expenditure of business firms, and this is determined by how profitable firms think investment would be – which is itself determined by their expectations of the return on a new investment on the one hand, and the cost of paying for it on the other. The level of output, then, and hence the level of employment, is determined by the total amount of money that families decide to spend on consumption, and firms decide to spend on investment. If it so happens that the sum total of families' consumption decisions and firms' investment decisions results in a level of output which it does not require the whole labour force to produce, then there will be unemployment. And until there is some change in either consumption or investment, this unemployment will continue.

This was the dramatic statement the book made – the earth-shaking message to the politicians and the public that if the unemployment problem was to be solved prevailing attitudes and policies must be radically changed. But Keynes had been issuing much the same advice for ten or fifteen years before the *General Theory* was published, and no one had taken much notice. The real importance of the book lay in the fact that the policy implications it contained were derived from a completely new and completely convincing theory of how the economy worked, and of how it was possible for there to be a permanent high level of unemployment.

This theory can best be understood by taking a close look at the statement that the total output of the economy is equal to consumption *plus* investment. This is true. But the total output of the economy is the same thing as the total income of the economy, and income *minus* consumption is saving. Therefore, by definition, saving must be equal to investment. But saving is determined by millions of individuals – it is the difference between their income and what they decide to consume. And investment is determined by tens of thousands of businessmen. Now why on earth should what millions of individuals decide to save just happen to be exactly equal to what tens of thousands of businessmen decide to invest?

The best way of answering this question is to assume that initially savings and investment are not merely *equal* (as by definition they always must be) but also *in equilibrium*, in the sense that the amount that businessmen *want* to invest is the same as the amount that families *want* to save. Now suppose that the equilibrium is broken – for example by businessmen deciding to increase their investment above the current level. In this case, said Keynes, the rise in investment will cause a rise in incomes which will cause a rise in consumption; this rise in consumption will in turn cause a further rise in other people's incomes, and so on. The exact extent of the rise in incomes will depend on the marginal propensity to consume – i.e. the proportion of their increased income that people spend on consumption. Eventually a new level of total output and incomes will be established, at which *desired* savings (as well as actual savings) will be exactly equal to the (higher) level of investment. There is nothing accidental about this. The reason why total incomes will increase to just that point where what families want to save is equal to the new level of investment is that the size of the increase in total incomes is governed by the proportion of their increased income that people consume – which is another way of saying the proportion of their income that they save. The smaller the proportion of each increment of income that they save, the further total incomes will have to rise until the total amount that they want to save is equal to the new and higher level of total investment that businesses are undertaking. But once it does reach that level a new equilibrium will be established, and there will be no further increase in the National Income.

The only trouble about this – to repeat the main point again – is that this level of National Income may not be sufficient to employ the whole of the labour force, in which case there will still be unemployment. In that case, Keynes concluded, it is the job of the government to raise the level of output and incomes further, by getting businessmen to invest more, or families to consume more, or simply by doing more public investment itself. By such actions any government is able to achieve, and maintain, full employment.

CHAPTER 5

THE ISSUES BETWEEN KEYNES
AND THE CLASSICS

NOT everyone recognizes a revolution when they see one, not even its principal victims. Orthodox economists continued to propound classical remedies after the publication of the *General Theory* in much the same way as Louis XVI had continued to sign royal decrees after the fall of the Bastille. Professor Pigou, for example, perhaps the most distinguished and authoritative exponent of classical economics* during the 1920s and 1930s, was not impressed by the book. 'Einstein actually did for Physics', he observed sourly, 'what Mr Keynes believes himself to have done for Economics. He developed a far-reaching generalization, under which Newton's results can be subsumed as a special case.'† Clearly the Professor did not take very seriously the possibility that the theories he had been propounding and embellishing all his life might have met the same fate as Newton's. Nevertheless, this is more or less what had happened.

Let us take a look at the way in which Keynes's theory differed from the classical theory, as represented by Pigou and others, and the implications of this difference for the economic policy of the 1920s and 1930s. In particular, let us look at the way in which Keynes, who said that full employment was not a normal and automatic feature of economic life, demolished the arguments of the classics, who said that it was.

---

*i.e. the economics originated by Adam Smith and Ricardo, and subsequently developed by Mill, Marshall and many others.

† *Economica*, May 1936.

ARE SAVINGS AUTOMATICALLY INVESTED?

As we have seen, the classical economists, though they did not use the same language as Keynes, had nevertheless been perfectly aware of one important logical point – that if there is to be full employment, then the whole of the output that the economy is capable of producing, when running at full stretch, has to find a buyer. Looking at it from the income side, the whole of the income generated by a fully employed economy must be spent either on consumption or on investment; or, more precisely, all savings (i.e. that part of total income which is not spent on consumption) must be invested. But of course, said the classics: this is exactly what happens. And so indeed it did – in the early nineteenth century, when the classical theory was being developed. At that time savings consisted largely of the profits which farmers, merchants and manufacturers had left over after providing for themselves and their families. These profits were usually all ploughed back into the business in order to expand it – i.e. savings were automatically invested. Indeed saving and investment, being done by the same person, were hardly distinguished as two separate activities. This conviction that savings will automatically be invested is to be found most strongly in the work of Ricardo and his immediate successors, and there is no reason to doubt that what they were saying was substantially true, at the time they said it. And precisely because it was true that at full employment levels of output everything that was saved was automatically invested, full employment remained (apart from the occasional interruptions of the trade cycle) a permanent feature of the economy. The difference between Keynes and the classical economists was that while they thought of this as the normal, universal state of affairs, he saw it as a special case.

But although the earlier classical economists were content, on the whole, simply to assert that savings were automatically invested, their successors went beyond this and argued that there were certain forces at work in the economy which made it *inevitable* that at full employment levels of output all savings would be invested.* They had to do this because as the nineteenth century wore on a marked distinction began to develop between those who did the investing and those who did the saving. The small manufacturer or trader who could only expand his business out of the savings he made himself became less typical. Instead, there began to emerge bigger firms, owned not by those who managed them but by large numbers of shareholders who in practice had little or no say in the firm's decisions. The managers decided how much the firm should invest, and the increasingly prosperous middle- and even working-classes decided how much they were going to save. The close link of earlier days between savings and investment had been broken: no longer were they essentially the same activity carried out by the same person – they were now different activities, often carried out by different people for different reasons.†

---

*The occasional bouts of unemployment associated with the downswing of the trade cycle were dismissed, in the words of John Stuart Mill, as a 'temporary derangement of markets', which did not alter the fact that there were certain forces at work which ensured that full employment was the normal state of affairs.

†This is very far from saying that *all* investment is nowadays done by business firms and *all* saving done by families; the situation is much more complex than that. In Britain in 1965, for example, total investment (and therefore total saving) was roughly £6,500 million (out of a Gross Domestic Product of a little over £30,000 million). About £2,700 million of this investment was done by private businesses in the company sector; and personal savings amounted to roughly £2,000 million. But this does not mean that business firms financed most of their investment by borrowing £2,000 million from the personal sector: on the contrary, business *saving*, i.e. retained profits, amounted to over £3,000 million – *more than* its own investment. (This was what happened in the aggregate; for individual firms experience was enormously varied, with some firms investing very much more than they could finance out of their own retained

There did not seem to be any obvious reason why the amount that thousands of managers decided to invest should happen to be the same as millions of people decided to save. But the later classical economists insisted that although the reason for this magical-seeming equality might not be obvious, it was nevertheless there. Savings and investment were brought into balance, they said, by changes in the rate of interest.

Their argument, if put rather crudely and explicitly, would go somewhat as follows. Suppose that one starts with an equilibrium situation, in which the economy is fully employed and the amount people are saving is just equal to the amount that businessmen are investing. Now suppose that for some reason people decide to save a larger proportion of their income, or that businessmen decide to reduce their investment. Will this not mean that some savings are unable to find an outlet in investment? And will this excess

---

profits, and others saving more than they themselves invested.) The excess of saving (by individuals and businesses taken together) over their own investment went to the public sector: investment by government and nationalized industries was about £2,800 million, whereas their savings were well under £2,000 million. Indeed, the complications do not end there, since the personal sector includes one-man businesses and partnerships which, just like their nineteenth-century counterparts, automatically plough the bulk of their profits back into the business, and are therefore credited with investment as well as saving: in the National Income accounts the personal sector is credited with investment averaging about £1,000 million a year.

But none of this affects the basic point, which is that there is no reason to suppose that nowadays (in contrast, on the whole, to the position in Ricardo's time) the sum total of all the decisions to invest which are made in the economy will happen to be the same as the sum total of all the decisions to save which are made in the economy. For simplicity of exposition in the text the complex pattern of investment and saving which actually exists is categorized as 'managers' or 'businesses' investing and 'people' or 'families' saving.

of savings over investment not lead to a fall in output and employment – exactly as Malthus had feared? No, said the classical economists. If there is a tendency for savings to exceed investment – i.e. a tendency for the *supply* of 'loanable funds' to exceed the *demand* for loanable funds – then the rate of interest will fall. And it will fall until savings and investment are brought back into balance. For the rate of interest is the price of these loanable funds – the price that one pays to borrow them, or receives if one lends them. If the supply of these funds is greater than the demand for them the same thing happens as in the case of boots or cabbages or anything else for which supply exceeds demand: the price, or rate of interest, falls.

This fall in the rate of interest has a double effect. It stimulates investment, because some projects that were not profitable before will become so now that money can be borrowed more cheaply; and it will tend to discourage saving, since the return on savings will now have fallen. Therefore any tendency for the savings of a fully employed economy to exceed investment will result in a fall in the rate of interest sufficient to bring savings and investment back into balance, either by reducing savings, or by increasing investment, or both. In fact, the rate of interest is a mechanism which will automatically ensure that whatever the level of savings generated by a fully employed economy, these savings will be invested.

The same point can be made in another way. Assume again an equilibrium position, in which the economy is fully employed and the savings being made by people are just equal to the investment being done by businessmen. What happens if people decide to reduce their consumption? Will this not result in a fall in output and employment? No, said the classics. A fall in consumption entails a rise in saving, and a rise in saving – i.e. an increase in the supply of loanable funds – will lead to a fall in interest rates and thus to a rise in investment. In fact any reduction in consumption will result in an exactly equal increase in investment; and since it is consumption and investment, taken together, which constitute the National Income this, and hence the level of employment, will be unaffected. In the same way, any fall in investment will be offset by a corresponding rise in consumption, and the National Income will remain unchanged.

In short, said the classics, full employment is the normal state of affairs. Full employment exists provided that all the savings generated by a fully employed economy are invested, and the rate of interest is a mechanism which ensures that this will happen. Just as a fall in the water level of a cistern will, by opening a valve, set in motion forces which will restore the water level, so any departure of the economy from full employment will, by its effects on the rate of interest, set in motion forces which will restore full employment.

KEYNES'S VIEW

This theory is simple, elegant and extremely plausible. Unfortunately, said Keynes, it is also complete nonsense. The main reason why it is nonsense is that it fails to see that what people *want* to save, and what they actually *do* save, are in certain circumstances quite different things. Let us take another look at the example we have just given, of an equilibrium full employment situation, in which what families want to save (and are saving) is exactly the same as what businessmen want to invest (and are investing); and let us assume that people are saving (and businessmen are investing) 20 per cent of the National Income. Families then decide, for some reason, to increase their savings to 25 per cent of their incomes. The classical theory assumed that these extra savings would actually be forthcoming, and would force down the rate of interest, thus leading to a corresponding increase in investment. But in practice, said Keynes, these extra savings would *not* be forthcoming. For in order to increase their savings people would have to reduce their consumption, and this would result in a fall in the incomes of those who made consumer goods. They in turn would reduce their expenditure, with further repercussions on other people's incomes – and so the process would go on, in accordance with the Multiplier analysis we discussed in Chapter 4. If people still stick to their new decision to save 25 per cent of their incomes, the National Income will fall (assuming that investment remains unchanged) to four fifths of its former level – for this will be the only level of income at which what families want to save is equal to what businessmen want to invest. To put this into numerical form, the situation was

$$\text{Actual } Y = £100$$
$$\text{Actual } C = £\ 80$$
$$\text{Actual } I = £\ 20$$
$$\text{Actual } S = £\ 20$$

People were content with a situation in which they were saving 20 per cent of their incomes. They then decide to save 25 per cent of their incomes. But this leads to successive falls in consumption and income, until a new equilibrium is established in which

$$\text{Actual } Y = £\ 80$$
$$\text{Actual } C = £\ 60$$
$$\text{Actual } I = £\ 20$$
$$\text{Actual } S = £\ 20$$

It is true that people have achieved their ambition of saving 25 per cent of their income. But this has happened not because their savings have gone up, but because their income has gone down. The *amount* they save is the same as before; their income has fallen by 20 per cent. This 20 per cent fall in the National Income will have been accompanied by a severe fall in employment – so that a new equilibrium has been established in which there is substantial unemployment.

In practice, said Keynes, the final position will probably be even worse than this, for against a background of falling income it is unlikely that investment will be sustained at its former level. Supposing it falls by a quarter (and that individuals still persist in their new desire to save 25 per cent of their incomes) the final position will look like this:

$$\text{Actual Y} = £60$$
$$\text{Actual C} = £45$$
$$\text{Actual I} = £15$$
$$\text{Actual S} = £15$$

Once again people have succeeded in saving 25 per cent of their incomes, but in the meantime the National Income has fallen by a catastrophic 40 per cent, and unemployment has probably risen to 20 or 25 per cent of the labour force – and the economy will remain in this situation until either consumption or investment starts to rise again.

So, Keynes concluded, classical theory provided a wholly misleading picture of how the economy reacted to an attempt to increase saving, or to reduce investment. Such attempts did not set in motion changes in interest rates which automatically preserved full employment. On the contrary, they led to falling incomes and rising unemployment.

Not only did Keynes disagree with this major element of classical theory; he also disagreed on the less important question of what causes interest rates to change, and what the effects of these changes are. It was true, he said, that interest rates do fall during the down-swing of the trade cycle, but this is not because the supply of loanable funds exceeds the demand for them. It is chiefly because of changes in liquidity preference:* as the national income falls, so does the need for money to satisfy the transactions motive – i.e. the amount

* For discussion of liquidity preference see pages 82 to 85.

of money needed for everyday purchases. This means that there is a fall in liquidity preference, i.e. less desire to hold money in the form of cash. As a result (assuming the supply of money to be unchanged) people will buy more government bonds, and this will cause bond prices to rise, and hence interest rates to fall. However, this fall in interest rates will not necessarily result in much of a rise in investment. On the basis of past experience people do not expect interest rates to fall below about 2 per cent, and for this very reason they do not fall below 2 per cent, even if the government increases the quantity of money. For at interest rates as low as this no one is going to buy government bonds, so that any increase in the supply of money is offset by an increase in liquidity preference, and there is no further fall in interest rates. And at a time when the business outlook is bleak and existing capacity under-utilized even the ability to borrow money at 2 per cent may not tempt businessmen to increase their investment. Nor will a fall in interest rates down to a level of 2 per cent or so result in a fall in saving and a rise in consumption, as the classics said (on the grounds that since there is now less return to be had on savings, people will spend their money instead). People's saving probably *will* fall, but not because of a fall in interest rates; their saving will fall, as will their consumption, because their incomes fall.

In brief, then, Keynes convincingly demonstrated that a desire on the part of families to save more than businesses were investing would not result, via a fall in interest rates, in a rise in investment and fall in saving which left the level of output and employment unchanged. On the contrary, it would lead to lower incomes and consumption, probably lower investment and saving, and certainly lower output and employment. And he added for good measure that even if interest rates did fall, the cause would be different from that given by the classics, and the effect very much less powerful.

FALLING WAGES AND RISING EMPLOYMENT

The discussion in the last few pages has dealt with the really crucial difference between the Keynesian and classical theories. But there was another aspect of the classical system which, though of rather less theoretical importance than the savings-investment analysis, assumed even greater significance during the inter-war period. This was the classical belief that quite apart from the flexibility of interest rates, the flexibility of wage rates would also operate to ensure permanent full employment. If there were any lapse from full employment, the story went, competition for jobs among the unemployed workers would drive wage rates down, and at lower wage rates more men would be employed. If by any chance unemployment persisted this could only be because something (such as trade union bargaining power) was preventing the necessary fall in wage rates. If employment was to be increased, the unions must agree to wage reductions.

This doctrine, which was the progeny of the union of the Law of Diminishing Returns and the Theory of Marginal Productivity (Chapter 2), and was the more or less explicit conclusion of the writings of such eminent economists as Pigou and Robbins (Chapter 3), became one of the more celebrated casualties left in the wake of the *General Theory*. This is the more remarkable, because looking back on the controversy from the 1960s one is inclined to feel that in his assault on this part of the entrenched theory Keynes unduly handicapped himself. For he started off by agreeing that both the Law of Diminishing Returns and the Theory of Marginal Productivity operated in the circumstances he was concerned with. That is to say, he agreed that as output and employment increase in the short run, output will increase less than employment, so that each additional man will produce less than the previous man, and average output per man will therefore fall.* And he also agreed that it was, roughly speaking, true that the last man taken on would be paid only the value of the output he produced, and that since competition operates reasonably effectively, and one worker is much the same as another, this means that all workers would be paid about the same amount as the last worker taken on.

Now if one agrees with both these propositions one must also, in logic, agree that if there is to be an increase in employment there must be a fall in average wages. Keynes's logic was generally pretty strong, and he did agree. But, he said, the classics had got it the *wrong way round*. One could not reduce wage rates and *as a result* get a rise in employment. The truth was exactly the opposite. One had to get a rise in employment first; this would result in a fall in average wages.

REAL AND MONEY WAGES†

Keynes's argument turned on two points: the fact that consumption is determined by income; and the difference between *money* wages and *real* wages. The first of these points was covered in the last chapter; the second is probably familiar to the modern reader, but should perhaps be briefly

*Nowadays one is more inclined to believe the opposite – that as output and employment increase in the short run (from an initial position in which unemployment is 10 or 15 per cent, which is what economists in the 1920s and 1930s had in mind) output will increase *more* than employment, and average output per man (i.e. productivity) will rise. This is chiefly because in a complex and capital-intensive economy the proportion of overhead labour (administrative, clerical and technical workers) tends to be relatively high, and in the short run the amount of overhead labour needed is much the same whatever the level of output. Had Keynes accepted this his task would have been easier, though his argument would have been fundamentally the same.

†Throughout this section (except where otherwise stated) we are talking about wages *per head* – i.e. the average wage, not the sum total of wages paid out.

explained. *Real* wages represent the amount of goods a man can buy with his pay-packet. Whatever happens to the amount of money in his pay-packet, he will only have had an increase in real wages if he can buy *more* goods than before. In other words, an increase in *money* wages is only an increase in *real* wages if prices stay unchanged, so that the extra money really buys something. A 10 per cent rise in money wages is a 10 per cent rise in real wages if prices stay the same; but if prices rise by 4 per cent real wages only rise by 6 per cent; and if prices rise by 10 per cent real wages are unchanged. Similarly, a 10 per cent fall in money wages will only be a 10 per cent fall in real wages if prices do not change; if prices fall by 10 per cent as well, real wages will not have fallen at all. According to Keynes, the classics had got into trouble over this bit of theory chiefly because they had failed to understand this distinction between money wages and real wages.

It is probably true, said Keynes, that if wages are cut in one firm or industry there will be a rise in employment of the workers concerned. Suppose that the money wages of shoemakers are cut by 20 per cent, for example, and that this leads (as is quite likely, given the way businessmen seem to price their products) to a 20 per cent reduction in the price of shoes. The incomes of everybody else in the economy will hardly be affected at all by the fall in the amount shoemakers can afford to spend on consumption, and now that shoes are 20 per cent cheaper the country will buy more shoes; employment of shoemakers will rise. The corollary of this is that there will have been a fall in the *real* wages of shoemakers as well as in their *money* wages, for all prices (apart from shoes) will have stayed the same, while shoemakers' money wages have fallen by 20 per cent. So the rise in employment of shoemakers has been accompanied by a fall in their real wages – as both Keynes and the classics agreed was necessary.

But the classics thought that what was true of shoemakers was true of everyone else; Keynes did not. What is true of the part, he said, is not necessarily true of the whole. If *everybody's* money wages are cut by 20 per cent, there is no reason to expect a rise in employment. For if, as in the example just given, a 20 per cent reduction in people's money wages leads to a 20 per cent fall in the price of what they produce, then if everybody's wages are cut by 20 per cent, all prices will be reduced by 20 per cent. In other words, real wages will be unchanged. And if real wages are unchanged then, according to the laws of the classical economists' own theory, employment must be unchanged as well. Or, to look at it simply in terms of common sense, if real wages are unchanged there can be no reason to expect any change in the actual amount families spend on consumption, or businessmen spend on investment. In fact there will be no change in output and therefore no change in employment either.* There will not have been any real changes in the economy; all that will have happened is that everybody's income, in money terms, is 20 per cent less than it used to be, so that someone who used to earn £20 a week now earns £16; and all prices will be 20 per cent less than they used to be – so that £16 will buy exactly the same amount now as £20 used to.

This, of course, is the simplest possible case and, according to Keynes, the most favourable one; in practice what happens will be much more complex and probably less desirable. Keynes discussed many of the things which might or might not happen in the *General Theory*, and indeed subsequently got involved in a long series of arguments about it with Pigou,

* In practice there would be some rise in output and employment because one kind of demand would rise – demand for exports; for, assuming a fixed exchange rate, these would now be 20 per cent cheaper to foreign buyers. However for present purposes we can ignore this complication.

which lasted into the 1940s. However we need not concern ourselves with the details. The main point, as Keynes saw it, was that people's consumption depends on their incomes, and if their incomes are cut they will have to reduce their consumption. While it is possible, as in the example above, that prices will fall so much that even though they are earning and spending less money than before people are still managing to buy the same amount of stuff, it is more likely that prices will not fall as much as money wages, and that there will therefore be a reduction in both *real* wages and *real* consumption. Or, to put the same point in a different way, it is likely that the total of non-wage incomes will fall less than the total of wages, so that there is a re-distribution of the National Income from wage-earners to those who receive incomes from dividends, interest and rent. Because this latter category of people tends to have a lower propensity to consume than wage-earners, this shift will result in a fall in consumption.

However one looks at it, in fact, a general cut in money wages, while it might possibly leave output and employment unchanged, is more likely to lead to some reduction in real wages and consumption and therefore, through the workings of the Multiplier, to some further fall in demand, output and employment. So at best, Keynes concluded, the classical remedy of wage cuts would leave unemployment unchanged, because reductions in money wages might be offset by reductions in prices, so that real wages stayed the same; and if real wages stay the same even the classical theory agrees there will be no increase in employment – as does Keynes's theory, though for different reasons. But at worst the classical remedy would result not in a *rise* but in a *fall* in employment, because the thing that determines output and employment is effective demand, and a fall in real wages would lead to a fall in consumption, which is the main element in effective demand. Just how far employment will fall depends upon the size of the Multiplier, and on whether falling consumption also leads to a fall in investment.

This line of argument, it is only fair to say, has provoked a counter-attack from adherents of the classical tradition. The most specific objection to this part of Keynes's analysis came originally from Pigou, and in more recent years has been taken up and developed by a group of economists in America sometimes known as the 'Chicago School'.* What Keynes had overlooked, it was argued, was the 'wealth effect' of a reduction in money wages. As money wages fell, prices would fall as well, and as prices fell the real value of a given sum of money would increase: £1,000 would buy more after prices had fallen than it had before. As a result, wealthy people with large stocks of money would find themselves wealthier still (in terms of what their money could buy) and would increase

* The Chicago School's attack on Keynes has broadened out beyond this particular point: it comes close to arguing that full employment depends not on effective demand (as determined by consumption and investment expenditures) but on the quantity of money created by the banking system (and non-banking institutions such as finance houses). This argument seems to be rather confused. Changes in the quantity of money can certainly affect consumption and investment, and affect them in more ways than Keynes bothered to discuss in detail. A credit squeeze in which the commercial banks are forced by pressure on their own cash reserves to restrict their customers' overdrafts will probably affect both consumers' expenditure and the investment expenditure of small firms which rely on bank credit: indeed this sheer unavailability of bank credit may be a more important influence in restricting investment than the (high) rate of interest to which Keynes perhaps devoted a disproportionate amount of attention. But none of this affects Keynes's basic argument that the level of employment depends on the level of effective demand, which in turn depends on consumption and investment (and, in the real world, exports and government expenditure). Just how, in the opinion of the Chicago economists, changes in the quantity of money are supposed to affect the economy except through the determinants of effective demand which Keynes discussed, is rather obscure. For this reason, perhaps, the number of economists who are convinced by the writings of the Chicago School is rather small.

their consumption. This increase in consumption would raise effective demand enough to bring the economy back to full employment.

In its extreme form, which purports to demonstrate that the economy really does return to full employment equilibrium of its own accord provided that wages and prices are flexible downwards, this argument is very difficult to take seriously. No one has ever succeeded in providing any empirical evidence – or indeed any sound theoretical reason – for supposing that the 'wealth effect' will not only be powerful enough to offset the fall in effective demand which will follow a fall in real wages, but will engender just enough expansion to bring the economy back to full employment. Indeed even in its weaker form – that the 'wealth effect' goes some way to offset the depressing effect on consumption of a fall in real wages – the argument is suspect, since it is not at all clear that an increase in the real value of their wealth will induce people to raise their consumption to any significant extent.

The 'wealth effect' criticism of this part of Keynes's analysis does not, therefore, seem to hold a great deal of water. Nevertheless, there is one remaining puzzle which needs to be resolved. As we have seen, Keynes agreed with the classics (unnecessarily, one would now tend to say) that if the economy is to move from 10 per cent unemployment to full employment there must be a reduction in average real wages, i.e. in the amount the average worker can buy with his wages. Yet here he is saying that a reduction in real wages either cannot be brought about (because prices fall as much as money wages) or, if it can be brought about, will lead not to a rise but to a fall in employment. How can this apparent inconsistency be explained?

The answer is that Keynes was demanding from his fellow-economists much the same sort of mental somersault that Copernicus had demanded from his fellow-scientists. The evidence, said Copernicus to his contemporaries, is consistent with your theory that the sun goes round the earth, and from this theory you have made many deductions. But the same evidence is also consistent with another theory – that the earth goes round the sun. This theory is correct, and your deductions are wrong. Similarly, according to Keynes, the agreed evidence of an association between rising employment and falling real wage rates was consistent with the classical theory that it was real wages which determined the level of employment – and from this theory they deduced that one must first reduce real wages, and that this would result in a rise in employment. But the same evidence, said Keynes, is also consistent with the theory that it is the level of employment which determines real wages. This theory is correct, and therefore the classical economists' deduction is wrong; the right deduction is that one should first increase the level of employment, and that this will result in a fall in real wages.

We have already seen how Keynes proposed that the level of employment should be increased: businessmen should be persuaded to spend more on investment, or families should be encouraged, for example by tax cuts, to spend more on consumption, or the government itself should increase its own expenditure, for example on public investment. If the Law of Diminishing Returns and the Theory of Marginal Productivity were both true and both in operation (as Keynes agreed with the classics they were) then this increase in employment would result in a fall in real wages, for as employment increased, output would increase less than proportionately and costs per unit of output would therefore rise. Rising costs would lead to rising prices and therefore, since money wages would not rise much if at all, to falling real wages.* One will therefore end up with full employment and

---

* Of course the fall in real wages (i.e. real wages per head of those in employment) is outweighed by the rise in the number of wage-earners in employment, which is why total consumption rises.

lower real wages, which is what the classics were trying to achieve. But one has only ended up here because one raised employment first; lower real wages followed. If one took the classical economists' advice one would probably succeed in reducing real wages (though not as much as they expected, because of the fall in prices) but what would follow would be lower employment and not higher employment (though of course this involves the Law of Diminishing Returns and the Theory of Marginal Productivity operating differently from the way the classical economists imagined).

CLASSICAL THEORY AS A SPECIAL CASE

It was not by accident that Keynes described his theory as a 'general' theory.* In his view it provided an account of how the level of employment was determined which could be applied with few qualifications to any economy, regardless of its form of organization or stage of development.† Classical theory, on the other hand, he thought relevant only to the special case of an economy in which everything that was saved at a full employment level of income was automatically invested. Where this particular condition was met he considered that some of the classical analysis was perfectly correct: he had no quarrel, for example, with the classical analysis of how the price of a particular product or the payment of a particular factor of production is determined; and therefore of what determines the distribution of the National Income between wages, profits and rents. The classical economists' main mistake, according to Keynes, lay in assum-

* The fact that he actually described it not as *a* general theory but as *the* general theory is a different point; Keynes never suffered from false modesty.

† Provided it was not so undeveloped that supply rather than demand was the limiting factor. The reasons why Keynesian theory is not so relevant to the less developed countries are discussed in Explanatory Note 5, page 259.

ing, and subsequently purporting to prove, that the special case was the normal case. This gave them a totally false conception of how the twentieth-century economy worked, and led them to offer advice to the government which was the exact opposite of what was needed.

When it becomes clear that a theory everyone had assumed to be of universal validity in fact only applies in particular conditions which have now passed away, it is obvious that a good many accepted notions will have to be revised. But the implications of substituting Keynesian for classical theory were particularly far-reaching; it was not only the techniques and advice of economists that now needed to be changed; a whole range of political and moral attitudes had become obsolete as well. Three of the changes called for are perhaps worth mentioning here.

SAVING AS A VICE

First, there is the question of the desirability of saving or, as many a Victorian good book put it, the virtues of thrift. From the beginning of time it has been an axiom of organized society that sensible people will put aside a bit of their current income in the form of savings; the Bible is full of parables driving the point home, and even today there are numerous children's books in which innocent-seeming stories about ants and grasshoppers are loaded with a deeper meaning. And if it is sensible for an individual to save, it must also be sensible for a nation to save; as Adam Smith put it, 'What is prudence in the conduct of every private family can scarce be folly in that of a great kingdom.' Now this attitude is right and proper in the case of a developing country, like nine-teenth-century Britain – or twentieth-century India – in which the opportunities for investment are so great that any savings which can be made are automatically swallowed up by businessmen's desire for more capital. In this kind of economy, in which incomes and therefore savings tend to be low, a shortage of savings is the great constraint on investment; people are consuming too much of the National Income, leaving too few resources available for investment. If only people saved more, more could be invested – and more investment would mean more factories and machinery to exploit new techniques, and therefore a faster rise in productivity and the standard of living. The more people save the better. Of course more saving means lower consumption today, but by promoting a faster growth rate it will lead to much higher incomes and consumption tomorrow.

But, as Keynes argued, as the economy becomes more developed, and the stock of capital grows bigger, opportunities for new investment may be harder to discern. There are already so many factories and pieces of machinery about that there seems no point in providing more, particularly if new products and processes are slow in coming forward. At the same time, because incomes are higher than they used to be, people may find it difficult to think of things to spend their money on, and so decide to save a larger proportion of their income. In fact Keynes seems to have much exaggerated the extent to which the growth and development of an economy over a long period reduces the incentive to invest and the propensity to consume. But it remains true in the short run that businessmen may reduce investment because of idle capacity, or families may try and save more because of the uncertainty of the outlook, and that the result of either act may be a rise in unemployment: this is precisely what happened in the 1930s. In the latter case (even, in a sense, in the former) it is perfectly legitimate to argue that this unemployment is the result of people trying to save too much. If they had been less anxious to save, their *actual* savings (as well as their incomes and consumption) would have been higher than they are now.* In this situation thrift is not a

* See the numerical examples on pages 112–13.

virtue; it is a vice.* It is not hard to see that a theory which carries a message like this is going to meet a good deal of resistance.

PUBLIC EXPENDITURE AS A VIRTUE

A second attitude which needed changing in the light of the *General Theory* was the attitude to public expenditure. In a developing economy in which a shortage of savings is the main constraint, public investment competes directly with private investment for scarce resources. Of course even the Victorians recognized that some public investment was necessary: roads, harbours and even a few schools and hospitals were necessary to enable private enterprise to operate. But if the government or local authorities invested in public libraries or swimming baths they were using up savings that would otherwise have been profitably invested in industry. In the interests of rising productivity and a rising standard of living public investment must therefore be kept to a minimum. Again, this attitude is logical provided the classical economists' special case, in which all savings are automatically invested, obtains. But if, at a full employment level of income, desired savings exceed desired investment, public investment is no longer an obviously bad thing; it may be a good thing. For in this situation one can maintain full employment just as well by increasing public investment or public current expenditure on goods and services as by increasing private investment or private consumption. Indeed if a society's provision of social services has fallen behind its provision of the goods and services that are bought by indi-

---

*This paradox had been intuitively grasped long before: as Keynes himself noted, a man called Bernard Mandeville had argued this in an allegorical poem called *The Fable of the Bees* in the early eighteenth century. Mandeville's book was convicted as a 'nuisance' by the Grand Jury of Middlesex in 1723.

viduals (e.g. if there are plenty of television sets but too few teachers or hospitals) an increase in public expenditure might be the best way to solve an incipient or actual unemployment problem.

GOVERNMENT INTERVENTION AS THE ULTIMATE EVIL

Finally, and most radically of all, the main message of the *General Theory* was that full employment could only be achieved provided the government was prepared to intervene – perhaps drastically and continuously – in the free working of the economy. To many people in the 1930s, casting an apprehensive eye on Stalin's Russia and Hitler's Germany, this proposition was very alarming. There was something ironic about this reaction: Keynes himself believed in a capitalist rather than a socialist society; and it has been argued that the only thing which saved Western countries from communist or fascist dictatorships was the *General Theory*. Nevertheless, Keynesian theory did demand a revolutionary change in the relationship between the government and the economy. Some people found this change very difficult to accept. In the United States, as we shall see in Chapter 11, effective acceptance of Keynes is very recent; even in Britain, where the battle was won some time ago, there are still sporadic outbreaks of guerrilla warfare.

CHAPTER 6

THE TWENTIES AND THIRTIES IN THE LIGHT OF KEYNES

In Chapter 3 we traced some of the history of the 1920s and 1930s, noting in particular the contemporary comments of a number of economists and politicians. It may be appropriate to round off the first half of this book by looking again at some aspects of the twenties and thirties in the light of Keynes's analysis. This will serve both to give a more precise indication of what went wrong during the inter-war years, and to provide an introduction to the kind of approach that successive governments have adopted towards the economy since the Second World War.

The most obvious question about the inter-war period was simply why there was so much more unemployment than there had ever been before. Why was the present so different from the past? During the century before 1914 unemployment in Britain probably averaged no more than 3 or 4 per cent; between 1919 and 1939 it averaged 13 per cent. The world economy as a whole had progressed quite happily throughout the nineteenth and early twentieth centuries – lurching about a bit from time to time, yet clearly on an upward trend; but at the end of the 1920s it plunged into a slump incomparably worse than any that had occurred before, and one which looked like going on for ever. What was the cause of this heavy and seemingly endless unemployment? According to Keynes, unemployment was a symptom of too low a level of effective demand. But this merely pushes the question one stage further back. Why should there have been too little effective demand in the 1920s and 1930s when presumably there had always been enough before?

To answer this question properly we need to break effective

demand down into a few more categories than we have done up till now. In our analysis so far we have broken down total demand (or total expenditure) into only two components, consumption and investment, since these were all that were necessary to demonstrate the essence of Keynes's argument. But we now need to take specific account of two other categories of demand – exports, and government expenditure.* These are both components of effective demand in exactly the same way as consumption or investment. Exports represent a purchase by someone (in this case a foreigner) of goods or services produced in Britain; so a fall in exports has exactly the same adverse effect on incomes, output and employment as a fall in consumption or investment. The same is true of government expenditure.

PRODUCTIVE POTENTIAL

But before we look in detail at the demand side, let us spend a moment on the supply side. The amount that a country can produce when its labour force is fully employed – let us call it the country's *productive potential* – depends on two factors. The first is the size of the working population – i.e. the number of people either in employment or looking for employment. The second is the average level of productivity, or output per head of working population. The bigger the working population and the higher the level of productivity the larger will be the economy's productive potential. Now in spite of the vast numbers killed and disabled during the war, Britain's working population was bigger in 1920 than it had been in 1914, chiefly because of a big wartime rise in the employment of

---

* Technically, government (central and local) current expenditure on goods and services. Government expenditure on transfer payments (such as pensions or family allowances) is not included here, since it is already allowed for under consumption; and capital expenditure by the government or other public bodies is included in investment.

women and older men. There was also some rise in productivity during the war years – output per man was perhaps 5–10 per cent higher during the early 1920s than it had been 10 years before. Taking these two factors – the rise in working population and the rise in productivity – together, one would estimate that in the early post-war period Britain's productive potential may have been some 10–15 per cent higher than it had been before the war, so that with full employment the economy would be producing 10–15 per cent more than before the war. The corollary of this was that if unemployment in the post-war period were to be as low as it had been in the years immediately before the war (when it averaged about 3 per cent) output, and hence effective demand, would have to be 10–15 per cent higher.

INADEQUATE DEMAND

Unfortunately, so far from being 10–15 per cent higher, demand was lower. The main villain was exports. As we saw in Chapter 3, Britain lost export markets during the First World War to other countries less involved in the fighting. Many of these markets were never recaptured, even when the economy moved off a war footing and industrial capacity again became available to meet export orders, because the rapid rise in British incomes and prices during the war had left many of our exports uncompetitive. As a result, exports of goods in the early 1920s were running at only about two thirds of the pre-war level; and since before the war exports had accounted for a fifth of the National Income the effect on employment was serious. Lack of competitiveness also affected employment, though to a much smaller extent, through the other side of the trade account: some manufactured imports were now higher than they would otherwise have been, thus displacing some domestic production.

A more favourable factor was government expenditure.

As one would expect, this had risen very sharply indeed during the war, and although it fell away again afterwards it remained at a higher level than before the war. Unfortunately, however, the beneficial effects on employment of this rise in government expenditure were swamped by government policy on the other side of the balance sheet, which was one of the factors responsible for keeping consumption in the early 1920s down to the pre-war level. As we saw in Chapter 3, in order to pay for war expenditure the government had increased taxation very sharply, but this did not nearly fill the gap, and there was also a big rise in government borrowing. After the war the government's expenditure fell off rapidly and so, correspondingly, did the need for taxation to pay for it. But orthodox financial practice required that each year there should be a Budget surplus so that some part of the money the government had borrowed during the war could be paid back. Therefore, it was argued, taxation must not be reduced as much as government expenditure, because a high level of taxation was still needed to finance these repayments. As a result the standard rate of income tax, which had stood at 1s. 2d. in the £ at the outbreak of war in 1914, remained at the peak wartime figure of 6s. until 1922, and only came down to 4s. in 1925.

The effects of a high rate of income tax on effective demand, and in particular on consumption, depend on what the government does with the tax revenue it collects. If it uses it to raise old age pensions or employ more primary school teachers consumption will probably rise, because the propensity to consume of these people is almost certainly higher than the propensity to consume of the people (roughly speaking the richer half of the community) who pay the great bulk of income tax. But to the extent that the government uses the proceeds of a high rate of income tax to redeem the National Debt, as it did in the early 1920s, the effect on consumption is almost certain to be adverse. Those who benefit from repayments of government debt are merely receiving one kind of asset (cash) in exchange for another (government securities); there is no particular reason why their expenditure on consumption should rise. Those from whom the money has come, on the other hand – the income tax payers – although the richer half of the community, will nevertheless in a great many cases have had to cut their consumption in order to pay the extra tax. There is no doubt that the government's policy of keeping taxes up in order to pay off some of the National Debt had a depressing effect on consumption in the early 1920s.

But probably the most important factor behind the stagnation of consumption in the early 1920s was not that because of higher taxes (or, perhaps, greater inequality in the distribution of income) people were spending less of a given income on consumption. It was simply that the level of incomes was relatively low – and incomes were relatively low because of too little demand, including demand for consumer goods. To make the point clear: the lower level of exports obviously reduced the level of employment and incomes in the export industries. Workers attached to these industries spent less on consumption, and this meant in turn (as we saw when discussing the Multiplier) that the incomes of those making certain consumption goods were depressed, and that they in turn had less to spend on consumer goods. But the chain did not end there. The fact that in the early 1920s consumption, for whatever mixture of reasons, was low in relation to the economy's productive potential had implications for investment: if existing capacity is underutilized there is little point in installing more. Not surprisingly investment during the early 1920s, like consumption, was no higher than it had been a decade before.

However we must not let ourselves get too tangled up in the cobweb of economic inter-relationships. The simple fact was that because of an increase in productivity, and in the size of the working population, the British economy was capable in the early 1920s of producing 10–15 per cent more than it had before the war. But consumption and investment were no higher than they had been before the war and exports were substantially lower, so that effective demand in total was 5–10 per cent lower than it had been. With actual demand and production therefore some 15–25 per cent lower than what the economy was capable of producing, heavy unemployment was inevitable. And whatever weight one assigns to different factors* it is clear that two of the basic causes of this heavy unemployment were the high price of exports, and the high rate of taxation.

GOVERNMENT POLICY

The unemployment consequences of excessive export prices were perfectly apparent in the 1920s – no Keynesian spectacles were needed to see them. Moreover although the mechanism by which high rates of taxation can result in unemployment was not properly understood, no community ever lacks those who ascribe the worst contemporary ills to high taxation; certainly there were plenty of influential businessmen in the 1920s who said that unemployment would never be reduced until taxes were reduced. One might have expected, therefore, that the government would aim to cope with the unemployment problem by trying to reduce export prices, or tax rates, or both. And so it did. But it did so in a way that certainly made things no better, and if anything made them worse.

As we have seen, in order to achieve the objective of lower export prices the government did not adopt the obvious course of lowering the exchange rate – for its avowed objective, eventually achieved in 1925, was to *raise* the exchange

* More technically, whatever value one puts on the Multiplier and the accelerator.

rate back to the pre-war level. Instead it tried to reduce wages and prices enough to ensure that even though the exchange rate went up the prices of British exports to foreigners would go down. In the event, resistance to wage cuts, culminating in the General Strike, prevented the reduction in wages and prices being carried far enough to restore competitiveness, and there was little change in the volume of exports for the rest of the decade, and hence little boost to employment.

But wage cuts were a more positive failure than that: although they did not go far enough to solve the export problem, they probably did go far enough to have an adverse effect on consumption. We have seen that the classical economists thought that general wage cuts would directly increase employment, and this was undoubtedly part of the rationale behind government policy; Keynes, on the other hand, thought the effects on employment would at best be neutral and at worst adverse. In this case consumption and employment almost certainly suffered from the effects of wage cuts: during the early 1920s prices fell less than wage rates so that there must have been a decline in real wages, and therefore in consumption and employment. One is therefore led to conclude that the government's policy was exactly the opposite of what was needed; had it supported *increases* in wages the effect on employment would probably have been better, at any rate as far as domestic demand was concerned. In practice, of course, the best way for a government to increase consumption is not to increase money wages, since much or all of this will before long be offset by a rise in prices, but to reduce taxation or increase pensions and other social security payments.

This brings us back to the second thing the government did, but did in such a way that the effect was almost certainly to reduce employment rather than increase it. It reduced taxation. But each time it reduced taxation it tried to follow the golden rule that in peacetime a government must avoid a Budget deficit as it would avoid the plague, and reduced its expenditure as well. The good effects on employment of higher consumption out of higher post-tax incomes were probably more than offset by the bad effects of lower public authority expenditure.

The story was not very different during the second half of the 1920s. It is true that effective demand rose quite strongly, mainly because of increases in consumption and investment. But this rise in effective demand was no greater than the rise in the economy's productive potential engendered by the growth of productivity and the working population. Consequently there was no narrowing of the gap between full employment output and actual output, and unemployment continued, year after year, at a high level of 10–12 per cent. None of the steps which Keynesian hindsight now suggests should have been taken, were taken. Government current expenditure was not significantly increased, for this would have meant an even larger Budget deficit than the one the government was already unwillingly running – and Budget deficits were simply assumed to be undesirable and indeed potentially disastrous. For the same reason, there was (after 1925) no cut in taxation which might have stimulated consumption. Nothing was done to cheapen the price of exports: the government was stuck as a matter of dogma with the pre-war, and therefore too high, exchange rate; and following the traumatic experience of the General Strike it was stuck as a matter of political reality with an inability to enforce wage reductions. It was unthinkable for a government to interfere with private enterprise by trying to persuade businessmen to increase their investment, except perhaps by reducing interest rates, and during the 1920s Britain was so dependent on short-term borrowing from abroad that interest rates could not safely be reduced very far. On the other hand public investment could not be increased (as Keynes and

Robertson were advocating in the later 1920s) because this would use up precious savings that might otherwise find their way into more profitable and productive private investment.

In short, nothing could be done. There was heavy unemployment in Britain throughout the 1920s because the economy had settled down into an equilibrium situation in which there was too little effective demand, and because the prevailing political and economic orthodoxy made it impossible for people to recognize that a shortage of demand was the root of the trouble, let alone to take steps to deal with it.

THE SLUMP: UNITED STATES

Throughout the 1920s Britain had been virtually alone in suffering from prolonged unemployment, but with the onset of the Slump she was soon to be joined by practically every other country on earth. The origins of the Slump lay in the down-turn in American investment which occurred at the end of the 1920s. This down-turn in investment was not in itself at all surprising – in the United States, as in Britain, the trade cycle had been a familiar phenomenon for over a century. What was surprising, and what past experience provided no precedent for, was the depth of the depression which followed this down-turn in investment; the severity with which many other countries were affected; and the refusal of the U.S. economy to recover. Some of this ground was covered in Chapter 3, and here we only glance at some of the more salient points in the light of Keynesian theory.

The severity of the down-swing in the United States (the fact that within a few years from the top of the boom, unemployment had risen to 25 per cent instead of the 6–10 per cent customary at the bottom of the trade cycle) can perhaps be attributed to two main factors (besides the confidence effects of the Wall Street Crash). Both of these factors had their ultimate origins in the First World War.

One was the sheer strength of the investment boom which developed during the 1920s. Between 1919 and 1927 American investment nearly doubled, rising so much faster than other kinds of expenditure that it increased from 16 per cent of the National Income in 1919 to 22 per cent in 1927. Such a rapid increase in investment meant that the country's stock of capital – the number of houses and factories, the amount of plant and machinery – was being added to at an unusually rapid rate. Sooner or later it would become clear that the capital stock was big enough – perhaps more than big enough – to meet current needs: factories would be easily able to meet all the orders they received, and builders would find new houses increasingly difficult to sell. When this happened, businessmen would stop adding to their existing productive capacity, and house-building would drop; in fact the 'accelerator' would go into reverse with a vengeance (see page 41), and there would be a sharp fall in investment – much sharper than it would have been had the rise in the stock of capital been slower, and kept more in step with the rise in demand.

This is precisely what happened. Investment flattened out in 1928, and turned down in 1929. As Keynes's analysis would lead one to expect, this fall in investment led, via the Multiplier, to a substantially bigger fall in the National Income. With a lower National Income there was less reason than ever to add to existing productive capacity, so that there was a further fall in investment; and this in turn led to a further fall in the National Income. One reason why the fall in the American National Income between 1929 and 1932 was so large was that the fall in investment was so large: National Income fell by about a third, investment by three quarters.

The other main reason why the American down-turn was so severe lay in the agricultural sector. The productivity of American farms had risen enormously under the stimulus of world-wide food shortages brought on by the war; and it continued to do so during the 1920s after pre-war sources of food and agricultural raw materials (such as Europe) had been restored. As a result world surpluses of many primary products began to emerge during the 1920s, and prices started to drop. This led to a vicious spiral, in which farm prices and farm incomes chased each other downward. Unlike an industrialist, a farmer who is faced by a lower price for his product tries to *increase* his output, for only by selling more can he offset lower prices and maintain his income; there was in fact a slight *increase* in American farm output between 1929 and 1933. But the consequence of millions of farmers trying to increase their output is a further fall in prices and farm incomes. When the over-supply which already existed in the late 1920s was accentuated by the fall in demand for food and raw materials that followed the downturn in investment in 1928–9 the situation became desperate. The prices of farm products fell by more than half in the three years after 1929, and American farm incomes suffered accordingly; and of course this fall in farm incomes itself brought the Multiplier into play, and led to a further decline in consumption and hence, as a result of the operation of the accelerator, in investment as well.*

THE SLUMP: REST OF THE WORLD

International trade and payments are fairly peripheral to the operation of the U.S. economy, and the cause of the severity of the American Slump must be sought internally in the kind of factors we have just been examining. But the same is not true in reverse; the American balance of payments was a major factor in the affairs of the rest of the world, and the origins of the world Slump lay in America. ('When America sneezes,' as someone once put it, 'the rest of the world catches pneumonia.') One factor we have already

* For a general discussion of the factors affecting primary product prices, see Explanatory Note 6, page 260.

examined in Chapter 3: the repatriation of American money from abroad, and the immense contraction in international lending to which this gave rise.

Another factor was the fall in American imports which accompanied the fall in the National Income. Foreign trade may have been unimportant to the American economy, but the U.S. was nevertheless, next to Britain, the world's biggest importer, and the 70 per cent fall in her imports between 1929 and 1933 brought bankruptcy and unemployment to export industries all over the world. Worse even than the direct effect on the exports of manufacturing countries such as Britain was the indirect effect on the value of primary producing countries' exports. Just as falling demand for primary products led (because of inelastic supply) to a big fall in their price within America, so a fall in the demand for these products on the part of Britain, Germany and other manufacturing countries led to tumbling primary product prices all over the world. The less developed countries whose exports consist very largely of primary products saw their export earnings fall catastrophically, and having little in the way of reserves were quickly forced to clamp down hard on their own imports of manufactured goods from the industrial countries. In the international sphere, just as within individual countries, falling incomes led to falling expenditure, and falling expenditure led to further falls in other people's incomes. But one difference was that in the international sphere the fall in incomes and expenditure was not entirely automatic. There may have been some cases in which a country's imports (and therefore other countries' exports) fell solely because National Income fell. But in many cases industrial countries took deliberate steps, by raising tariffs or imposing quotas or foreign exchange restrictions, to reduce imports, with the idea of diverting expenditure from foreign goods to home-produced goods, and thus giving a boost to employment. Such measures came to be known, not surprisingly, as 'beggar-my-neighbour' policies: countries were trying to solve their unemployment problem by passing it on to some other country. With nearly everyone forced to pursue these policies (for a country which failed to do so would soon find itself with few exports, huge imports and vast unemployment) no one benefited very much; indeed in a sense everyone suffered, for many of the benefits of greater specialization, which are the underlying reason for international trade, were inevitably lost. Yet import restrictions, however self-defeating, seemed to many desperate governments the only quick and practical step that might alleviate a little the unemployment that threatened to swamp them.

In Keynesian terms, then, the Great Slump was a reflection of too little effective demand on a world-wide scale. Expenditure was too low; therefore incomes were too low; therefore expenditure was too low. The initial cause of this was a big decline in investment in the United States, which was not offset by a rise in consumption or any other category of expenditure, and therefore led to a progressive slide in output and employment. Partly as a result of special factors owing their origins to the war the great American contraction convulsed countries all over the world. Banks failed, businesses went bankrupt, incomes plummeted and tens of millions of men were thrown out of work. By 1933 there were probably 30 million unemployed in the industrialized countries alone.

NO RECOVERY

This down-swing in world economic activity was not only much more severe than any previous down-swing; it was not succeeded by an up-swing. In the U.S. unemployment rose from 3 per cent in 1929 to 25 per cent in 1933, but then fell very little, to 22 per cent in 1934 and 20 per cent in 1935. The U.S. economy – and with it the world economy – had got stuck at the bottom of the down-swing. What was supposed to happen in this situation, according to all the trade cycle literature, was a recovery in investment, induced by the emergence of profitable opportunities on the one hand, and lower costs, including lower interest rates, on the other. Keynes broadly agreed with this. But, as we saw in Chapter 4, he believed that the yield of new investment was largely determined by the amount of existing capital equipment in the economy and the extent to which it was being used. In the U.S. in 1933 there was a very large amount of capital equipment and a great deal of it was not being used. The yield to be obtained by installing yet more capital equipment seemed likely to be pretty low. But what about the other determinant of investment, the rate of interest? This, said Keynes, was determined by liquidity preference and the quantity of money, and it seemed that when interest rates got down to a certain level (perhaps $2-2\frac{1}{2}$ per cent) it proved impossible to force them down any further, because any increase in the quantity of money (which should have the effect of reducing interest rates) was offset by an equal increase in liquidity preference. It could therefore happen, said Keynes, that the yield of new investment was lower than the rate of interest: a man might be unable to borrow for less than 2 per cent, yet be unable to find an investment project that yielded more than $1\frac{1}{2}$ per cent. When this happens no sane businessman will invest. According to Keynes, this is precisely what happened in the United States, and to a lesser extent in Britain, in the 1930s.

If investment is very low then savings will have to be equally low, and given a fairly normal propensity to consume among the population this will only happen if the National Income is low. An equilibrium gets established in which the National Income is much lower than the economy's productive potential, and unemployment is high. Until either consumption or investment or exports or government expenditure rises this low-level equilibrium will persist. It is virtually impossible for consumption to rise of its own accord, for incomes and savings are now so low that even if people cut their propensity to save in order to increase their consumption it would not make very much difference. And as long as consumption stays so low there is no particular reason why businessmen should chance their arm by increasing investment. And exports are unlikely to rise as long as there is heavy unemployment in other countries. If anything is to be done, therefore, it must be done by the government, which can stimulate consumption by cutting taxation, or (the remedy Keynes preferred) can create employment by itself spending large sums on public works.

THE NEW DEAL

Curiously enough, it was not in Britain, the country most exposed to Keynes's views, and one which had a supposedly left-wing government for the first two years of the Slump, that an attempt was made to alleviate unemployment by public works, but in the United States, supposedly the last bastion of capitalism. The 'New Deal' which Roosevelt introduced in 1933 got off to rather a shaky start, by trying simultaneously to raise wages, in order to increase consumption, and to raise prices, in order to provide businessmen with an inducement to invest; obviously one or other of these measures might have had some effect, but the two together were self-defeating. But after a year or two the public works programmes which are now thought of as the essence of the New Deal got under way. The Administration started to spend large sums of money *over and above what it received in tax revenue* on roads, dams, harbours, irrigation and land reclamation works, public buildings, housing estates and projects of many other kinds. Thus the Administration directly provided a large amount of employment, and indirectly a lot more; for the men it paid to build the roads and dams spent the money on goods and services and thus provided employment for others. The increase in government expenditure put the Multiplier into operation in exactly the same way as a rise in investment or consumption would have done.

The counterpart of this policy, under which the Administration spent more than its income, was of course a Budget deficit of the kind so dreaded by orthodox economists and politicians. In 1929–30* the federal Budget had been in modest surplus, as was considered correct and necessary to help pay off the National Debt: expenditure was $3·4 billion and tax revenue $4·2 billion. By 1935–6 expenditure had risen to over $8·5 billion, though tax revenue was only $4·1 billion; as a result there was a deficit of nearly $4½ billion. Every year throughout the rest of the 1930s there was a Budget deficit (indeed the next time there was a surplus was 1946–7) and by the time the U.S. again found itself at war the National Debt, which had stood at some $20 billion when Roosevelt became President, was over $50 billion. In fact the National Debt, which in the eyes of the faithful is only supposed to increase in wartime, and then only if really necessary, had more than doubled in eight peacetime years. This fact was – and indeed still is – held bitterly against Roosevelt by many people in the United States. Yet looking back today any economist or politician who has assimilated Keynes must feel that the only trouble with the U.S. Administration's deficit spending in the 1930s was that it did not go nearly far enough. Under the stimulus of large government expenditures there was a substantial rise in employment, but the total labour force was also rising, and unemployment only fell to 14 per cent (in 1937) and actually rose again (to 19 per cent) in 1938. A large part of the trouble was that despite the rise in consumption resulting from government spending, private investment still refused to revive properly; even in the later 1930s, though there was some recovery from the very

* American financial years run from 1 July to 30 June.

low levels in the depth of the depression, investment was still much lower than it had been immediately before 1929. Those hostile to Roosevelt claimed at the time that this was because his policy of deficit spending had destroyed confidence among the business community; more sophisticated (though now seen as sadly pre-Keynesian) critics advanced the old theory with which Keynes had been confronted in the 1920s by the British Treasury, that expenditure on public works uses up savings that would otherwise have been used to finance private investment. In fact a much more compelling explanation seems to have been the excessive amount of idle productive capacity referred to earlier. Until demand was high enough to call existing capital equipment into use there seemed no point in installing more. Only an even greater increase in government expenditure could have led at all quickly to this. As it was, it was only with the massive re-armament programme on which the United States embarked at the end of the 1930s that any real impact was made on unemployment; and so vast were the numbers out of work that it was not until 1941 – the year of Pearl Harbor – that unemployment fell below 10 per cent.

GERMANY

Another country whose heavy unemployment was tackled by large-scale public expenditure was Germany. When the Nazis came to power in early 1933 they started a vigorous spending campaign: roads and railways were built and rebuilt, large-scale land improvement schemes were embarked on and, in the private sector, businessmen were given subsidies to encourage them to invest. These measures effected a drastic reduction in unemployment, which was carried further when re-armament got under way in 1935. By 1936 or soon after, while Britain and America were still struggling with unemployment rates of 15 per cent or more, the problem had virtually disappeared in Germany. Within three or four years Hitler's policies had resulted in a big enough rise in effective demand to re-employ most of the six million men who had been out of a job when he came to power. No wonder he enjoyed a certain popularity. Of course he also incurred very large Budget deficits, but what is an unbalanced Budget or two to set against the building of an Empire that will last for a thousand years?

BRITISH POLICY IN THE 1930S

Britain, of course, had long since left the Empire-building business; it might have suffered less in the 1930s if it had not. Throughout most of the decade the principal aim of the British government was not world domination but prudent housekeeping. From about the middle of the 1920s, as we saw in Chapter 3, the Exchequer had suffered from a small but growing deficit. After the onset of the world Slump in 1929 this deficit leaped alarmingly. The government reacted like any worried housewife. On one side of the account steps were taken to cut back expenditure – steps that faltered a little at first but became much firmer after the formation of the National government in August 1931: public expenditure was reduced in 1932 and continued to fall for several years. On the other side of the account steps were taken to increase the government's revenue: the standard rate of income tax was raised, and so were various indirect taxes, notably the duties on tobacco, beer and petrol. These tax increases did not, in fact, succeed in raising government revenue very much: higher rates of income tax were offset by lower incomes, and higher taxes on expenditure by falling expenditure. Nevertheless the combination of cuts in public expenditure and increases in taxation did put the Exchequer back on the road to the black: the Budget deficit started to fall and by 1934 there was again a small surplus. The government's satisfaction with this state of affairs was summed up in 1935 by the Chancellor of the Exchequer, Neville Chamberlain. Speaking with the air of a man recalling some arduous but in the end victorious military campaign he said, 'By cuts, by economy and by severe taxation the Budget was balanced.' He failed to add that in the meantime unemployment had doubled. Yet in the light of Keynes's analysis one can see that this was bound to be the result: cuts in public expenditure, and increases in taxation which force individuals to reduce their consumption, both lead to falling incomes and further reductions in expenditure. In Britain, even more than in the United States, where at least government policy was aimed in the right direction, it was only the onset of re-armament and finally of the Second World War itself that really solved the unemployment problem.

THE INTER-WAR YEARS IN RETROSPECT

We have seen that during practically the whole of the inter-war period Britain suffered from too low a level of effective demand; during much of the second half of the period the disease afflicted the rest of the world as well. Some of the immediate causes of this deficiency of demand we have traced – for example, the weakness of exports in the case of Britain, and the slump in investment in the case of the United States. Yet unemployment as severe and long-lasting as this was an entirely new phenomenon, and prompts the question of whether there was some more fundamental force at work which had permanently upset the balance of supply and demand; or, to put it in Keynesian terms, which made people want to save more at full employment levels of income than businessmen wanted to invest.

Keynes himself made some play with the notion that in the industrial countries of the West, and most notably in Britain and the United States, a 'mature society' had been achieved.

In a mature society, he suggested, most people's demands for goods and services are pretty well satisfied – given the existing distribution of income. There is therefore a chronic tendency towards under-consumption, in the sense that people buy less consumer goods than the economy is capable of producing; and since this means that capital equipment stands idle, there is a correspondingly depressing effect on investment, particularly if there is a slowing-down in technological innovation. Keynes took the view that this situation could be coped with, and full employment restored and maintained, but only at the cost of fairly drastic action in the way of increasing public expenditure, reducing the inequality of income (and so raising the average propensity to consume) and keeping interest rates as low as possible. A number of other economists who accepted Keynes's analysis took a much gloomier view of the possibility of coping with the problem, arguing that the British and American economies were settling into a state of permanent stagnation, and that government action of the kind recommended by Keynes would never be able to increase demand sufficiently to employ the country's resources to the full.

Today this latter appraisal is difficult to comprehend; even Keynes's own views, with their implication that in such countries as Britain and America it would for evermore be a hard and unremitting struggle to maintain full employment, seem absurdly gloomy. They almost suggest that in the face of the apparent hopelessness of the situation in the mid-1930s he suffered a momentary lapse of faith in his own analysis. It is true that in most Western countries people's incomes were higher in the 1920s than they ever had been, but it was surprising for someone who appreciated the good things of life as much as Keynes did to infer from this that people would now save a lot more because they would have more money left over after satisfying their basic needs. There is in fact very little evidence that a society's propensity to consume falls significantly as its income rises – though some no doubt think that the story might be different in the absence of advertising. Moreover, it is quite untrue that there has been a slowing-down in the pace of technological innovation – during the past twenty-five years it has been proceeding faster than ever. The sluggish rate of investment in the 1930s was not the result of a lack of new products or processes; it reflected the fact that incomes were so low and idle plant and equipment so plentiful that most of the new ideas, however good, simply looked too risky to invest in.

This is not to say that the Great Slump had nothing to do with some of the changes which had taken place in the economies of Western countries over the previous fifty or a hundred years. The emergence, for example, of a situation in which savings were not automatically invested (partly because to an important extent saving and investment were now different activities carried out by different groups of people) was, as we have seen, a crucial factor in the mechanism of prolonged unemployment. But the search for some great cosmic factor which decreed that although great slumps had not been a problem in the past they would, unless one was very cunning in countering them, be a continual problem in the future – such a search, even though Keynes himself showed some disposition to join in it, seems to have been a wild goose chase. The more prosaic kind of investigation we have been engaging in, of examining the specific factors which influence particular components of demand at particular times, seems a better guide to the truth. Or so post-war experience would suggest.

It is to some aspects of post-war experience that we now turn.

Part Two · After

CHAPTER 7

UNEMPLOYMENT SINCE THE WAR

FULL EMPLOYMENT GUARANTEED

WITH stunning suddenness, the Second World War transformed Britain from a great power to a minor one, from a creditor to a debtor, from the ruler of an Empire to a member of a Commonwealth. But the war had other, more parochial, effects as well. It acted on the nation's values and attitudes like a pressure cooker on a potato. Changes that would normally have taken decades were compressed into a few years. It would have seemed inconceivable in 1939 that within five years the government would have passed the 1944 Education Act, and made a start on implementing Sir William Beveridge's report on *Social Insurance and Allied Services*. It would have seemed equally unlikely that in 1944 the government would publish a White Paper on *Employment Policy* in which it pledged itself to maintain full employment after the war was over by regulating effective demand. 1939, after all, was the nineteenth consecutive year in which unemployment had averaged 10 per cent or more. Was it possible that only five years later the government would have found both the will and the weapons to maintain full employment?

As far as the will was concerned there was no doubt. The same national mood which demanded that after the war everyone should receive a secondary education and everyone should be protected by a comprehensive system of social security also demanded that everyone who wanted to work should have a job. There were plenty of jobs in wartime; there had better be plenty of jobs in peacetime too, and woe betide the government that failed to provide them.

And by 1944 the weapons were there as well. For by this

time the economists and civil servants, and even some of the politicians and businessmen and trade union leaders, had absorbed what Keynes had been saying. It was accepted that the government could and should regulate its own expenditure so as to maintain a level of effective demand sufficient to preserve full employment. In the words of the White Paper,* 'The government accept as one of their primary aims and responsibilities the maintenance of a high and stable level of employment after the war. . . . Total expenditure on goods and services must be prevented from falling to a level where general unemployment appears.' It is true that not everyone believed in the government's willingness to preserve full employment, as was perhaps demonstrated by the massive defeat in 1945 of the senior partner in the Coalition government. It is also true that some economists were still doubtful about the government's ability to control demand in such a way as to maintain full employment; some of them predicted that the Second World War, just like the First, would be followed by a temporary boom which gave way to a prolonged depression. But such worriers and sceptics were proved totally wrong. Full employment has been maintained year in and year out. Since the war unemployment has averaged little more than $1\frac{1}{2}$ per cent. This is a good performance even by the apparently optimistic standards laid down during the war by Beveridge, who said that if unemployment could be kept down to 3 per cent the country would be doing very well. By the standards of the inter-war period, when unemployment averaged about 13 per cent, the achievement is monumental. Moreover this achievement has not been confined to Britain. In the two countries hardest hit by the Slump in the 1930s – the United States and Germany – there has also been, by pre-war standards, permanent full employment. It is true that in the U.S. unemployment has been somewhat higher than in Britain, and we shall be

* *Employment Policy*, Cmd 6527, May 1944.

looking at this more closely in Chapter 11. In Germany, on the other hand, unemployment has for many years been substantially lower even than in Britain. In fact in no highly developed country has there been anything remotely like a recurrence of the unemployment of the 1930s. Although one would not want to apply the statement to all countries equally, the basic reason for this is quite simple. Within a decade or so of the publication of the *General Theory* Keynes's analysis of how the economy worked had become widely accepted, and his prescriptions, insofar as they were required, widely administered. Even on timing, Keynes's prediction to Shaw had been right.

PENT-UP DEMAND

This brings us to a point which we shall examine more closely in the next chapter, but must touch on here. During the war the main economic feature in Britain, and indeed in all the countries involved in the war, was not a *shortage* but an *excess* of demand. So far from having to increase demand in order to maintain full employment, the government was faced with the problem of holding demand down to prevent it erupting in uncontrollable inflation. To some extent this was done by increasing taxation, but the main weapon the government used was rationing and various other physical controls. This meant that however much money people had they could only buy a certain amount of food or clothing – and because of the operation of subsidies and price controls they got these pretty cheaply. The result was that after the war consumers had accumulated large savings they were longing to spend on something. The same was true of businessmen, particularly in less essential industries, many of whom had accumulated idle funds which, because of the allocation of labour and materials, they had not been able to spend during the war on new machinery or buildings.

This huge amount of pent-up demand, combined with the physical destruction and dislocation caused by the war, meant that for several years after the end of the war the problem remained one of too much demand rather than too little. Consequently it continued to be necessary for several years to restrain demand by keeping on with rationing and high taxation. But although this was the opposite of the situation Keynes had been concerned with, in doing this the government was in fact pursuing a Keynesian policy. Instead of concentrating on balancing its Budget, and allowing the economy to behave as it liked – as governments had done before the war – it was deliberately regulating demand in order to keep it in a desired relationship to what the economy was capable of producing. The fact that in the early post-war years government intervention was directed at holding demand down rather than pushing it up was in a sense a detail; the thing that must have been immensely encouraging to those who had feared a relapse into heavy unemployment was that the government *was* intervening. If it took steps to restrain demand when it was excessive there must be a strong presumption that it would also take steps to increase demand when it was inadequate. And indeed when demand did first show signs of beginning to wilt, in the early 1950s, the government did intervene in order to increase it.

CONTINUOUS GOVERNMENT INTERVENTION

As time went on the character of government intervention became somewhat more sophisticated. The 1944 White Paper had tended to envisage, in rather a crude way, that once the war was over the trade cycle would go on much as before, but that the government would fill in the troughs, chiefly by timing its own investment to coincide with the periods when private investment was slack. There was, it is true, some discussion of the possibility of influencing business investment and private consumption in a counter-cyclical direction; but this was thought of mainly as a long-stop in case variations in public investment failed to iron out fluctuations. However this conception of government as a kind of businessman's water-spaniel did not hold sway for very long. The government soon got into the habit of controlling – or at any rate trying to control – private investment and consumption, as well as its own expenditure, in the interests of economic stability. It would begin by making a forecast of how demand seemed likely to move, and then compare this with the likely increase in productive capacity or potential output – i.e. what the economy was capable of producing if there was full employment. If there appeared to be a discrepancy between the two it would then take action to bring them into line. This action was mainly directed towards demand, since the government has little power to affect the rate of increase of productive capacity in the short run. It consisted partly in altering government expenditure plans, for example by speeding up or slowing down the rise in public investment; and partly in boosting or restraining the amount spent by businessmen on investment, or families on consumption, by altering taxes, interest rates, hire-purchase regulations, and so on.

The crucial point about all this was that changes in taxation and public expenditure were made not with an eye to balancing the Budget but in the interests of the government's overriding economic objectives – of which full employment was one of the most important. This meant that when there was too little demand taxes would be cut and public expenditure increased, despite the fact that this would obviously lead in the direction of a Budget deficit; similarly, if there was too much demand, taxes would be raised and public expenditure would be held back – but this would be done in the interests of preventing inflation, and not of achieving a Budget surplus.

An example of the latter situation occurred in 1955. By the summer of that year it was clear that the economy was seriously over-heated. Demand was so intense that wages, profits and prices were rising very rapidly – as indeed were imports, since little more output could be squeezed out of factories in Britain. The government announced cuts in capital investment by nationalized industries and local authorities, and increases in profits tax and purchase tax. This was done not in order to improve the government's own Budgetary position – which was in fact unusually favourable at the time – but in order to reduce the pressure of demand. An example of the other kind occurred at the beginning of 1963, when unemployment had risen to more than 3 per cent for the first time since the war. The government increased old age pensions and other national insurance benefits, a significant part of the extra cost falling on the Exchequer; and in the Budget in April introduced substantial reductions in income tax. This was done in order to increase demand and employment; the effect on the Exchequer accounts must have been regarded as a very minor aspect of the situation.

The simple and overwhelming fact, then, is that since the war every British government has manipulated demand in order to maintain full employment. The conversion to Keynes's once-heretical ideas has been complete. But having said this one must immediately qualify. Some of the wider qualifications are dealt with later in the book. But first of all we must look at two respects in which there have been lapses from full employment in Britain during the past twenty years. There have been lapses in particular *places*; and there have been lapses at particular *times*. We shall take them in that order.

REGIONAL UNEMPLOYMENT

Although unemployment in Britain since the war has averaged only 1·6 per cent, this is the figure for the country as a whole; in some places it has been consistently higher than this and in others consistently lower. In the northern region, for instance, the average unemployment rate has been 2·8 per cent, and in Scotland 3·4 per cent. In Northern Ireland (which of course is not included in the statistics for Great Britain, but is nevertheless to a large extent the responsibility of the British government) the position has been even worse than this, with an average unemployment rate of over 7 per cent. By contrast, unemployment in the Midlands and south-east has only averaged about 1 per cent. Even within the individual regions there have been wide variations. In Scotland, for example, unemployment has tended to be quite low in Edinburgh, but very much higher in the High-lands. In the south-east some of the coastal resorts have suffered from a persistently high rate of unemployment, while in light engineering centres such as Slough or Acton unemployment has tended to be virtually non-existent. How far post-war governments have succeeded in maintaining full employment is therefore a question that will elicit differ-ent answers from a tool-maker in Slough and a labourer in Inverness.

Exactly why unemployment has persistently been so much higher in some regions than others remains something of a mystery – though the phenomenon is not a new one: through-out the 1920s and 1930s unemployment was particularly heavy in the north and west. Part of the answer, it is true, lies in the way different industries are spread around the map of Britain. Largely because the Industrial Revolution started in the north rather than the south it is in the north that the bulk of the country's older, slower-growing industries are located. Since the war, and in many cases since long before that, there has been a big fall in the number of people em-ployed in certain traditional industries for whose products demand has been growing slowly, or which have been meeting increasingly severe competition from new products and other countries. Industries which have suffered most have included agriculture, mining, shipbuilding and textiles. These industries tend to be located in the north and west: the northern region, for example, has a relatively high proportion of employees in mining and shipbuilding; Scotland and Northern Ireland in agriculture and shipbuilding; the north-western region in textiles; and Wales in mining.

Nevertheless a preponderance of declining industries, although a factor of considerable importance, does not provide an adequate explanation of the persistence of high unemployment in certain regions, because if one looks closely one can see that employment *in the same industry* has grown more slowly, or declined more rapidly, in some regions than in others. Fast-growing industries such as engineering, distribution and many kinds of services have tended to grow faster (in terms of number of employees) in the Midlands and south than in the north and west; declining industries such as those listed above have tended to decline more slowly. The reasons for this are complex, but seem to lie in a combination of factors unfavourable to the older industrial areas of the north and west: the younger and more energetic people often leave and look for better opportunities elsewhere; those who are left behind tend to be less adaptable and, precisely because of the legacy of heavy unemployment (since these were also the regions that suffered most between the wars), unusually resistant to the introduction of new techniques they fear might throw them out of work; the amenities in these areas are often inadequate compared with those available in the south, and the best managers and key workers who are needed if a firm is to expand rapidly are unwilling to go there.

Whatever the precise mixture of reasons, the fact is that despite a level of employment in Britain as a whole that most people would agree to be 'full employment', relatively high unemployment has persisted in parts of the north and west throughout much of the post-war period. This kind of regional unemployment does not really fall within the scope of Keynes's analysis. It is true that unemployment in the regions has tended to move roughly in proportion with unemployment in the country as a whole, so that a doubling or halving of national unemployment has been accompanied, roughly speaking, by a doubling or a halving of unemployment in the north and west. Thus with national unemployment of $2-2\frac{1}{2}$ per cent (as it was in 1952, 1958-9 and 1962-3) government action along Keynesian lines to increase effective demand and bring unemployment down to $1-1\frac{1}{2}$ per cent (as happened in 1953-5, 1960-61, and 1964-5) was bound to have a substantial effect also on unemployment in the relatively depressed regions. Nevertheless, with national unemployment down to $1-1\frac{1}{2}$ per cent, unemployment in some of the regions will still be $2\frac{1}{2}-3$ per cent, and in the more depressed areas of these regions considerably higher. Many of those remaining unemployed in these areas will be unskilled or in possession of an old skill learned many years ago and now made obsolete by technical change. No amount of increase in the *general* level of demand can make much difference to these men: lower taxes would enable consumers to buy more, but not more of whatever these men can produce; nor are incentives to businessmen likely to result in much rise in the demand for these men's services. What happens instead is a further intensification of demand in the industries of the Midlands and south – the industries producing capital equipment or cars or whatever it is that businessmen and consumers decide to spend the extra money on. Not all this extra demand can be met by firms which are already going flat out, and the result is not higher output but either higher prices and wages or higher imports (matters we shall be discussing more fully in the next chapter). In either case the outcome is not much help to unemployed miners in the

Welsh valleys or unemployed building-workers in Greenock.

It is true that a high level of demand in the country as a whole, particularly if it is expected to last indefinitely, will have some *indirect* effects on unemployment in the depressed areas. Businessmen in the Midlands and the south who find it very difficult to get labour may be prompted to move workers down from the north, or to open a branch factory in the north, and to provide whatever training or re-training is necessary to enable these workers to do the job. Unfortunately all the indications are that left to themselves business-men will not do this on nearly a large enough scale: they fear that if they spend money on moving and training workers these workers will be poached from them by other firms who have saved their money for poaching rather than training, and no British firm wants to be more poached against than poaching. As for opening a branch factory in the north, businessmen claim that there are all sorts of disadvantages about starting up in an unknown and far-off location, and these often outweigh the advantages of the ease of getting labour, unless generous inducements are offered.

To generalize, then, it would seem that the Keynesian technique of creating enough effective demand in the economy as a whole is a necessary condition of full employment in every part of the country, but not a sufficient condition. There is no hope of maintaining full employment in what have been euphemistically termed the 'less fortunate' areas of an advanced industrial country – which in contemporary Britain happen to lie mainly in the north and west – unless a full employment policy is pursued deliberately at the centre; but such a policy will not by itself reduce unemployment in all parts of the country to reasonable proportions. There is also a need for selective policies aimed at creating employment in particular areas, or in some cases at moving people out of these areas to places where jobs are easier to provide.

Since the war successive British governments have pursued

such policies, though with varying degrees of energy and success. The 'Special Areas' which had originally been designated in 1934 (in central Scotland, the north-east coast, west Cumberland and south Wales) were somewhat expanded and added to in 1945 and again in later years. Within these 'Development Areas' (as they were now called) the government built factories which were then leased or sold relatively cheaply, and various other grants and loans were provided to firms expanding or setting up there. This approach, of providing incentives in a relatively small number of large areas, was reversed by the Local Employment Act of 1960, which designated instead a large number of small areas in which there was persistently high unemployment as 'Development Districts'. The idea behind the change was that many places in the large development areas were perfectly prosperous and needed no special help, while on the other hand there were a number of stubborn pockets of unemployment in the south that were not getting any help at all under the existing system. The same assistance was available in the new development districts as had previously been available in the old development areas, though the incentives were strengthened in the 1963 Budget.

However even when reinforced by these further measures the development district approach seemed inadequate. Too many of the development districts were small, isolated places in which few go-ahead businesses wanted to set up, however seductive the purely financial terms on which they could do so. What was needed instead, it was argued, was to concentrate on building up a number of *growth points* in the north and west to which people in places of high unemployment could either move permanently without being too far away from family and friends, or commute on a daily basis. These growth points could be based on suitably located existing towns, or new towns could be built from scratch. Over a period of time they could be developed into fair-sized cities with all the amenities that a city can provide, and into flourishing industrial complexes offering external economies such as closeness to customers and suppliers, facilities for sub-contracting, a wide choice of employment opportunities, and a whole range of other advantages difficult to provide in smaller places.

Over the past few years policy has been moving in this direction. In central Scotland and the north-east region, for example, assistance is being concentrated not so much on isolated pockets of high unemployment as on places where the opportunities for future expansion look brightest. In particular, these areas are now getting a more than propor-tionate share of public service investment, so that there can be some speeding-up in the provision of the amenities – houses, schools, hospitals, roads, parks, libraries, swimming baths and so on – in which many of the older industrial areas are so disproportionately and depressingly lacking. More generally, the Labour government abandoned the 'Development District' approach at the beginning of 1966 and reverted to the earlier concept of 'Development Areas'. Virtually the whole of the northern half of Britain, most of Wales and much of the West Country are now scheduled as development areas. This means that businessmen get sub-stantial assistance (also amended and improved in 1966) for setting up or expanding anywhere in these areas; they no longer have to confine themselves to the particular places where unemployment happens to be highest at the moment. A further step forward was taken in the summer of 1967, when the government announced that in addition to sub-sidizing *capital* in manufacturing industry in the develop-ment areas it would in future also subsidize *labour*,* thus providing a direct incentive to business to set up or expand in these areas.

Another advance has been the increasing recognition of

* By paying employers an extra 'selective employment premium'.

the need for training and re-training. One of the main characteristics of those who are unemployed nowadays (other than those who are merely changing jobs) is that they are either unskilled, or possess skills that technological change has rendered obsolete. This is particularly true of those in the development areas, and it is clear that many of these men will not get jobs again until they receive some form of training. Facilities for training and re-training in this country are still seriously inadequate by the standards of some other countries, a fact for which employers and unions are probably more to blame than the government. Nevertheless some progress has been made during the past few years both in expanding the amount of training done in industry and in enlarging the government training centres, and it is to be hoped that this will gather momentum.

But perhaps the main advance on the regional front during the past few years has been the increasing acceptance that hit-or-miss methods are not good enough. It is no good simply pushing certain buttons (labelled *cash grants* or *tax allowances* or *cheap loans*) in a random sort of way and hoping that the resulting stimulus will just happen to create the right amount of employment in the right places. What is needed is a detailed assessment of the needs of individual regions (and areas within regions) and carefully planned action to remedy these needs. The location of new factories or offices must be influenced by the distribution of population, and by travel-to-work distances. The siting of new social investment in houses, roads, schools and so on must be related to plans for the expansion of employment. The kind of employment provided must be the kind that is needed: it is no good creating plenty of jobs for typists or shop assistants in an area where technical change is displacing coal-miners or farm labourers.

The coordination of decisions that this approach requires probably needs to be handled on a regional basis: it is too detailed to be manageable by the central government, but too large in scope to be within the functions of local authorities. It is still too early to pronounce a final verdict on the new regional planning machinery set up by the Labour government in 1964–5, and there is still a multitude of problems to be solved. But the new approach seems full of promise.

However we must not lose sight of the fact that specific measures aimed at reducing regional unemployment will only work in the context of a generally full employment economy. Businessmen will not invest in the development areas, and neither they nor unions will cooperate in re-training programmes, if the overall level of demand is too low and men and machinery are idle in the Midlands and south. Regional incentives are not a substitute for Keynesian policies; they are a supplement to them.

CYCLICAL UNEMPLOYMENT

We have seen that although in a broad sense Britain has enjoyed full employment since the war, a miner in the Welsh valleys or a labourer in Greenock might have good reason for taking a different view. But even such apparently favoured categories of worker as skilled tool-makers in Reading and semi-skilled car-workers in Coventry might be forgiven for questioning whether it was true that with the publication of the 1944 White Paper full employment had come to stay. For during the past twenty years unemployment has not only been present for a good deal of the time in particular *places*; it has also made an appearance practically everywhere at particular *times*. In other words the old pre-war trade cycle has not been altogether eliminated. It has, it is true, been tamed almost out of recognition. In the past, unemployment during the cycle would not generally fall below 2–3 per cent, and would rise during the down-swing phase to 8–10 per cent. Since the war the variations have been very much smaller, with unemployment occasionally falling as low as 1 per cent, but rarely rising above 2 or 2½ per cent. But even this latter degree of unemployment, which occurred in 1952, 1958–9, 1962–3 and 1966–7, is obviously undesirable. Were the Keynesian tools too clumsy to regulate the economy with more precision than this?

A large part of the answer, at any rate as far as the first ten years after the war were concerned, must be yes. It was not always possible to foresee developments which could change demand: and even if they could be foreseen they could not always be compensated for sufficiently quickly. One of the chief villains of the piece was the same as it always had been – business investment (including investment in stocks, a very volatile item). Even in the much more stable and fully employed post-war world, businessmen's attitudes can oscillate alarmingly. At times they feel that the outlook is good and that high profits can be earned from new investment, and in these circumstances – optimism being infectious – investment can rise very rapidly – by 10 or 15 per cent a year. At other times all can be gloom, and businessmen pull in their horns and wait and see; in this situation there can be a marked fall in investment. Furthermore the one set of attitudes can give way quite rapidly to the other. This makes the forecasting of business investment a very tricky affair.

Another example of a category of expenditure which behaves rather unpredictably is exports. Exports depend not only on the price and quality of British goods but also on conditions in the rest of the world. As we saw in connexion with the experiences of the 1930s, falling demand or the emergence of a balance of payments problem in other countries can hit British exports quite hard and suddenly, and with exports accounting for more than a fifth of total production a setback to exports can have major repercussions on employment.

Thus changes in exports or investment can occur fairly suddenly and unexpectedly, and can have quite significant effects on the economy before any government counter-measures have time to come into play. Consequently there are bound to be short periods now and again when the economy suffers from a bit too much demand, or a bit too little. A couple of quick examples may illustrate the point. In 1952 British exports, which had risen rapidly, even dramatically, since the end of the war, turned sharply down. This fall was concentrated particularly on textiles which, although their importance in the exports picture had been falling for decades, were still a significant part of the exporting effort. This drop in textile (and other) exports, which was compounded by a simultaneous decline in stock-building at home, was not foreseen (or, to any great extent, foreseeable); as a result demand and employment fell below the levels predicted and intended by the government, and there was a sharp, though fairly short-lived, rise in unemployment, particularly in the textile areas.*

Another failure of effective demand to behave in the desired way was seen in 1955, though this time the failure was in the other direction. Business investment, after remaining flat in the early 1950s, suddenly started to accelerate, and by 1955 was rising at the unexpectedly rapid rate of 15 per cent a year. Other kinds of expenditure were also rising quite fast, and further fuel was added to the flames by the 1955 Budget, which reduced the standard rate of income tax by sixpence. Production rose, but not nearly enough to match the rise in demand, so that an excess demand developed which was met partly by rising imports and partly by rising prices. We shall be saying more about this kind of situation, where the problem is not one of too little demand leading to unemployment, but too much demand leading to inflation

---

* The full story of the 1952 recession is much more complicated than this, of course; in particular the period was influenced by the Korean War and the re-armament programme. But the fall in textile production was a very noticeable feature.

and balance of payments difficulties, in the next two chapters. The point to note here is that certain kinds of expenditure can move rather suddenly either above or below the level expected of them, and however quickly the government acts once this becomes apparent, it will be too late to avoid some temporary excess demand or some temporary unemployment.

Indeed some people would take this argument a good deal further and say that by the time it is agreed that expenditure is misbehaving (for statistics are always out-of-date and often conflicting) and by the time the government has decided to act (for there are always those who want to wait and see) and by the time such action has started to bite (for it takes a long time to put some tax changes into effect, and even longer to change public expenditure) the original situation will probably have disappeared, and may even have been replaced by its opposite. In other words, steps to raise demand may not take effect until the next boom is already under way, and steps to reduce it may coincide with the next recession: government intervention may be intensifying the cycle rather than smoothing it out.

It has been argued, for example, that this is what occurred in 1961–3. In 1958 unemployment had risen to what was then the highest level since the war, and to counter this hire-purchase controls were removed and Bank Rate brought down to 4 per cent; and in the 1959 Budget the Chancellor announced big reductions in both income tax and purchase tax. As a result, demand rose rapidly in 1959 and 1960, imports soared, and the balance of payments worsened dramatically. By the middle of 1960 people were beginning to talk of the dangers of another 1955, with an excess of demand intensifying the rise in prices and making the balance of payments worse than ever. Demand must be reduced, it was urged, to prevent this from happening. But the government did not get around to taking action until July 1961, when indirect taxes were raised by 10 per cent, Bank Rate was increased and government expenditure was cut back. But in the meantime, as is now clear, the economy had gone right off the boil. Exports had flattened out and private investment was already turning down. Some of the government's measures – notably the cuts in public expenditure – did not really start to bite until well into 1962, and by this time the economy was already sliding into recession, with consumption pretty flat and investment falling fast. In fact the government's measures did not hit the economy on the head until it was already on the way down. Consequently the rise in unemployment was, by post-war standards, quite marked; even allowing for the temporary effects on the building industry of the particularly severe winter of 1962–3, unemployment in early 1963 was over 3 per cent.

Insofar as cyclical unemployment results from a failure to foresee changes in some category of expenditure, or failure to offset such changes quickly enough, one can obviously hope for improvement in the future. Although short-term forecasting techniques are now very sophisticated in comparison with the first efforts of twenty-five years ago, there is still plenty of scope for improvement. We have not yet reached the stage, for example, where a computer can provide very helpful predictions about the future behaviour of different kinds of expenditure, chiefly because we are not yet able to feed it with sufficiently accurate or up-to-date information about economic relationships in the very great degree of detail required; but econometric models are beginning to play an increasing part in forecasting. Similarly there is room for improving the effectiveness of government measures to offset changes in expenditure: it would be very useful, for example, if the Chancellor could alter direct taxation whenever it seemed necessary, without having to wait until his next April Budget. Indeed there is no reason why one should not develop more sophisticated methods of reducing the fluctuations in some of the elements of demand which are the source of the trouble. Obviously fluctuations in exports will always remain to some extent outside our control – though even here international forecasting and planning could assume a bigger role; but fluctuations in private investment could probably be reduced by giving grants or tax credits which varied according to the pressure on the capital goods industries. This was in fact done late in 1966, when the government announced a *temporary* increase in investment grants, to apply only to investment expenditure incurred before the end of 1968.

However it would be quite wrong to give the impression that cyclical unemployment since the war has resulted solely from errors of forecasting and sluggishness of government response. For the same reason, it would be idle to imagine that improvements in forecasting or regulatory techniques will necessarily lead to smaller fluctuations or a lower average level of unemployment. For on every occasion since the mid-1950s that unemployment has risen it has done so because the government *took decisions which it knew would have this effect*. This is not to say that unemployment was always expected to rise as far as it did – in 1962–3, as we have seen, the recession was deeper than expected. Nor is it to say that once a higher level of unemployment has been reached the government has been content to leave it there: in periods such as 1958–9 and 1963–4 steps were taken to increase demand and thus bring unemployment down again. But the fact remains that the rise in unemployment in 1957–8, in 1962–3, and again in 1966–7, was the result of deliberate government policy.

Here we have a paradox. During the 1920s and 1930s the government wanted full employment but had no idea how to get it. But it now seems that in the 1950s and 1960s it has known how to get it but has not always wanted it. This is, of course, to exaggerate, and indeed to raise the semantic question of exactly what is meant by 'full employment' (see

Explanatory Note 1, page 255). No government since the war has ever wanted unemployment to rise above 2 or at most $2\frac{1}{2}$ per cent – less than a fifth of the average between the wars. Nevertheless it remains true that since the war the job of the Greenock labourer or the Coventry car-worker has been at risk not only from regional decline and technical progress, or fluctuations in private investment and other countries' imports; it has also been at risk from deliberate government policy. To the explanation of this paradox we must now turn.

CHAPTER 8

PRICES

RISING PRICES SINCE THE WAR

WE have seen that if there is too low a level of demand in an economy the result is unemployment: during the 1920s and 1930s there was too little demand in Britain, and the consequence was prolonged unemployment. But what happens if there is too *much* demand in an economy? What is the opposite of unemployment? Naturally enough Keynes did not devote a great deal of the *General Theory* to this question, but nevertheless he did answer it quite clearly. What one means by saying that there is too much demand in the economy is, to put it rather loosely, that the economy is already going flat out, with full employment of men and machinery, so that output is at its highest possible level – and that there is then an increase in demand. This increase in demand cannot call forth more output. All it can do is one of two things. Either it can pull up the price of the goods and services that are already being produced – the consequence of a larger amount of money being spent on the same amount of stuff. Or, in an economy which trades with other countries, it can increase the quantity of goods available – but only by sucking in more imports and diverting to the home market goods that would otherwise have been exported. In practice, an excessive level of demand will probably result in some of each: there will be some rise in prices; and imports will be higher, and exports lower, than they would otherwise have been.

Now anyone who has lived in post-war Britain in even moderate possession of his faculties will observe that there is something familiar about this. Rising prices; too low a level of exports; too high a level of imports; surely these are at the heart of our post-war economic problems – as characteristic of the 1950s and 1960s as unemployment was of the 1920s and 1930s? If Keynes's analysis showed us how to prevent unemployment by ensuring that there is *enough* demand in the economy, why has it not also shown us how to prevent rising prices and balance of payments crises by avoiding *too much* demand?

There is certainly cause for complaint. Over the past fifteen or twenty years retail prices have risen at an average rate of about 4 per cent a year. This is in sharp contrast with the twenty-year period between the wars, when there was a significant fall in prices, and with the century before the First World War, when prices remained roughly stable – not because they never rose, but because during the down-swing of the trade cycle they usually fell. The continuous rise in prices of the past twenty years has been a new phenomenon. Similarly, the series of balance of payments crises we have suffered since the war has also been a new phenomenon: occasional crises had of course occurred in the past, but to have five or six within twenty years certainly sets a new record.

But although the complaint about rising prices and balance of payments crises is amply justified, one must approach the explanation of these phenomena with extreme caution. Aristotle pointed out a long time ago the dangers of the kind of logical sequence which runs:

Excessive demand causes rising prices and balance of payments difficulties;

Britain has suffered from rising prices and balance of payments difficulties;

Therefore Britain has suffered from excessive demand.

Unfortunately this ancient warning sometimes falls on stony ground, and many people, including some economists, have tended to suppose that excessive demand must have been the cause of rising prices and balance of payments problems in the post-war period. It has been assumed, in fact, that the persistence of these evils has been due to the government's failure to apply Keynes's analysis in a situation of too much demand, just as the persistence of unemployment between the wars was due to the government's failure to understand what was needed in a situation of too little demand. There was some excuse for the unemployment of the 1920s and 1930s, because Keynes had not yet supplied the key; there could be no excuse for the rising prices and balance of payments crises of the 1950s and 1960s – Keynes's key worked in reverse, but was simply not being used. So at any rate ran (and in some places still runs) the argument.

EXCESS DEMAND DURING THE WAR

One compelling reason for supposing this argument to be wrong is that the war years demonstrated convincingly that the corollary of Keynes's analysis – i.e. that too much demand leads to rising prices – had been pretty well understood. Indeed one could say that the first signs that the real signifi- cance of the *General Theory* had been grasped by the govern- ment came not with the promise in the 1944 White Paper to keep demand *up*, but with the government's action from the early days of the war to keep demand *down*. Although un- employment was still above 10 per cent in 1939, it was obvious that in the all-out war that looked like developing this unemployment would soon disappear and be replaced by a condition of excess demand. Millions of men would be drafted into the armed forces; millions more would be en- gaged on war production. What would the wages and salaries of all these people be spent on ? Only a relatively small pro- portion of the labour force would be engaged on the produc- tion of the consumer goods and services on which individuals spend their income, and not much shipping capacity could be spared for consumer imports. The attempt by individual families to spend their incomes on the usual consumer goods would constitute a very large degree of excess demand, and result in a very rapid rise in prices which could prove highly damaging to the war effort. It was clear from the analysis in the *General Theory* (and the point was hammered home in *How to Pay for the War*, which Keynes published early in 1940) that if this were to be avoided demand must be reduced. Just as when there is unemployment the government must increase demand by cutting taxes or persuading businessmen to invest more, so in this situation the government must reduce demand by increasing taxes or persuading businessmen to invest less. And this was in fact done: income tax went up to 10s. in the £, drink and tobacco duties were put up very sharply, and purchase tax made its first appearance. Taxes had, of course, risen during the First World War, though much less sharply; but the reason then had been to balance, as far as possible, the government's own accounts; now it was to balance demand and supply in the economy as a whole.

In *How to Pay for the War*, however, Keynes went further than this and argued that it would be impossible to eliminate excessive demand simply by higher taxation: the necessary rise in taxes on wage-earners would have been politically unacceptable. Therefore there should be a scheme of compulsory savings – people would have money deducted from their pay-packets, but this money, instead of going to the Exchequer in the form of taxes, would be kept for them and given back after the end of the war. Expenditure on consumption would be reduced in exactly the same way as by higher taxes, but people would have the comfort of knowing that they would get the money back, and be able to spend it on consumer goods, after the war. This scheme was adopted ('post-war credits'), though not on nearly as large a scale as Keynes would have liked, and the main weapons used to reduce excess demand were rationing and physical controls.*

NO EXCESS DEMAND SINCE THE WAR

Nevertheless, in spite of the use of rationing and physical controls, and in spite of the fact that prices did rise quite substantially (by nearly 50 per cent) between 1939 and 1945, it is clear that the Keynesian conclusion that excess demand causes rising prices had a significant influence on wartime economic policy, and helped to prevent prices from rising much faster than they did. Therefore it cannot plausibly be argued that rising prices in the post-war period have been due to a failure to realize that excess demand leads to rising prices. The explanation must be either that the government was unable or unwilling to eliminate excess demand, or that rising prices in the post-war period have been caused not by excess demand but by some other factor.

There is a little bit of truth in the first explanation. There

* Rationing and physical controls are alternatives to higher taxes and compulsory savings as a method of preventing rising prices in a situation of excess demand. Taxes and compulsory savings reduce the amount of money that people have to spend until it is equal (at the existing level of prices) to the amount of consumer goods being produced. Rationing, on the other hand, limits the amount of goods that people can buy, irrespective of how much money they have to spend. The price of these goods can be fixed by the government, since people cannot obtain more of them by offering to pay a higher price. This leaves many people with money to spend on other things, but if physical controls over the allocation of materials (or labour) to industry prevent other goods from being produced this money cannot be spent. The end-result is much the same as Keynes's compulsory saving scheme – at the end of the war people will have large accumulated savings which they will want to spend. The main difference is that once consumer goods come back into the shops they will find it easier to spend the money if they have saved it themselves than if the government has saved it for them in the form of post-war credits (as many of those with post-war credits have discovered). But if the government continues to control the level of demand even this distinction is more apparent than real.

has been excess demand from time to time for particular kinds of goods; for quite long periods for particular kinds of skilled labour; and in 1955, as we saw in Chapter 7, throughout much of the economy. In many, though not all, of these cases excess demand has developed because of the forecasting errors we discussed in the last chapter, and not because of a willingness to tolerate it. But this kind of excess demand has been of a very partial and peripheral kind compared with the kind of widespread and general excess demand that threatened during the war, and to which Keynes's analysis is relevant. Most economists would now agree that the measures appropriate in a situation of general excess demand – higher taxes and interest rates, cuts in public investment and discouragement of private investment – would not have eliminated or even significantly reduced the rise in prices; they would simply have led to a fall in output and employment, and a rise in unemployment. Indeed this is no theoretical proposition: measures appropriate to a general excess demand *have* been adopted from time to time during the past ten or fifteen years, and *have* resulted in unemployment without significantly slowing down the rise in prices.

This is because it is the second of our two possibilities that contains the main part of the truth. The factor mainly responsible for rising prices in the post-war period has not been excess demand, but something quite different – rising costs. In fact, it has been less a question of a *pulling up* of prices from above, than of a *pushing up* of prices from below. Or, to use the generally accepted terms, it is not 'demand' or 'demand-pull' inflation that has been the real trouble, but 'cost' or 'cost-push' inflation.

It is not always easy in practice to tell the difference between demand and cost inflation, but in principle they are quite different processes. In the demand inflation case, the demand for a commodity exceeds the supply at the existing level of prices, and prices are therefore pulled upwards until they reach a level at which supply and demand are once again in balance. (An analogy of an extreme sort would be an auction, at which people bid against each other in order to get possession of an object in limited supply.) In the case of cost inflation, on the other hand, what happens is that the cost of producing a commodity rises, and as a result its price is raised, even though there is no excess demand for it. If, for example, there is a rise in the cost of producing a ton of coal, either because narrower seams have to be worked, or simply because miners are given a wage increase, and this leads to a rise in the price of coal, this is cost-push inflation at work.

Now one crucial element in the operation of cost inflation is that producers should be able to raise their prices without suffering much, if any, loss of sales. Normally, the only producer with this kind of control over prices is a mono-polist – i.e. someone who is the sole producer of a commodity, such as salt or electric light bulbs, for which there is no close substitute. One can see how a monopolist could increase the price of his product to cover higher costs (resulting perhaps from paying his workers more) without suffering much loss of sales. But monopolists are fairly rare. How, it may be asked, can cost inflation operate in an economy which is for the most part made up of producers who compete with each other? How can any one producer pass on higher costs by raising his prices (if there is no excess demand for his pro-duct) without badly losing sales to his competitors?

The answer, in brief, is that although *one* employer in-curring higher costs will probably not be successful in passing them on in higher prices, if *all* employers incur higher costs, they *can* pass them on in higher prices – for the price of all the goods in competition with each other will have risen, and there is no reason for any particular producer to suffer. But, it might be argued, if all goods have risen in price because all employers have passed on higher costs, surely many of these goods will remain unsold? Where is the money to come from to buy the same quantity of goods as before at a higher price? The answer, again in brief, is that the extra money is there – in the form of the higher wages (and profits) that were responsible for prices being pushed up in the first place. In fact higher wages and profits lead to higher prices, and then higher prices can be paid out of the higher wages and profits.

This analysis underlies much of the economic policy of the last ten years, and it may be as well to look at some of the salient points in a little more detail.

INCOMES AND PRICES

The money income of an economy, the output of that economy, and the price of that output, are all related to each other in a fairly simple and obvious way. We saw in Chapter 4 that the total output of the economy is the same thing as the total income of the economy.* Prices are the link between the two.

In a simplified economy, if total money incomes are a thousand pounds a year, and the output of the economy consists of a hundred chairs a year, then the price of each chair must be £10. If money incomes are two thousand pounds a year, then the price of each chair will be £20. And if (getting closer to home) each year money income rises by 7 per cent, and the output of chairs by 3 per cent, then each year the price of chairs will rise by approximately 4 per cent; for a rise in money incomes to £1,070 is only consistent with a rise in the output of chairs to 103 if the price of each chair rises to approximately £10 8s.

This is, in essence, what has been happening in post-war Britain. The facts about the behaviour of the economy during the past fifteen or twenty years are simple: on average, output has risen by about 3 per cent a year, incomes by about 7 per cent a year, and prices by about 4 per cent a year. What we

* And see Explanatory Note 3, page 256.

are saying is this: given that output rose by 3 per cent a year, prices rose by 4 per cent a year *because* incomes rose by 7 per cent a year, and not the other way round.

For this to have happened in this way, there must have been sufficient of a monopoly element in existence to enable producers who hand themselves and their workers bigger incomes to cover these bigger incomes by raising their prices without suffering any loss of sales; and people's incomes must be rising enough to enable them to buy the same quantity of goods even though prices are higher. In particular, there must be some monopoly element at work which ensures that in the main incomes and prices are determined by the deliberate decisions of workers and employers, and are not shaped in an impersonal way by the pressure of market forces.

One such factor is fairly clear. There are still some areas in the economy where something like perfect competition prevails, and prices are determined by impersonal market forces, with each buyer and seller being too small to influence the price: Covent Garden fruit and vegetable market is an example. But such cases are very much an exception to the general rule. Throughout most of the economy decisions on incomes and prices are now taken by far fewer groups of people, each representing a much larger share of the market, than was the case in the last century or even before the last war. The basic pay of three million engineering workers, for example, is negotiated by one group of men; the price of nearly all the flat glass produced in Britain is determined by one board of directors. In this kind of situation there is clearly scope for wages and salaries to be pushed up without regard to how fast output is rising, and for prices to be pushed up without this resulting in much, if any, reduction in sales.

RISING PRICES AND FULL EMPLOYMENT

But although the influence of this sort of monopoly element is important, one cannot say that it has grown enough since the war to account fully for the difference between the stable or even falling price level of the early decades of the century, and a price level which rises by around 4 per cent a year. The truth is that the real monopoly element lies in the existence of full employment itself. With the maintenance of full employment, employed labour as a whole now enjoys a monopoly that it did not enjoy before the acceptance of the *General Theory*, when it was in actual or potential competition with the unemployed. 'If you ask for large wage increases you may become unemployed, either because those at present unemployed are willing to do your job at your present wage, or because your firm cannot afford higher wages and would have to close down.' This would have been a very potent threat to make to a trade union negotiator in the 1920s and 1930s, and even in the less depressed conditions before the First World War. But once the government knew how to maintain full employment, *and had pledged itself to do so*, the threat became meaningless. Whatever the size of wage increases that unions asked for or got there was no reason to fear that unemployment would result.*

Exactly the same monopoly status was conferred on employers, as a class, by the guarantee of full employment. Before the war the employing class as a whole might fear that if they pushed up prices in order to maintain or increase their profits they might be unable to sell their output at the higher price, so that a general recession might develop in which their output and profits would be badly hit. But now that permanent full employment was guaranteed by the government, although this might be the fate of an individual firm, it could not happen to output and profits as a whole.

One can see how these two factors – the guarantee of full employment and the size of bargaining units – can operate

---

* Though it is fair to add that – as is illustrated by the continuance of many restrictive practices – unions have not always behaved as though they accepted that full employment was here to stay.

to push up incomes faster than output, and therefore raise prices, if one looks at a particular example. Take the case of engineering, where basic wages are fixed over a table by negotiations between two sets of men, one representing 3 million workers and the other the thousands of firms which employ these 3 million workers. Each year (for these negotiations have become something of an annual event comparable to the Boat Race or the Grand National) the proceedings might be characterized as follows. The unions start off by asking for a 12 per cent wage increase. The employers offer 4 per cent. After prolonged negotiations and a series of virtuoso displays of brinkmanship which give everybody a feeling of importance and provide industrial journalists with a livelihood, British compromise ensures that wages are actually increased by 8 per cent. Assuming that productivity in the engineering industry rises by about 5 per cent a year this will mean a rise in labour costs per unit of output of 3 per cent.* Employers normally fix their prices (and maintain their profit margins) by adding a mark-up to their unit labour costs. They will therefore raise their prices by 3 per cent. With a 5 per cent increase in output this will ensure that profits, like wages, will rise by 8 per cent.

Now no explanation is needed of why the unions should want a large wage increase. But it may seem puzzling that the employers should be willing to grant it. Are they not running rather a risk in granting a wage increase so big that they have to put up their prices by 3 per cent in order to pay for it? Quite simply, no. There is no particular risk. No individual employer need fear that by increasing his prices he is going to lose business to his competitors, for his competitors (i.e. other engineering firms) have granted the same wage increase as he has and will therefore have to raise their prices too. Nor is there much need to fear that people will reduce their

* Each man produces 5 per cent more each year, but earns 8 per cent more. Therefore the cost of each item he produces rises by 3 per cent.

purchases of engineering goods *as a whole* because they now cost more. There are three reasons for this. First, there are no close substitutes for engineering goods as a whole – a rise in the price of machine tools or cars or record-players will not normally cause a massive switch of expenditure towards food or clothes or foreign travel. Secondly, if by any chance people *did* do this, and the engineering industry found itself faced by falling sales and rising unemployment, the government would have to step in and do something about it. Thirdly, and perhaps most compelling of all, it will not only be in engineering that wages (and profits) will have risen by 8 per cent; this kind of wage increase will have occurred in many other industries as well. This has a double effect: the prices of other goods and services will also have risen, thus reducing any incentive to switch expenditure from engineering goods to other things; and people's incomes will have risen enough to enable them to pay higher prices for engineering goods.*

In this situation, then, an engineering employer has no strong incentive to resist a demand for an 8 per cent wage increase. Indeed there is a positive incentive *not* to resist it. If he grants it he can raise his prices at little or no risk to his sales, and his profits will rise accordingly; but if he resists it and his workers go on strike his sales and profits can be badly, perhaps even fatally, affected. The line of least resistance, in fact, is also the line of greatest prosperity. And although we have been discussing a case (engineering) in which there is a monopoly element on each side of the bargaining table, the existence of a number of such cases ensures that the same moral applies throughout most of the rest of the economy as well. Even the small employer bargaining on his own is likely to grant big wage increases and push up his prices rather than

*A qualification to all this, of course, is the possibility that people may switch to buying engineering goods from other countries whose prices have not risen. We come on to this problem in the next chapter.

risk a strike. For he will reckon that his competitors, even though they are acting quite independently of him, will be facing the same pressures as himself and are also likely to concede wage increases and raise their prices; and with everybody's wages, salaries and profits rising in this way, there should be no great difficulty in selling his output at a higher price.

This, then, is a brief and simplified account of how one gets continuously rising prices in an economy in which there is full employment but no general excess demand. But it should be noted that although, for convenience, we started the process off with a large increase in wages, this does not necessarily mean that rising prices must be blamed on the unions. This is a chicken and egg problem. It is true that an increase in wages which outstrips an increase in productivity will, in the typical case, lead to an increase in prices. But one can equally say that an increase in prices, by reducing real wages (i.e. the amount that can be bought with a given money wage) will inevitably lead to a demand for higher money wages. It is hardly surprising that a demand for higher money wages will be aimed not merely at restoring real wages to what they were before prices rose, but at actually increasing real wages and thus participating in the growing prosperity of the economy. If prices have risen by 3 or 4 per cent since the last wage increase this is bound to mean wage demands of 6–8 per cent or more.

TRADITIONAL DIFFERENTIALS

It has been a notable feature of the post-war scene in Britain that big increases in wages have not been confined to particular industries in which the unions happen to be large and well organized. Big wage increases have tended to be an annual or near-annual event for most workers in the economy. One reason for this lies in the complex network of traditional differentials that has grown up over the past half-century or so. Over a large part of the economy this has meant that if workers in one industry get a 6–8 per cent wage increase, workers in many other industries will soon get 6–8 per cent wage increases as well.

In the post-war period, for example, an increase in wages in the engineering industry has also tended to be applied in railway workshops, which employ a number of engineers. This in turn has spread to railwaymen in the workshops, then other railwaymen, then the London Underground, then London busmen, then provincial busmen. There is no way of breaking the chain short of disrupting traditional relativities. As long as the unions insist on maintaining these relativities, and employers are unwilling to face a prolonged strike in order to upset them, it will be inevitable that an increase in wages granted to one set of workers in the chain will be applied pretty automatically to others. Nor does the process stop there. If a third of the workers in the economy have had a 7 or 8 per cent wage increase in the past six months, the other two thirds will tend before long to be granted increases of the same sort of size: trade union officials have the same desire as the rest of us not to appear noticeably feebler than their colleagues.

WAGE DRIFT

As we have emphasized earlier, the kind of process we have been describing ('cost-push' inflation) can and does operate in the absence of general excess demand. But we must not throw excess demand completely out of the window. Cost-push inflation has undoubtedly been accentuated in post-war Britain by *specific* kinds of excess demand in particular places and for particular types of labour. This again has resulted in part from the system of traditional differentials. There is, for example, a long tradition about the right kind of differential that should exist between the pay of skilled and unskilled engineering workers. Throughout much of the post-war period there has been excess demand for particular types of skilled engineering workers, particularly in parts of the Midlands and south-east, in the sense that such men have been relatively scarce, and employers have been willing to pay more than they are actually paying in order to get or retain them. This has led to employers bidding against each other for such men: many skilled fitters have had a good time in recent years moving around from one firm to another getting an extra twopence or threepence an hour on each occasion. This is one aspect of what has been called 'wage drift'. But because of the existence of traditional differentials the increased pay of skilled men for whom there is excess demand has resulted in semi-skilled and unskilled men, for whom there is *not* excess demand, claiming higher wages in order to restore the differential. This they do by the kind of industry-wide bargaining we discussed above. But the process does not end there either. In engineering, for example, an 8 per cent wage increase agreed on by the collective bargaining process will also raise the wages of the skilled men (though by less than 8 per cent, since the 8 per cent is calculated on the basic rate and not on their, much higher, level of earnings). And so before long the whole cycle starts again.

Even if excess demand for particular types of skilled labour in particular places were a major contributory factor to rising prices one could hardly hope to deal with it by measures aimed at the general level of demand in the economy. As we have seen, such measures would tend to produce unemployment among unskilled workers in the north and west before they had a great deal of impact on the demand for tool-makers or bricklayers in London or Birmingham. In other words such measures would have more effect in increasing unemployment than in slowing down the rise in prices. The steps needed are specific ones, aimed at training more skilled men and evening out the demand for labour in different parts of the country.

But we must not exaggerate the part that excess demand for certain skills has played in post-war inflation: it has had an effect, but a relatively minor one. The most important factor has been 'cost-push' – the pushing up of wages by unions and of prices by employers. This being so, there is no hope, as long as the government is committed to full employment, of stopping prices from rising by manipulating the general level of demand. One can only do it by attacking the problem at source, by ensuring that total incomes – both wages and profits – do not rise by 6–8 per cent a year, but only in line with the rise in total output. It is a matter of judgement how far one attacks the problem from the incomes end, by preventing wages from rising by more than 3 or 4 per cent a year, and relying on the normal 'mark-up' method of pricing to ensure that profits also rise by only 3 or 4 per cent and the overall level of prices therefore remains stable; or, on the other hand, how far one attacks the problem from the prices end, by making it difficult for businesses to increase prices, and thus forcing them, if they want to maintain their profit margins, to resist wage increases that are bigger than the rise in productivity. In practice what has now come to be called the 'prices and incomes policy' attempts to operate on both ends of the problem simultaneously.

Efforts are also being made to increase the growth of productivity, and it is of course an arithmetical fact that the faster production and productivity can be made to grow, the less is the need to slow down the rise in incomes to get stable prices. But a faster rise in productivity cannot be counted on to provide a great deal of help as far as the prices problem is concerned, because of the relative orders of magnitude of the factors involved. It will be a substantial achievement if the British growth rate can be increased from around 3 per cent to around 4 per cent, but this will obviously not go very far towards closing the gap if incomes continue to rise by 7 or 8 per cent a year – particularly since a faster rise in productivity may to some extent carry with it a faster rise in incomes because of methods of payment – such as piece-rates – which are geared to productivity.

It may be worth summarizing in a few words the main point we have been making in this chapter. In the *General Theory* Keynes showed governments how, by controlling the level of demand, they could ensure full employment. Governments, in Britain and most other developed countries, have used the weapon of control of effective demand deliberately and successfully to achieve this objective. But the very success with which the weapon has been used has created conditions from which has sprung another problem – rising prices – against which the weapon is largely ineffective. Sensible use of Keynes's analysis to ensure that the level of demand is not excessive is a precondition of stable prices, for if demand is excessive, prices will certainly rise. But controlling the level of demand will not by itself do the trick. The problem must be attacked more directly by a 'prices and incomes policy' aimed at persuading individual unions to moderate their wage claims and individual firms to stabilize or reduce their prices.

CHAPTER 9

GROWTH AND THE BALANCE OF PAYMENTS IN THE POST-WAR PERIOD

In the last chapter we looked at the problem of rising prices in a purely domestic context. This being so, an intelligent visitor from outer space who had followed the argument to date might be expected to inquire what all the fuss was about. Why are post-war rising prices implicitly being treated as an evil of the same order of magnitude as pre-war unemployment? Surely what really matters in an economy is the standard of living, which can be quickly defined as the level of output per head? What was really evil about the pre-war situation was that because over a million men were unemployed, output was much lower than it need have been. But throughout the post-war period there has been virtually permanent full employment, and total output has therefore been as high as the economy's slowly growing productive potential allowed. No doubt one can criticize the way in which this output, or National Income, has been distributed between different groups of people in the community, and also the rate at which it has risen, but what is the sense in bewailing the fact that prices have not been stable? How is this relevant to the standard of living?

One must have a great deal of sympathy with this line of argument. Certainly the standard section in the standard seaside constituency speech to the effect that post-war rising prices constitute the same kind of evil as pre-war unemployment is complete rubbish. Of course rising prices create serious problems for those who do not participate in the annual rise in wages, salaries and dividends. Pensioners and others on fixed incomes are the hardest hit. But the fact that they suffer from rising prices is not an act of God. As a society we are perfectly well able to insulate them against rising prices if we want to. There is no reason whatever why retirement pensions and other National Insurance benefits paid out by the state should not rise automatically, at yearly or half-yearly intervals, in line with prices, or indeed earnings. Those on private fixed incomes are a more difficult case, but can still be helped indirectly in a variety of ways; and many of them can and do help themselves by investing their savings in equity shares (or unit trusts holding equity shares) instead of fixed-interest bearing assets. Rising prices also create other, more technical problems, for example in connexion with the management of the National Debt – but none that are beyond the wit of man to cope with. In short, as far as the domestic scene is concerned, no suggestion that rising prices constitute a major social and economic problem comparable to mass unemployment will bear serious examination.

THE BALANCE OF PAYMENTS

But when we turn to the international scene things are rather different. Consider the balance of payments – the King Charles's head of any discussion on the British economy. The British balance of payments is a monstrously complicated affair, and those who understand it in its full glory are probably as rare and privileged as those who understood the mysteries of the Delphic oracle. However for present purposes we can confine ourselves to aspects of it which are, at any rate in outline, fairly simple.

The balance of payments on *current account* is just what the term suggests: it is the difference between payments made, and payments received, for current transactions. These mainly comprise exports and imports of goods and services, but also include military and diplomatic expenditure overseas, and current grants to less developed countries. Since the war it has been a continuing major objective of British economic policy to have a surplus on current account in order to finance various capital payments overseas (chiefly investment in foreign countries by private firms) and to build up the reserves. The size of the desired surplus has been put at different times at various figures between £300 million and £450 million. In fact the average surplus since 1948 has been only about £25 million, and in many years there has been a deficit.

In a world of fixed exchange rates (i.e. in which the British government is committed to keeping the value of sterling in a fixed relationship with other currencies, so that for example there are $2·80 to the £ and no more and no less) the relevance of what happens to the prices of British goods is fairly obvious. *If British prices rise faster than other countries' prices* the British balance of payments will tend to move from surplus into deficit. British goods on sale in Germany, for example, will become more expensive compared with goods made in Germany or goods imported into Germany from France, and British export sales will suffer accordingly.* The same thing happens in reverse in the home market. British-made goods rise in price compared with goods imported from Germany and France, so people switch increasingly to foreign-made goods and the import bill rises. The current account surplus (if there was one in the first place) gets eaten away from both directions.

---

*It is theoretically possible for the British balance of payments actually to benefit from this, if the Germans are so keen on British goods that they buy the same quantity of them, even though their prices have risen (technically, if the price elasticity of demand for British goods is zero). For in this case Britain would be selling the same quantity of goods but getting a larger quantity of deutschmarks in return. Unfortunately British goods do not appear to be as marvellous as that.

RESERVES AND LIABILITIES

When this has happened – and it has happened often during the past twenty years – the British government has always, after a shorter or longer period of vacillation, taken action. But the action has not always been dictated solely by a virtuous desire to earn a modest surplus on current account. British policy is hedged in by more sinister constraints than that. Briefly (we shall be dealing with this in more detail in Chapter 10) sterling is a *reserve currency*, which means that many other countries hold their international reserves in the form of sterling – i.e. they hold large sums of money in London in the form of bank accounts, Treasury Bills and other government securities. They are entitled to convert this sterling into gold or other currencies such as dollars or deutschmarks whenever they like; in other words to present their pound notes to the Bank of England and demand gold or foreign currencies in return. Moreover it is not only foreign governments which hold sterling in this way; sterling is also a widely used *trading* currency, meaning that an Argentine firm buying steel from a Japanese firm may well pay in sterling. Consequently there are banks and private firms all over the world which hold substantial amounts of sterling.

Now this would be perfectly all right as long as Britain had enough gold and foreign exchange to meet all demands for conversion of sterling. Unfortunately she has not. Throughout most of the post-war period Britain's gold and foreign exchange reserves have averaged something like £1,000 million, while her sterling liabilities have averaged more like £4,000 million. In normal times this 4 to 1 ratio is perfectly adequate: foreign governments and banks hold sterling because it suits them to do so, and there is normally no particular reason why a large number of them should suddenly decide to convert this sterling into foreign currencies.

But the position changes when Britain's current balance moves into deficit. Since it is Britain's openly proclaimed objective to achieve a reasonably large surplus on current account, even a fairly small deficit represents a marked failure of policy. When the deficit is a large one – as it has been on several occasions in the last ten or fifteen years – the failure of policy becomes very pronounced. Now when a country's current account is in deficit, because its exports are too low or its imports too high, there is one ultimate step which might be expected to put things right. This is a devaluation of its currency. By altering its rate of exchange with other currencies it can at one stroke make its exports cheaper and its imports more expensive. The presumption is that its exports will rise, its imports will fall, and its current account move swiftly back into surplus.

Every time Britain's current account has moved heavily into deficit, then, there has been a tendency for foreign holders of sterling to be afflicted by doubts. Will Britain be forced to devalue in order to put things right? If Britain did devalue, reducing the dollar value of the pound from $2·80 to, say, $2·40, foreign holders of sterling would feel rather foolish. At one stroke the value of their sterling in terms of gold, dollars and any other currency which had not been devalued would have been reduced by 15 per cent. Not unnaturally, many of them tend to take precautions against this possibility by exchanging their holdings of sterling for other currencies before Britain has time to devalue. This presents the British government with an urgent problem. At a time when they are already having to dip into their reserves (or borrow abroad) in order to finance a current account deficit, they are now faced with a 'run on sterling'. Large amounts of sterling are presented to the Bank of England for conversion into gold or foreign currency, and this accelerates the fall in the reserves or the need to seek short-term assistance from abroad. And, as is the case with any run on any bank, the knowledge that it is happening itself gives the process a further twist.

The international monetary system is so complex that the extent and timing of a run on sterling cannot always be directly related to the behaviour of Britain's current balance. In 1957, for example, current account was in quite a healthy condition, yet there was a run on the pound partly because people were looking beyond the actual trade figures to the threat posed for the future by the rapid rise in incomes and prices, and partly because whether or not sterling might have to be *de*valued there seemed an imminent prospect of the German mark being *re*valued. Thus while one might not lose money by staying in sterling, one might make some by getting into deutschmarks. In 1964, on the other hand, a very large deficit on current account (and on capital account) did not lead to a run on sterling until nearly the end of the year because the effect on our reserves of the British deficit was masked for a long time by a big inflow of funds from abroad, the result in part of the favourable balance of payments position of the overseas sterling area countries which keep their reserves in London in the form of sterling. However we must not lose sight of the wood for the trees. The basic fact is that when rising prices in Britain cause the current account to worsen markedly, the government must act quickly if it is to prevent a cumulative loss of confidence which could quickly lead to the exhaustion of our reserves.

DEVALUATION AND PHYSICAL CONTROLS

What action can it take? The problem is to do something which will increase the growth of exports, slow down the rise in imports and, either in this way or more directly, restore confidence in sterling. Broadly speaking, there are three things the government can do. First, it can devalue. This was in fact done in 1949. At a stroke of the pen export prices can be reduced, import prices raised, and thus a powerful stimulus imparted towards the improvement of current account. But any suggestion that devaluation might be the answer always releases a flood of objections ranging from the coldly economic to the wildly pathological. It is argued, for example, that a rise in import prices will raise the cost of living, and thus stimulate bigger wage claims which in turn will reduce the advantage gained by devaluation. As a qualitative argument this is clearly correct, but a reasoned estimate of the size and spread of the effects is often conspicuously lacking. Another argument is that a devaluation of sterling is unjust to foreign holders of sterling, and might fatally damage the precarious structure of international liquidity, of which sterling is at the present time one of the main supports. Some people find these and other arguments against devaluation convincing; some people do not. Suffice it to say that since 1949 all governments have firmly rejected devaluation as a remedy.

The second thing the government can do is to act directly on imports and exports (insofar as this is permitted by our international obligations to the General Agreement on Tariffs and Trade – GATT, the European Free Trade Association – EFTA, and so on). Imports can be restrained by quotas, thus physically limiting the amount that importers are allowed to bring in, or by raising their price by imposing a surcharge or higher duties or tariffs. Exports can be encouraged by a series of measures to rebate certain internal taxes on goods exported, by providing information to potential exporters about foreign markets, improving credit terms and other facilities and so on. (Direct subsidies to exports are ruled out under GATT.) This kind of rather direct and specific approach was used a great deal in the immediate post-war period when the government had the advantage of the continued existence of much of the wartime apparatus of regulations and controls, but it went out of favour in the early 1950s. It came back into favour in the mid-1960s, particularly with the return of a Labour government in October 1964.* But it was not the approach the government adopted in face of most of the balance of payments crises of the last ten or fifteen years.

DEFLATION

If the government is unwilling to devalue or make use of rather direct and physical measures to improve an ailing current balance, it must fall back on a third method. This is a reduction in the level of demand, or, in one word, deflation. As we have seen, a reduction in demand (assuming there is no general 'excess demand' in the first place) leads to unemployment. At last we are getting to the explanation of the paradox with which we closed Chapter 7 – the paradox that in the 1920s and 1930s the government presumably wanted full employment but did not know how to get it, while in the 1950s and 1960s it knew how to get it but apparently did not always want it.

The government deflates by taking a whole series of measures designed to reduce consumption and investment. (Strictly speaking, in a growing economy, these measures are generally aimed not at reducing the *absolute* level of consumption and investment, but the rate at which they are increasing. In other words the aim is to prevent consumption and investment from rising to the level they would otherwise have reached. But for the sake of simplicity we shall talk of 'a reduction in consumption' when what we really mean is 'a

* The Labour government also took a number of steps to improve the other part of the balance of payments – the capital account – by reducing the outflow of private capital. The basic idea was to lessen the improvement needed in the current account if the overall balance of payments position was to be made viable.

reduction in the *rate of increase* of consumption'.) Consumption can be hit by increasing income tax or purchase tax, or tightening up on hire-purchase conditions; private investment can be affected by raising company taxation or squeezing credit; and public investment and certain kinds of public current expenditure can to some extent be directly controlled by government decision. This deflation is supposed to help the balance of payments current account in two ways. By far the most important effect is on imports. If consumption and investment fall, so will imports: if people buy fewer shoes, they will (one hopes) buy fewer Italian shoes, and if businessmen buy less machinery, imports of machinery and raw materials will be reduced. In fact the effect of deflation on imports is more powerful than this, for when demand falls the first instinct of many producers and distributors is to run down their stocks, and the import content of stock-building is much higher than the import content of consumption or fixed investment. Between 1960 and 1961, for example, the total output of the British economy rose by 2 per cent, but the volume of imports (which until then had been rising much faster than output) actually fell by 2 per cent. The deflationary measures taken in mid-1961 had by the end of the year done no more than slow down the rise in output, but, chiefly because of a big fall in stock-building, they resulted in an actual fall in the volume of imports.

The second way in which deflation is supposed to help the balance of payments – by increasing exports – is much more questionable. The idea is simple: as businesses find it more difficult to sell in the home market, they are supposed to go out and search more aggressively for markets abroad. How far this actually happens is difficult to say. British exports have in fact tended to do rather badly after deflationary action has been taken at home, but this is partly because such deflationary action has often coincided with periods of rather slow growth in world trade. Some people argue that exports would have done well had they been given time – had deflationary action been firmer and more prolonged. But this is an aspect of a more general question to which we shall be returning in a moment. All one can say is that the various studies made on the subject have had pretty inconclusive results.

Whatever the effect on exports, however, the effect of deflation (or what has come to be called the 'stop' part of 'stop-go') on imports has in the typical case been sufficiently dramatic to solve the immediate problem. Imports fell, or at any rate rose much more slowly than before, the current balance improved, foreign holders of sterling felt better about the outlook and sent their funds back to London, and everyone breathed again. But in the meantime the growth of output had flattened out and unemployment had risen – in the typical case from around $1\frac{1}{2}$ per cent (350,000 people) to $2\frac{1}{2}$ per cent (575,000 people). What was to be done about this? Presumably if the government turned round and reflated (i.e. increased the level of demand) the old trouble would start all over again. The inevitable crash would have been postponed but not averted, and in the meantime output would have been needlessly low and unemployment needlessly high.

But in the late 1950s there crystallized a substantial body of opinion with other ideas. It believed that once unemployment has risen to a level of $2-2\frac{1}{2}$ per cent it should be kept there.

There were two schools of thought among those who believed this. One of them can be dealt with very quickly; the other must be looked at a little more closely. The first school of thought was represented, to put it a little crudely, by those who had absorbed Keynes but never got any further. They accepted the theory that we attacked earlier, that since unemployment was a symptom of too little demand, rising prices and balance of payments problems must be a symptom of too much demand. Therefore demand must be reduced, and once it had been reduced to a level at which it was not excessive, all would be well: prices would not rise, and the balance of payments would be all right. Therefore the government should reduce demand from a level at which unemployment had been about $1\frac{1}{2}$ per cent to a level at which it was $2-2\frac{1}{2}$ per cent, and once unemployment had reached this higher level (by definition, the level at which demand was no longer excessive) it should be kept there. As we have seen, this theory was wrong simply because post-war rising prices have not on the whole been due to excessive demand – a conclusion suggested, to put it no higher, by the fact that when unemployment has risen to $2\frac{1}{2}$ per cent, and by no stretch of the imagination could demand have been said to be excessive, prices have continued to rise.

The second school of thought was more realistic. It accepted that post-war inflation has been of the 'cost-push' rather than 'demand-pull' type, and argued that the only way to eliminate cost-push inflation was to maintain a permanently lower level of demand and higher level of unemployment than had obtained in the late 1940s and early 1950s. In this way not only would prices be prevented from rising but, by the same token, the basic causes of the recurrent balance of payments crises would be removed. In support of this argument a series of complicated econometric models was shoved under the noses of ministers and civil servants, who, perhaps because they were unable to understand them, were visibly impressed. But it is fair to add that strong arguments were also adduced in verbal form. If there was rather more unemployment about, it was said, trade unions would be less aggressive in demanding big wage increases. Similarly businessmen, finding it more difficult to sell their output, would be much tougher in their attitude to wage claims. Together these forces would reduce the size of wage increases, and increases in profits, to something more in line with the rise in productivity, and so would lead to a stable level of prices.

There is a prima facie plausibility about this argument which many people found attractive. Most unfortunately, this plausibility was reinforced at the time this argument was gaining currency by a wholly extraneous set of circumstances.

Imports account for about a fifth of total expenditure in Britain. Therefore the overall domestic price level is determined to the extent of about a fifth by what happens to import prices. Between 1954 and 1957 import prices rose by 7 per cent (a bit of the rise, though not a great deal of it, being accounted for by the effects of the Suez crisis on world commodity prices); in consequence import prices exerted an upward influence on the final prices of British goods and services. But between 1957 and 1959, chiefly because of a marked slowing-down in the growth of world trade, the movement of import prices was reversed, and they fell by nearly 10 per cent. Other things being equal, this fall in import prices might have been expected to lead to a fall in retail prices in Britain of something like 2 per cent. It was in a sense unfortunate that this fall in import prices occurred when it did, for Mr Thorneycroft, then Chancellor of the Exchequer, inaugurated a deflationary policy in September 1957. Between 1957 and 1959 retail prices rose by less than 2 per cent a year – about half as fast as usual – and this was hailed as evidence of the success of a reduction in demand as a method of slowing down the rise in prices. But if allowance had been made for the effect of falling import prices it would have been seen that the real underlying upward trend of prices was about 3 per cent – a bit lower, but not all that much lower, than the post-war average.

One must not overstate the case. There is evidence that when the level of demand is falling, and unemployment is rising, there is some effect on the vigour with which unions press wage claims and employers resist them. But the effect does not seem to be strong enough to slow things up very much. Moreover it can be argued that although unions and employers may pull in their horns a bit while unemployment is actually rising, because of the general uncertainty that rising unemployment creates, once it has stabilized at a level of $2-2\frac{1}{2}$ per cent (and anything higher must be deemed inconsistent with the full employment pledge) they will revert to their bad old ways. A $2\frac{1}{2}$ per cent rate of national unemployment, as we saw in Chapter 7, may have pretty unpleasant effects in the Welsh valleys and the Scottish Highlands, but may not do a great deal to temper union militancy or employers' complacency in London or the Midlands.

Many economists are scientists *manqué*, and would love to conduct controlled experiments on the level of demand and employment. What would happen if one kept unemployment at a rate of $2\frac{1}{2}$ per cent for a few years? Or allowed it to rise gradually to 3 per cent and then brought it slowly down again? Would the rise in incomes be kept down in line with the rise in productivity, so that prices were stable? Or would unemployment have to be kept at 4 or 5 per cent before this happened? Fortunately, perhaps, politicians are less detached. They have their seats to consider, and an M.P.'s seat is a much flimsier piece of furniture than a professor's chair. When unemployment gets up to a level of $2\frac{1}{2}$ per cent or so they call not merely for a halt but a reversal. The first great deflationary experiment of 1957–8 was called off towards the end of 1958, when unemployment was approaching $2\frac{1}{2}$ per cent; and the second, of 1961–2, early in 1963, when unemployment, accentuated by a particularly hard winter, had gone over the 3 per cent mark. Thus sooner or later the government has always got around to reducing the unemployment it had deliberately created, though not before several hundreds of thousands of people had suffered shorter or longer spells out of work.

But there have been other unfortunate aspects of the 'stop-go' policy of recent years, quite apart from the periodic unemployment and loss of output involved. First of all, except in the most temporary sense, the policy simply has not worked: it has done nothing to cure the underlying problem. Each time the government has reflated the economy by allowing demand to rise again the balance of payments problem has re-appeared – and it has re-appeared in a more critical form on each occasion. The figures of the overall deficit (i.e. on current account and capital account taken together) for each of the last three crisis years tell their own story:

Year	Deficit (£ m.)
1955	277
1960	467
1964	763

It is hardly surprising that by late 1964 foreign holders of sterling should have been asking themselves whether Britain could solve her balance of payments problem except by devaluation.

THE EFFECTS ON GROWTH

The second unfortunate aspect of 'stop-go' is even more serious; indeed it represents what is probably the most fundamental criticism that can be directed at British economic policy since the war. The object of all economic activity is to provide people with the highest possible standard of living, or National Income per head.* During the 1920s and 1930s *actual* National Income was much lower than *potential* National Income: men and machinery were idle, and output therefore well below what it could have been. Naturally the

* This is another sacrifice of precision to simplicity. 'National Income' must be taken as shorthand for 'Gross Domestic Product at constant prices'. See Explanatory Note 3, page 256.

main objective of economic policy was to make full use of existing resources – in other words to achieve full employment. But once Keynes had shown governments how to achieve full employment, and full employment (at any rate by pre-war standards) had become a permanent feature of economic life, attention began to shift to the other side of the equation. If resources were fully employed, the only way to increase the standard of living was to increase the size of the resources. In other words, assuming that most people's standard of living, or real income, is not yet as high as they would like it to be, this means that an important, if not over-riding, objective of economic policy must be to ensure that the National Income (or total output) grows as fast as possible. In brief, we must have a fast rate of growth.

Britain's growth rate over the past fifteen or twenty years has averaged about 3 per cent a year.* This is not bad by the standards of the earlier years of this century, or even most of the nineteenth century; but it is not good by the contemporary standards of other countries at roughly the same stage of economic development. Since the early 1950s (when post-war reconstruction was more or less complete) other European countries such as Germany, Italy and France have had average growth rates varying between 4 and 6 per cent. It is true that not all of the difference between Britain's 3 per cent growth rate and other countries' 4–6 per cent growth rates can be said to be Britain's 'fault'. For the growth of output can be broken down into two parts: the growth in the number of people in the working population, and the growth in output per head of the working population

---

*i.e. total output has grown by about 3 per cent a year *on average*. In some years output has risen much faster than this; in others it has hardly risen at all. This is the result of the variations in demand (either autonomous, or induced by the government) that we discussed in Chapter 7. But the concept of a 'growth rate' involves abstracting from the year-to-year fluctuations associated with changes in the pressure of demand, and measuring the rise in output over a longer period.

(i.e. in productivity). Other things being equal, the faster the rise in the working population, the faster the growth of output, and part of Britain's relatively slow growth rate can be attributed to the fact that the working population has grown more slowly than in a number of other countries. Nevertheless, the main part of the difference lies in the slower growth of productivity in Britain, and it is with this that we are mainly concerned.

The difference made by a high rate of growth can be very big. If, for example, Britain had had a rate of 4 per cent a year over the past decade (instead of about 3 per cent), the National Income would now be about £3,500 million higher. Pensions, family allowances and expenditure on the Health Service could all be doubled, and there would still be a good deal left over.

Just what it is that gives a country a rapid growth rate rather than a slow one has for many years been the subject of enormous amounts of thought, argument, research and dogma. A distinguished American economist has written a book in which he not merely analyses the American growth rate in terms of thirty-one different determinants, but actually quantifies the importance of each of them. It is not within our terms of reference to embark on this particular battlefield, but we must make one very brief foray into it.

Few economists would deny that one very important influence on growth is investment. Attempts to demonstrate close correlations between a country's growth rate and the proportion of its National Income that it devotes to investment have not always been completely convincing; but there is undoubtedly some connexion. Of course it makes a great deal of difference what form the investment takes. Investment in houses or hospitals, or alternatively bowling alleys or gambling casinos, may illustrate something about a society's values, but will not do much to increase its growth rate. The kind of investment that does this (to over-simplify again) is investment in productive and distributive industry, and particularly investment which takes the form of the most up-to-date plant and machinery. If such plant and machinery is to be installed and effectively operated, employers must want to install it, and workers must be willing to work it as efficiently as possible.

The real trouble about 'stop-go' is that it drastically weakens the necessary incentives to both groups of people. When the government deflates the economy, and unemployment starts rising, employers are provided with a double reason for not putting in new machinery. First, as we saw in earlier chapters, if they are unable to sell what they can produce with their existing capacity, they ask themselves what is the point of installing more. (Of course it is possible for them to argue the other way – if the market is going to shrink they will only be able to maintain their sales by using the most efficient and up-to-date methods; but in practice this argument seems to carry much less weight.) Secondly, even if they do want to go on investing they will find it much more difficult to do so: interest rates will be high, credit will be tight and the Stock Exchange too depressed to make new share issues attractive. Similarly, rising unemployment is bound to make workers less cooperative in their attitude to new machinery, which is almost always labour-saving – i.e. it enables the same amount to be produced with less men. A time of rising unemployment is no time to be made redundant by a new machine. Even if new plant and machinery is installed in such circumstances, workers will tend to insist, in an endeavour to preserve employment, that it is overmanned – thus losing much of the advantage in installing it. Moreover these timid and restrictive attitudes – on the part of both employers and workers – do not simply disappear when the government decides to increase the level of demand again, and unemployment starts falling. If the government has deflated once in the face of rising prices and a balance of payments crisis, what is to stop it doing so again? Any businessman or trade union official who had argued this in the later 1950s would have been amply justified by subsequent events.

Just how far the cautious and restrictive mentality engendered by periodic deflation has slowed down the British growth rate below what it otherwise would have been is anybody's guess. Some experts calculate that over the past ten or fifteen years there has been some acceleration in the 'underlying' growth rate – i.e. the rate at which output would grow if the pressure of demand were kept constant, and not continuously raised and lowered. It is now put at something over 3 per cent. It can be argued that but for 'stop-go' it might now be more like 4 per cent – and the kind of difference this could have made was illustrated above. Not only would a higher rate of growth be a thoroughly good thing in itself; it would probably have reduced, though admittedly rather marginally, the rise in prices. (It is noticeable that the fact that other countries' prices have risen less than ours is not only due to the fact that their incomes have risen more slowly – in some cases this has not been so – but also to the fact that their output has risen a good deal more rapidly.)

VICIOUS CIRCLE

This leads to the thought that throughout much of the post-war period the British economy has been trapped in a vicious circle. Because incomes have risen rather fast and output rather slowly, prices have risen; because prices have risen there have been balance of payments crises; because there have been balance of payments crises the government has deflated; because the government has deflated the growth rate has continued to be rather low, and since incomes have continued, in spite of periodic deflations, to rise rather fast, prices have continued to rise; and so on. If this vicious circle is to be broken our prices will have to stop rising faster than other countries' – which means either that other countries' prices must rise faster, or ours must rise more slowly. (This appears to be a minimum requirement; one could argue, in view of the upward trend of balance of payments deficits illustrated on page 201, that to get the balance of payments right our prices will actually have to *fall* in relation to other countries'. If this were true, either the moral being pointed out here would be more imperative than ever, or one would have to envisage some alteration of exchange rates.)

It is just possible that other countries' prices will rise some-what faster in the future than they have done in recent years, either because incomes rise rather faster or output grows rather more slowly; some people claim to have detected bits of evidence that point in this direction. But it would be very unwise to count on it; we must rely mainly on slowing down the rate at which our own prices rise. Some help may come from speeding up the growth of output, but as we pointed out earlier the relative orders of magnitude are such that this could be no more than a small part of the answer. The main attack must be on the incomes side: the objective must be to bring down the rate at which incomes rise from around 7 per cent a year to something more like 4 per cent a year. It is precisely because an analysis of the performance of the British economy since the war drives one so inevitably to this conclusion that such enormous emphasis has been placed over the last few years on a prices and incomes policy; and why finally, in July 1966, the government took drastic action to 'freeze' incomes and prices.

A final word may help to put the subject matter of this chapter in perspective. Keynes showed how a government could maintain full employment. But the very success with which this lesson has been learned and applied has had two consequences. First, with the disappearance of periodic bouts of severe unemployment there disappeared also the forces which kept incomes from rising faster than output: with full employment came rising prices. Secondly, as permanent full employment (by pre-war standards) came to be taken for granted, economists and politicians started to perceive another economic objective: growth. The same importance is now attached to growth as was attached to employment between the wars.

Keynes did not live long enough to get to grips with the problem of achieving faster growth and more stable prices; though it is fair to add that the theoretical work done on both these questions is largely based on concepts and relationships which he developed. But Keynes himself would have been the first to recognize that a slower rise in prices and a faster rate of growth are, at any rate for contemporary Britain, closely connected; and that the management of effective demand along Keynesian lines, though a necessary condition for solving both problems, is not a sufficient solution of either of them.

CHAPTER 10

THE PROBLEM OF
INTERNATIONAL LIQUIDITY

A SHORTAGE OF RESERVES

WE have seen that one of the major causes of such unemployment as has existed in post-war Britain has been deflation undertaken by the government with the intention of slowing down the rise in prices and improving the balance of payments; and that one of the major reasons why the government has had to do this so often and so drastically has been a shortage of reserves. Had the reserves been bigger, deflationary action might have been less frequent and less severe. Overseas observers might have been less nervous about Britain's ability to meet her commitments at the existing exchange rate, and the government might have been able to sit out temporary balance of payments deficits instead of always reacting to them, sooner or later, by deflation.

The argument should not be pushed too far in the case of Britain, for as we have seen her post-war balance of payments crises have increasingly suggested a fundamental disequilibrium requiring drastic measures, rather than a series of essentially temporary deficits which, given the inevitable fluctuations of economic life, might happen to anybody. But in the case of a number of other countries it is this latter picture which seems the true one. A temporary fall in exports because of some change in an important overseas market; a temporary surge in imports because of some change in fashion at home; a sudden rise in private investment or government expenditure overseas – some combination of these and other factors can cause a sharp worsening in anybody's balance of payments. If a country's reserves are adequate it can ride out such temporary fluctuations, confident that within a year or two other changes will restore its balance of payments to health. But if its reserves are too small (or thought to be too small) it may react to such temporary fluctuations by deflating so as to force the pace at which imports fall (and, perhaps, exports rise). Such deflation may have a fairly rapid effect in improving the balance of payments, but it will cause a rise in unemployment – and not only at home: the fall in imports will tend to reduce production and employment in other countries and this may cause them to deflate in turn, for as we saw in Chapter 6, in a freely trading world the Multiplier operates internationally. Moreover, as we saw in the last chapter, deflation can have more far-reaching effects than the unemployment and loss of output immediately involved. By reducing firms' incentive to invest, and reinforcing restrictive attitudes among employers and employees, it can have an adverse effect on the longer-term rate of growth.

This shortage of reserves is essentially what is meant by 'the problem of international liquidity'.* It is a problem with which Keynes was particularly concerned during the last years of his life, and one which appears to be coming to a head in the late 1960s: some observers believe that it is one of the major threats to full employment and a reasonably fast rate of growth that exist in the post-Keynesian world. In this chapter we take a look at it.

THE NEED FOR RESERVES

A simple analogy may help to illustrate what many economists would regard as the basic problem. Suppose that on average, over a period of time, a family both earns and

---

*This is a rather Anglo-Saxon way of looking at it. As we shall see, many Continentals feel that the problem of international liquidity is that there is too *much* liquidity rather than too little.

spends £20 a week. In the long run earnings and expenditure are equal, and the family will neither save nor dis-save (i.e. use up existing savings). But in any given week there may be fluctuations in both earnings and expenditure: earnings may be either higher or lower than £20, because the wage-earner does a bit of overtime, or alternatively loses a day's work through sickness; similarly expenditure may be higher or lower than £20, because of the sudden need to replace some expensive item of household equipment, or alternatively because the family gets invited out to a lot of meals. If a week in which earnings are only £18 coincides with a week in which expenditure needs are £23, the family will only be able to cope if it has savings that it can dip into. If it has a reserve of £5 in a teapot, well and good; it can spend it on bridging the temporary gap between earnings and expenditure, confident that within a week or two earnings may be higher than £20, and expenditure lower, so that it can build up its reserve again. But if it has a reserve of only £1 it will be in trouble: it will only be able to spend a total of £19 and it will have to cut its expenditure well below the £23 it wants to spend. If the extra £3 of expenditure is absolutely unavoidable, this will mean that it has to make very drastic cuts in its normal expenditure on such items as food or tobacco. This in turn will tend to make things difficult for the local shopkeepers. Thus if the family has an average reserve of £5 it will be able to weather temporary fluctuations in income and expenditure in reasonable comfort; but if its average reserve is only £1, there will be occasions when both it and others will suffer.

There is one further point to note before we leave this analogy. Over a period of years the family's weekly income and expenditure will rise; we saw in Chapter 8 that in post-war Britain total incomes and total expenditure have risen (in money terms) by about 7 per cent a year. This means, such is the power of compound interest, that income and expenditure will double in about ten years. After ten years, then, the family may be earning and spending £40 in an average week, and the presumption must be that fluctuations in income and expenditure will have increased in proportion. The difference between income and expenditure in a bad week will be the difference not between £18 and £23 but £36 and £46 – a gap that can only be bridged if the family's reserve has also doubled, from £5 to £10. In short, to preserve the same degree of protection against temporary fluctuations, the family's reserves must rise in line with its income and expenditure.

Broadly speaking, what is true of an individual family is also true of a country. A country must have enough reserves to cope with temporary fluctuations in its foreign income or expenditure without having to react by making drastic changes in its normal expenditure pattern. And there must be some way in which, as time goes on, its reserves can be increased broadly in line with the rise in its income and expenditure. The way in which an individual family creates and builds up such reserves is simple: it does a bit of saving, or gets left something by a rich aunt. But the way in which the reserves of a country get created and increased is a good deal more complicated.

THE WORLD LIQUIDITY SYSTEM

A country's reserves must be kept in a form which other countries will accept in payment for goods or services. If a country has a balance of payments deficit because its imports are greater than its exports it can normally bridge the gap (i.e. pay for the extra imports) only by handing over something that the country from which it is importing will accept. In practice, this means gold and foreign currencies – and in fact the only two currencies widely used as 'reserve currencies' are dollars and sterling. This system of 'reserve currencies' is of fairly recent origin; in the nineteenth century most countries held their reserves exclusively in the form of gold. But as time went on countries came to realize that there was no need to hold gold directly; it was just as good to hold reserves of a currency, such as sterling, which could be exchanged for gold at the Bank of England, at a fixed rate, whenever one wanted. Indeed there was a positive advantage in holding sterling rather than gold, for gold yielded no return. Sterling, on the other hand, being held not in the form of pound notes (which would have yielded no return either) but in the form of interest-bearing short-term British government securities (e.g. Treasury Bills) which could be sold in exchange for pound notes at any time, did yield a return.

Essentially, the same system is still in operation today. Britain and a number of other countries hold their reserves in the form of gold and dollars (more exactly, various interest-bearing dollar assets which can be sold for dollars at any time); while a number of countries in the 'overseas sterling area' hold their reserves mainly in the form of sterling. Just how far a country holds its reserves in the form of dollars or sterling rather than gold depends mainly on how it assesses the advantage of holding an asset that yields interest against the disadvantage of holding an asset that may be devalued in terms of gold. (In fact some countries' assessment of this does not appear entirely rational: sterling or the dollar would have to be devalued by 20 per cent every 4 or 5 years to offset the advantage of holding sterling or dollar assets which yielded a return of 4 or 5 per cent a year rather than holding gold.)

Now the question is, how do countries get hold of these reserves in the first place? And what, if anything, causes these reserves to rise fast enough to ensure that there is no shortage of international liquidity?

As far as gold is concerned, the position is fairly straightforward. The non-Soviet world (mainly South Africa) pro-

duces a certain amount of gold each year in exactly the same
way as it produces a certain amount of coal or pig-iron. The
amount of gold produced, just like the amount of pig-iron
produced, depends basically on profitability – on the relationship between how much it costs to produce, and how much it
can be sold for. Other countries buy gold from South Africa
(paying in sterling or dollars) in exactly the same way as they
buy diamonds or uranium. Some of this gold is used indus-
trially, or by jewellers and dentists; some of it is hoarded by
canny or superstitious individuals (India, for example, is a
great place for gold-hoarding); and some of it is bought by
monetary authorities and becomes an addition to the world's
gold reserves. At the present time gold production in the non-
Soviet world is worth something like $1,500 million a year,
of which well over half usually goes for non-monetary purposes. On the other hand every now and then the Soviet
Union (whose gold production is, for obscure Marxist-
Leninist reasons, a closely guarded secret) sells a few hundred
million dollars' worth of gold to the West (though some of
this, for equally obscure Maoist reasons, is then bought back
by the Chinese). The net result is that in an average year the
amount of gold becoming available to add to the non-Soviet
world's gold reserves is around $500 million, though the
figure fluctuates very substantially from year to year, and
since about the mid-1960s has been very small.

The creation of the other component of the world's international reserves is equally simple, if considerably more
arbitrary. It depends essentially on the balance of payments
deficits of the countries whose currencies are reserve currencies – in the contemporary world Britain and the United
States. A glance at the recent history of the U.S. balance of
payments will serve to illustrate the point.

The United States, unlike Britain, always has a large
surplus on her balance of *trade* – that is to say her exports
always comfortably exceed her imports. But in recent years

this surplus has been more than eaten up by her other international transactions, such as private investment overseas, and government military and aid expenditure in foreign countries. As a result, in every year but one since 1951 the overall U.S. balance of payments has been in deficit, the total deficit between then and 1967 amounting to roughly $30 billion. Now in this situation how far the rest of the world's dollar reserves will rise depends on how the U.S. deficit is financed. At one extreme the whole of the deficit may be financed in gold. In that case the U.S. will lose $30 billion of gold and the rest of the world will gain $30 billion of gold, and there will be no increase at all in the world's reserves. At the other extreme the rest of the world may decide that it does not want $30 billion of gold, which yields no return; it wants to receive the $30 billion it is owed in the form of dollars (which, if held in the form not of dollar bills but of New York bank deposits or U.S. Treasury Bills, will yield a return). In this case the *gold* reserves of both the United States and the rest of the world will have remained unchanged, but the rest of the world's *dollar* reserves will have increased by $30 billion; so *total* world reserves will rise by $30 billion.

Now it makes no difference to the liquidity of the rest of the world whether it holds its extra reserves in the form of dollars or in the form of gold. In either case its reserves have risen by $30 billion. But it makes a great deal of difference to the United States. In the one case its gold reserves stay the same (though its dollar liabilities rise by $30 billion); in the other its gold reserves fall by $30 billion. In other words how far a U.S. deficit results in an increase in world liquidity depends on how the deficit is financed: at one extreme it may result in an increase in liquidity equal to the size of the deficit; at the other extreme it may result in no increase in liquidity at all. Indeed there could, in theory, be an actual *fall* in world liquidity. If a large U.S. deficit causes a loss of confidence in the dollar, the surplus countries may not merely demand that the whole of the deficit be financed in gold; they may insist on exchanging some of their *existing* dollar holdings for gold. In this case the rest of the world's reserves will have risen by $30 billion, but U.S. reserves will have fallen by more than $30 billion, so that total world liquidity is reduced.

There is thus an enormous degree of arbitrariness in the way in which world liquidity is created. There is first of all the arbitrariness affecting the amount of gold that is produced, the amount that is sold by the Soviet Union to the West, and the amount that is used for industrial purposes, for decoration and (an extremely fluctuating factor) for private hoarding. Secondly, there is the arbitrariness attending the size (if any) of the deficits run by the two reserve currency countries – the U.S. and the U.K. And finally there is the arbitrariness of how much of these deficits is financed by gold outflows and how much by an increase in dollar and sterling balances. Taking all this together, it would be pretty amazing if the amount of international liquidity created each year happened to be just right.

Just how much is 'just right' is itself a controversial question, and in any case the total amount of world liquidity cannot be treated in isolation from the way in which it is distributed between different countries. We shall be returning to these questions a little later on. Here we need merely note that if the value of world trade rises by about 7 per cent a year (as it has over the past 10 or 15 years) and if the world's gold and foreign exchange reserves rise by only about $2\frac{1}{2}$ per cent a year (as they have) then, unless there was far too much liquidity about in the first place, there may well have been an increasing shortage of liquidity. In other words countries may have been forced to adopt increasingly deflationary policies, with adverse effects on employment, and on the growth of world trade and production, because they had too few reserves to be able to ride out temporary balance of payments fluctuations.

KEYNES'S PROPOSALS

Not surprisingly, Keynes became aware of the problem at a very early stage: the man who first grasped that there was no reason at all why millions of individual investment and consumption decisions should automatically lead to full employment within a country was hardly likely to miss the fact that there was no reason at all why the millions of decisions which ultimately determine the amount of international liquidity should automatically result in the creation of just enough to finance the optimum increase in world trade and production. He had been thinking in the 1930s about the need for an international credit-creating institution; by 1941 he was pondering deeply on the international liquidity problem that would arise after the end of the war. His immediate concern was with the question of post-war reconstruction. He could see that the United States would emerge from the war in an immensely strong economic position compared with the devastated countries of Western Europe, and that it would be many years before Britain and other countries had built up their war-shattered economies enough to be able to resume normal trading and financial relationships with the U.S. In the meantime there would have to be a galaxy of physical and financial controls in Europe, aimed at building up exports and restricting the use of precious foreign exchange (particularly dollars) for all but the most essential imports.

However Keynes was a firm believer in the virtues of a free system of international trade and payments, and was aware that the Americans held the same views even more strongly, and would press hard for Europe to liberalize her trade and payments system at the earliest possible moment.

But if European countries were to dismantle their import and exchange restrictions fairly quickly it was imperative to provide a long-stop to ensure that if they were driven into temporary balance of payments deficits by a flood of imports from America they should not be forced to deflate in order to solve the problem. They should have enough reserves to ride out the storm until their own economies were strong enough to compete with the Americans on equal terms.

But although in 1941 this was Keynes's immediate preoccupation, he really had his eye on the longer-term problem we were discussing earlier. He believed that quite apart from the transitional difficulties of post-war reconstruction it was important to ensure that there would always be enough liquidity to finance the growth of world trade, so that countries would not be forced by temporary balance of payments deficits into the kind of deflation and competitive devaluations that had plagued the 1930s. It was no good providing countries with the key to full employment if they were going to refuse to use it because of perpetual anxiety about the size of their reserves.

The solution to the problem which Keynes proposed was the establishment of a kind of world central bank, which should ensure that there was enough liquidity in the world as a whole in the same way that a country's central bank ensures that there is enough liquidity within the country. The world central bank (which he called a 'Clearing Union') should create for each country a deposit of a new and internationally acceptable currency (which he called 'bancor'). Countries' deficits with each other would be settled by a transfer of bancor from the accounts of the deficit countries to the accounts of the surplus countries: if, for example, Britain had a £100 million balance of payments deficit with the U.S., £100 million worth of bancor would be deducted from Britain's bancor deposit with the Clearing Union, and added to the bancor deposit of the U.S. As time went on, and the value of world trade increased, the absolute size of temporary balance of payments deficits would increase as well, and so would the need for bancor. The Clearing Union could take care of this by increasing the size of bancor deposits – probably broadly in line with the growth of world trade, so that the ratio of total bancor deposits to world trade remained about the same.

As we shall see below, this proposal was not adopted, though a good many economists would now argue that something like it is inevitable eventually. But the fact must be faced that there are certain difficulties about this – or indeed any other – scheme for ensuring enough liquidity to prevent countries from reacting to a temporary balance of payments problem by deflating.

One difficulty is inherent in economic life: how do you know the deficit is temporary? A deficit does not usually emerge from a surplus carrying a placard saying 'Temporary'. If the deficit *is* temporary it is obviously silly for the country concerned to deflate or devalue and cause unemployment or other disturbances at home and abroad, in order to cope with it. But if the deficit is *not* temporary it may be equally silly to provide the country with enough liquidity to finance it, for this may merely postpone the action – such as a reduction in the pressure of demand, or changes in exchange rates or long-term capital movements – needed to cure a fundamental disequilibrium, and perhaps make such action, when it comes, particularly severe.

There is no simple answer to this problem. Perhaps the best one can do is to try and ensure that in whatever system is established to control the level of international liquidity there is provision for an objective examination of individual countries' deficits, and not too much scope for a country to live on its reserves unless such examination suggests that the deficit is temporary. There can be no hard-and-fast formula; the answer in each case is essentially a matter of judgement.

Nevertheless, although in practice the line may be very difficult to draw, the principle to be followed is fairly clear: countries should have enough reserves to be able to ride out a temporary balance of payments problem without deflating, but not so much as to enable them to run a large deficit year after year without bothering to do anything about it.

DEFICIT COUNTRIES AND SURPLUS COUNTRIES

So far, so good. But now we start to enter rather choppier waters. Up till now we have been assuming that although a country should be able to tide over a temporary deficit by dipping into its reserves it should deal with a more permanent or fundamental deficit by other means, and that it should not have so many reserves as to be tempted off this path of rectitude. But is it necessarily the case that a country with a fundamental deficit has the responsibility of doing something about it? Prima facie this would certainly seem to be so; but we must not be dogmatic. There is another side to the medal.

As a matter of definition, if some countries have a balance of payments deficit, other countries must have a balance of payments surplus: for the world as a whole, the sum total of balance of payments deficits must be equal to the sum total of balance of payments surpluses.* If the world consisted of only two countries, and country A had a balance of payments deficit of £500 million, then country B must have a balance of payments surplus of £500 million. One of the points Keynes was particularly concerned to establish was that it is by no means clear that the responsibility for restoring balance of payments equilibrium rests on country A; it may rest on

* At any rate in theory, and subject to a small qualification because of new gold production going into reserves. In practice, the figures of individual countries, if added up, show that the sum total of balance of payments deficits is markedly greater than the sum total of surpluses. The fact that the error goes in this direction rather than the other is perhaps an indication of countries' desire not to appear too flagrantly in surplus.

country B. It may be the case that country A is behaving in an obviously profligate way, with a level of demand which is clearly excessive, making no attempt to restrain the growth of money incomes, and content to suck in imports from B while making no attempt to increase its exports. In this case one could reasonably say that the imbalance in international trade is the fault of A.

On the other hand A may be conducting its affairs in a perfectly responsible fashion, maintaining a pressure of demand which is not excessive, but just high enough to preserve full employment, trying to operate an incomes policy, encourage exports and so on. Yet it may be unable to reduce its balance of payments deficit because of the anti-social policies of country B, which may insist on maintaining a level of demand too low for full employment, or an exchange rate which is undervalued, or restrictions on imports or hidden subsidies to exports. If this is the situation it is clearly wrong that balance of payments equilibrium should be restored by deflation in country A; it should be restored by reflation or other appropriate policies in country B. But if country B refuses to take appropriate action it will be very difficult for any rational method of creating sufficient international liquidity to operate properly. Country A will lose reserves to country B and sooner or later be forced to deflate, devalue or take other measures designed to eliminate its deficit. Whatever it does it runs the risk of creating the kind of international unemployment and restrictions on trade that Keynes, looking back at the experience of the 1930s, was so concerned about in the early 1940s.

Over the past decade or so the world has in fact experienced the kind of imbalance just outlined: one group of countries has had a fairly persistent balance of payments deficit and another group a fairly persistent surplus. But both the causes and the effects of this situation have been rather different from those Keynes envisaged. However before we go on to examine this we should pause for a moment and look at the sequel to Keynes's original ideas for a solution to the general problem of liquidity.

THE INTERNATIONAL MONETARY FUND

As we have noted, Keynes's own idea of a world Central Bank which would create 'bancor' deposits for individual countries, and keep adding to these deposits as time went on so that international liquidity would rise roughly in line with world trade, was not accepted. The idea proved much too strange and radical for the Americans. By the early 1940s it was clear that after the war the Americans were going to be in a very strong economic position compared with Britain and the other Western Allies. Consequently it was what they wanted that really counted, and the outcome of international discussions on the subject – the International Monetary Fund, set up under the terms of the 1944 Bretton Woods agreement – was much closer to American ideas than British.

It was, for one thing, much smaller – the total amount of resources initially available in the Fund was around $8 billion, whereas Keynes had been thinking in terms of $25 billion. The resources were also created in a quite different way: instead of being deposits *created by* the Fund, they consisted of subscriptions *made to* the Fund by member-countries, a quarter of each country's subscription being in gold and the other three quarters in its own currency. Each country's quota was equal to its subscription; ultimately it could draw out the whole of its quota in the form of gold or foreign exchange – i.e. four times as much gold as it had subscribed (this being, in essence, the way in which the operations of the Fund added to international liquidity). But although a country could draw on the first slice of its quota (which was equal to the amount it had subscribed in gold) quite freely, each subsequent slice could be drawn on only after increasingly critical scrutiny by the Fund. In practice the Fund could be said to lend money to individual countries, for a certain period and on certain conditions; under Keynes's Clearing Union plan, countries would in a real sense have owned the deposits created for them. Moreover subscriptions to the Fund (and therefore the value of countries' quotas) did not increase automatically; they could only be increased by deliberate decision of the member-countries. Such increases have become distinctly difficult to negotiate.

This is not to say that the Fund has proved a failure. It was certainly not adequate to cope with the immense trade and payments problems of the immediate post-war period, which were mainly dealt with by direct U.S. assistance – e.g. Marshall Aid; but it has proved much more useful in more recent years, as Britain in particular has reason to know: on several occasions during the past decade assistance from the Fund has enabled Britain to avoid the choice between devaluation and much more severe deflation than we have actually experienced. Nevertheless the Fund has by no means provided a complete solution to the problem Keynes had in mind in the early 1940s.

For one thing, as was mentioned above, there is the problem of persistent creditor countries – even though their balance of payments surpluses have tended to result from an undervalued currency and various factors on the capital side rather than a persistently low level of demand and high level of unemployment, which was what Keynes was chiefly afraid of. The Bretton Woods agreement contained a 'scarce currency' clause, which said in effect that countries were entitled to discriminate in their trade and payments policy against any country whose currency was scarce (i.e. which persistently had a large balance of payments surplus and was therefore earning more foreign currency from exports or capital imports than it was paying out in the form of its own currency for imports or other expenditure overseas). But the scarce currency clause has proved ineffective, chiefly because of the technical conditions that must be satisfied if a currency is to be declared 'scarce'; no currency has ever in fact been declared scarce.

More serious have been the effects of the relatively small amount, and slow rate of growth, of the resources available in the Fund. Quotas were in fact increased by 50 per cent in 1959, and a further increase of 25 per cent (rather more for a number of countries) came into force in 1966. Nevertheless the effect of this has not been very great: total world liquidity (i.e. including the resources in the Fund) has risen by less than 3 per cent a year on average over the past fifteen years – not much faster than the $2\frac{1}{2}$ per cent increase in holdings of gold and foreign exchange alone. And, as was stated earlier, these increases in quotas have not been negotiated without considerable difficulty.

DIFFERENCES OF VIEW

This difficulty is not a reflection on the particular set of arrangements agreed at Bretton Woods and incorporated in the International Monetary Fund. It is a symptom of fundamental differences of view about the whole liquidity problem. Indeed it could be argued that these differences are so deep that there has never been any real possibility of working the kind of supranational system envisaged by Keynes: to allow a world central bank, even working within certain constraints, to determine the size and speed of increases in international liquidity would represent a considerable surrender of sovereignty on the part of individual countries, and one for which they are not yet ready. International liquidity can only be increased by agreement of all the major countries, for liquidity, whether it takes the form of gold, dollars, bancor or cowrie shells, is no good unless most countries are prepared to accept it in payment for goods or services.

The main difference of view about international liquidity in recent years has been (to use a rather broad brush) between Britain and the United States on the one hand, and most of the Common Market countries on the other. The Anglo-Saxons argue that there is too little liquidity – or at any rate a grave danger of there being too little in the very near future; the Common Market countries tend to argue that there is too much. One reason for this difference of view is fairly obvious – certainly no cynic would miss it. In recent years Britain and America have tended to have balance of payments deficits; the Continentals have usually had balance of payments surpluses. The former have seen their reserves drain away (or their external liabilities rise); the latter's reserves have been large and increasing. Small wonder that the U.S. and the U.K. say there is too little liquidity, while the Continentals profess themselves unable to see any problem.

Another explanation of the difference lies in history. As we saw in Chapter 6, both Britain and the United States were very hard hit by the unemployment of the 1920s and 1930s, and are particularly sensitive to the deflationary possibilities which stem from a shortage of liquidity. Many of the Common Market countries, on the other hand (despite the very severe but relatively short-lived depression in Germany in the early 1930s) are much more sensitive to the inflationary possibilities inherent in an excessive amount of world liquidity, chiefly because of the very big inflations they suffered during and after both World Wars.

But there is more to it than this. Embedded in the difference of view is the argument we mentioned earlier on, about whether persistent imbalances are the fault of the surplus-countries or the deficit-countries. Britain and America argue, in essence, that the large Continental balance of payments surpluses are the result of anti-social policies. They agree that these policies do not take the form (as Keynes had feared) of unemployment, which keeps imports low. They take the form in some cases of exchange rates which are too low; in others of a refusal to remove trade barriers against imports from other countries (particularly the less developed countries); in other cases again of a failure to offset a large current account surplus, or a large inflow of capital, by investment and other expenditure overseas. Unless these policies are changed, and Western Europe stops hogging so large a share of international liquidity, either more liquidity must be created, or else Britain and America will be forced either to deflate or drastically to cut overseas military or aid expenditure. Whichever of these two happens, so the argument runs, the consequences could be very undesirable – not least, in the long run, for the Common Market countries themselves.

The Continentals, on the other hand, argue that it is not their responsibility to get rid of their surpluses; it is the Anglo-Saxons' responsibility to get rid of their deficits. They do not, they say, *like* having balance of payments surpluses – a large balance of payments surplus, after all, means that the country is enjoying a lower standard of living than it might, since some of the goods and services the country produces are in effect being exchanged for lumps of gold instead of being consumed at home or swapped for consumer goods from abroad. The trouble is that Britain and America have for years been pursuing inflationary policies which inevitably result in balance of payments deficits (and by the same token a higher standard of living than they have earned); and they are able to go on doing this, instead of being forced to get their balance of payments back into balance, precisely because there is so much liquidity about. If there were less liquidity about they would soon find themselves unable to finance their deficits, and be brought to their senses.

This is the general Continental indictment, though a close examination of the facts and figures of international trade and payments does not suggest it is particularly compelling. But the Continentals (and especially the French) do not rest the case there; they still have an ace up their sleeve. The reason why Britain and the United States can go on running a deficit year after year without bothering to do anything about it, they say, is that *sterling and the dollar are reserve currencies: Britain and America can finance their deficits with their own currencies*. Any other country which has a balance of payments deficit has to finance it with gold or foreign exchange, either from its own reserves or by temporary borrowing from the International Monetary Fund; and there is obviously a limit to this process which must serve to concentrate the mind wonderfully. But Britain and America can finance a balance of payments deficit by printing and handing over pound notes or dollar bills (or rather, as we saw earlier, interest-bearing sterling or dollar assets). There is no obvious limit to this process.*

This is the major paradox at the heart of the international liquidity problem. The purpose of international liquidity is to enable countries to weather temporary balance of payments deficits; persistent deficits are supposed to be dealt with by other means. Yet one of the main elements in international liquidity can only be created if Britain and the United States are in persistent deficit. A related paradox is that Britain and America tend to regard the ultimate solution to a persistent deficit – devaluation – as out of court precisely because their currencies are reserve currencies and devaluation would reduce the value of that part of the other countries' reserves held in the form of sterling or dollars. But the possibility of sterling or dollar devaluation is one of the factors impelling these other countries to exchange their sterling or dollars for gold. Thus a large part of the creation

* One aspect of the situation that has been particularly abhorrent to the French is that part of the U.S. deficit has reflected a large amount of investment in France by American firms. In effect, France has been losing control of substantial chunks of her major industries and getting nothing better than U.S. Treasury Bills in return. The fear of neo-colonialism is not confined to ex-colonies.

of world liquidity depends on a disequilibrium situation which is difficult to cure and inherently unstable.

The Continental argument, in fact, has very serious implications: it is not just an attack on excess liquidity or balance of payments deficits in general; it is an attack on the whole principle of reserve currencies – and holdings of the reserve currencies at present constitute a third of world liquidity (excluding IMF quotas). To look at it from another angle: we saw earlier that the cumulative U.S. balance of payments deficit since 1951 has been around $30 billion, and noted that had this all been taken in the form of dollars world liquidity would have risen by $30 billion, while if it had all been taken in the form of gold world liquidity would have remained unchanged. In fact about a third of the deficit was financed by an outflow of gold, and the remainder by an increase in other countries' holdings of dollars (and to a small extent IMF assistance). Had the Common Market countries (with whom in the main the deficit was contracted) followed the logic of their present attitude, and demanded that the whole of the deficit be financed in gold, world liquidity would have risen much less than it did. U.S. gold holdings would have fallen to a lower level than Britain's – an outcome that no U.S. Administration could conceivably have permitted. The U.S. would have had to make drastic changes in policy – and although this is what the Continentals appear to want, the consequences for the rest of the world could hardly have failed to be very severe, and might have been disastrous.

Although these dangers have not overtaken the world yet, there are some grounds for anxiety about the future. Over the past few years a number of countries (notably France and Germany) have been reducing the proportion of their reserves held in dollars and increasing the proportion held in gold, thus in effect reversing their previous willingness to let the U.S. finance a large part of her deficit in dollars. This not only results in an actual destruction of world liquidity (for it leaves the size of French and German reserves unchanged, while reducing the size of American reserves); it also – as it is intended to do – gives the Americans an even greater incentive to reduce their deficit. The Americans have indeed been trying to reduce their deficit for some years, with a certain measure of success: it fell from a peak of $3·9 billion in 1960 to about $1·4 billion in 1966. But the hardening of the European attitude has made them look at the problem more seriously than ever, and increasingly tough measures have been taken, particularly on U.S. private investment overseas. As we noted earlier, the U.S. trade balance is always in substantial surplus, and there is little doubt that the Americans could eliminate their overall deficit if they really tried – but in the process a number of desirable items of overseas expenditure, such as aid to the less developed countries, might suffer badly. And if the American deficit is eliminated, one of the main sources of increased world liquidity will be eliminated too.

There is nothing at all unreasonable about the Continental demand that reserve currencies should gradually cease to be one of the elements of world liquidity – even if some of the motives behind the demand may not always be creditable. The whole reserve currency system stems from a time when Britain and even the United States were in a much stronger international economic position than they are today, and is not necessarily appropriate to the modern world. Certainly Britain, as we observed in the last chapter, suffers severe constraints on her economic policy from the present use of sterling as a reserve currency, and should welcome any further move towards reducing the dependence of world liquidity on the currency of particular countries. But it is of vital importance that any such move should be an orderly one, and that any reduction in the use of sterling and dollars as reserve currencies should be accompanied by an increase in liquidity of other kinds.

POSSIBLE SOLUTIONS

One possibility that is sometimes mooted is to build on the one hopeful feature that has emerged in the last few years. Over the past five or six years there has grown up an *ad hoc* system of international support based on currency swaps and central bankers' assistance. The main feature of these arrangements is that a country in severe balance of payments difficulties is lent foreign exchange by the other main industrial countries. But this assistance is of a very temporary nature, being made available, in the typical case, for only three months, and is chiefly appropriate to a situation in which a reserve currency country is under heavy speculative pressure: it was in these circumstances that Britain obtained such assistance in late 1964 and again in the summer of 1965 – and the 1964 assistance was essentially a tiding-over operation until Britain could draw on her full IMF quota. Moreover this kind of assistance has the great disadvantage of uncertainty – it is usually unclear until the last minute whether one is going to get it or not. It is as if – to go back to our family analogy for a moment – the family, faced by a temporary fall in income and rise in expenditure, might be able to get a loan for a few days from a rich neighbour, and then again might not. It cannot therefore be regarded as a satisfactory or permanent solution to the liquidity problem.

As far as more permanent solutions are concerned, there is certainly no shortage of ideas. One possibility, of course, is to enlarge IMF quotas and perhaps increase the proportion of its quota that a country can draw on automatically. However, the difficulty of negotiating the most recent increase in quotas suggests that long-term progress along this road may be limited: the EEC countries sometimes seem to regard the IMF as an Anglo-Saxon creation still largely dominated by the Americans, and inappropriate to the new balance of power between the United States and Europe. Another possibility is to increase the price of gold: if the Americans were to announce that in future they would buy and sell gold at $70 an ounce instead of the present price of $35 an ounce the value of world gold holdings would be doubled overnight. Moreover it would almost certainly result in a substantial rise in gold production, and might even tempt a good deal of existing gold out of private hoards. But there are disadvantages in this course of action. The countries that would benefit most are those with the largest gold holdings at the moment – almost by definition those least in need of extra reserves – and those countries (notably South Africa and the Soviet Union) which are major gold producers. Moreover the fact that the price of gold had been raised once (after decades of categorical refusals 'ever' to increase the gold price) might lead before long to the expectation that it might be increased again, and this could make the scramble for gold worse than ever. (The expectation that the price might be raised has probably been a factor – though much less important than the one we discussed earlier – in the recent tendency for some Common Market countries to raise the proportion of their reserves held in the form of gold.) In any case, it is high time the world grew up and stopped regulating its affairs by reference to the production of one relatively useless mineral.

THE LESS DEVELOPED COUNTRIES

A number of other, more imaginative, possibilities have also been canvassed. One – usually known as the Triffin Plan – is very similar to Keynes's original scheme for a Clearing Union, except that the management of the proposed supranational central bank would seemingly have more freedom than under the Keynes plan to increase members' deposits in line with the growth of world trade. Another (the Stamp Plan) aims to kill two birds with one stone: the IMF would distribute to less developed countries certificates which the advanced industrial countries would agree to accept in payment for exports. Thus the less developed countries would get a boost to their development programmes, since they could use the certificates (which they had obtained free) to pay for imports of capital goods; while industrial countries, once they had received these certificates in return for exports to the less developed countries, could add them to their reserves: the fact that other industrial countries had agreed to accept them in payment would by definition make them an element in international liquidity.

The Stamp Plan, and a number of other even more ingenious plans with the same basic objective, do well to draw attention to the plight of the less developed countries. For it is they who suffer most from a shortage of international liquidity. Indeed, they suffer doubly.

They suffer in the first place because their own reserves are usually low, and much of their production is at the mercy of the weather. A failure of the cocoa crop in Ghana can drastically reduce the country's export earnings; a failure of the rice harvest in India can divert precious foreign exchange to emergency food imports. In either case existing reserves may be hard put to it to cushion the impact, and imports of capital goods needed for the country's development programme may have to be slashed.

But the less developed countries also suffer from a shortage of international liquidity in a less direct way. By a horrible irony, they tend to suffer more from a shortage of reserves *among industrial countries* than the industrial countries do themselves. As we have seen, if the industrial countries of North America and Western Europe are short of reserves, they may react to temporary balance of payments fluctuations by deflating the level of demand. There will be some rise in unemployment, and a slowing-down or even a flattening-out of the increase in output. These consequences are very unpleasant, but they do not kill anybody. Political pressure will not permit unemployment to rise very far, and a year or two in which output rises more slowly than usual, or even remains flat, is an object of concern and criticism rather than a matter of life or death.

But to the less developed countries deflation in the industrial countries can be a matter of life or death. When an industrial country deflates, its imports fall – indeed this is one of the main objects of the exercise.* The imports most affected are likely to be imports of primary products, particularly agricultural and mineral raw materials, because these are the commodities that tend to be stockpiled, and deflation has a drastic effect on stock-building. Moreover these products are mainly in inelastic supply, so that a small fall in the demand for them can have disproportionate effects on their price – as we saw when examining the early 1930s.† Thus the value of the less developed countries' exports of primary products – and hence their ability to finance vital imports of capital goods – can be drastically affected by a relatively small measure of deflation in the industrial countries.

There is another way in which a shortage of reserves among industrial countries, which leads to some deflation, can hit the less developed countries. Either as a result of the contraction of the market, or as a result of deliberate policy, the industrial countries' imports of simple *manufactured* goods from the less developed can fall. Quantitatively the effect of this may not be very great – exports of manufactured goods from the poorer countries are still fairly small. But from a longer-term point of view the importance of these exports of

* As before, a 'fall' in imports does not necessarily mean that there is an *absolute* fall in imports (though there may be) but rather a fall in the *rate of increase* of imports – i.e. a fall below what they otherwise would have been. Treating the processes involved in static rather than dynamic terms helps to simplify the argument without affecting its substance.

† And see Explanatory Note 6, page 260.

manufactured goods is crucial. If the less developed countries are to industrialize, they must be able from an early stage to sell their manufactured goods. In many cases the domestic market cannot absorb them, and they can only be made if they can be sold abroad. There is no reason, for example, why India should not manufacture a relatively simple product like transistor radios – but she cannot do so unless she can export them: Indians cannot afford them. Thus anything which impedes the manufactured exports of the less developed countries also impedes one of their best hopes of raising their production faster than their population.

In short, any method of increasing international liquidity would be important to the less developed countries; and if any increase in liquidity can first be channelled to them, so much the better.

However the trouble about all the plans to increase liquidity is that they can only be put into operation with a wide measure of international agreement.* As long as persistent surplus countries (notably those in the Common Market) profess themselves unable to see any shortage of liquidity the prospects of further progress will remain dim. Pessimists go so far as to say that the problem will not be solved until the Common Market countries go into deficit on their balance of payments and begin to realize what a shortage of reserves is like. Since this is unlikely to happen until the U.S. (and perhaps even Britain) starts earning a substantial surplus, and one of the main sources of liquidity is therefore eliminated, there could be an unpleasant interregnum in which a number of countries were forced to take severe deflationary action or to resort to competitive devaluations.

But perhaps this is too pessimistic a view. The fear of

* With the exception of an increase in the gold price, which could be decided by the Americans alone: the world gold price is set by the fact that the U.S. Federal Reserve system is willing to buy and sell gold at $35 an ounce.

inflation (which the Common Market countries see as one of the results of too much world liquidity) is widespread, but so is the commitment to full employment and a fast rate of growth. There are signs that the Common Market countries, though as firm as ever in their opposition to the reserve currency system, are beginning to appreciate that there may soon be a liquidity problem, particularly if the Americans succeed in getting their balance of payments out of the red, and thus remove the Continentals' immediate objection to the reserve currency system. How quickly progress will be made remains to be seen, though it is encouraging that during 1966 and the first half of 1967 a good deal of 'contingency planning' (or, at any rate, discussion about the need for contingency planning) was conducted by the main industrial countries. Certainly some way must be found of ensuring enough liquidity to prevent countries having to deflate or take other harmful measures in order to cope with essentially temporary balance of payments difficulties; and the faster Britain and the U.S. succeed in reducing their balance of payments deficits the greater the urgency will be.

SUMMARY

The field of international liquidity is a distinctly treacherous one, and easy to get bogged down in. It may therefore be worthwhile restating very briefly the bones of the argument.

Any country which pursues a policy of full employment and a reasonably fast rate of growth is likely to find from time to time that it has a balance of payments deficit. If it is to avoid over-reacting to the deficit in a way that may harm itself and other countries (by deflating, devaluing or imposing a network of controls) it must have enough reserves to tide it over until its balance of payments recovers. (This is particularly true of a reserve currency country like Britain whose deficits, as we saw in Chapter 9, may be compounded by speculation leading to a flight of capital.) Unfortunately there is no mechanism which ensures that world liquidity will increase at the necessary rate (which may be broadly related to the rate at which world trade increases). The two main elements in world liquidity – gold and foreign exchange (sterling and dollars) – are provided in an essentially arbitrary way; and the resources of the International Monetary Fund have often seemed too small to fill the gap, and too difficult to increase.

In recent years the problem has been aggravated by the fact that some countries (mainly in Europe) have had persistent balance of payments surpluses while others (notably Britain and the United States) have had persistent deficits. The international liquidity system is not intended to deal with this sort of problem; it is meant to deal with *temporary* deficits. Persistent surpluses and persistent deficits should be dealt with by more fundamental re-adjustments, such as alterations in exchange rates or long-term capital flows. But in recent years these maladjustments have not been dealt with in this way. The surplus countries have not been willing to reduce their surpluses – and there is no easy way of forcing them to do so. And the deficit countries have not been forced to reduce their deficits because of the accident that they happen to be the countries which run reserve currencies: the United States in particular has been able to finance a large part of its deficit by paying its creditors in dollars. Thus the existence of the reserve currency system has caused the provision of international liquidity to become inextricably entangled with the quite separate problem of fundamental maladjustments.

During the last year or two the problem of international liquidity has become, at any rate potentially, more acute. The surplus countries have shown no real signs of ceasing to be in surplus; but they have shown increasing unwillingness to agree to the provision of more liquidity through the IMF, or to accept dollars in lieu of gold in settlement of the U.S. deficit. In response to this the U.S. is bound to redouble its efforts to eliminate its deficit, and its very success in doing this will in itself slow down the growth of world liquidity even further.

Unless new measures to provide adequate liquidity are agreed on fairly soon, therefore, there is a danger that countries will increasingly have to react to temporary balance of payments deficits by deflation, leading to unemployment and a slowing-down of growth. In the advanced industrial countries political pressures are likely to prevent these reactions from becoming intolerably severe; but in the less developed countries the effects could be grim. Such an outcome would certainly be a poor tribute to Keynes, who diagnosed the problem and offered a possible solution a quarter of a century ago.

CHAPTER 11

THE UNITED STATES:
UNEMPLOYMENT AND AUTOMATION

DURING the last four chapters we have implicitly taken the view that for Britain at any rate heavy and persistent unemployment is a thing of the past. Such unemployment as has occurred since the war has mainly been either the mild and temporary result of errors of forecasting; or the consequence of deliberate government action (always reversed before long) aimed at stabilizing prices or improving the balance of payments. There has been no hint of general and persistent unemployment of a kind the government was unable to cope with. Keynes's lessons have been learned and applied; and they have worked. But to some this may appear too smooth and facile a judgement. Heavy and hopeless unemployment lies within the lifetime of anyone over thirty; to many people in their fifties and sixties the whole post-war period has been no more than an overture to the next slump. We may have had reasonably full employment so far, but what of the future? What happens if there is disarmament? What about the government's inability to cope with regional unemployment? What about automation? Do not all these unresolved issues suggest that full employment may prove to have been no more than a lucky interlude?

The earlier chapters of this book have tried to provide some support for the view that most economists would now take about such questions – namely that this sort of anxiety is basically misguided, and displays a failure to grasp what happened in the Keynesian revolution. Nevertheless it may be appropriate, in this final chapter, to come back to some of these questions in a rather more specific way, and to do so in the context of the United States. For it is to the U.S. that the doubters most readily point – and not without reason, for what happens there must be something of a touchstone of the success of Keynes's theories. The U.S. still accounts for nearly half of world industrial production outside the Sino-Soviet bloc, and if Keynesian theories do not work there the rest of the world will not be safe: as we have seen, it was in the U.S. that the Great Slump started. But, by the same token, America is still the most capitalist of the industrial countries, and if Keynes's answers do work there they should work anywhere. Again, the U.S. suffers from bigger structural problems than most other countries: if regional and racial maladjustments do not inhibit the maintenance of full employment by Keynesian techniques there, they should not do so anywhere else. And finally, America is the country in which automation has proceeded fastest and farthest. If the Keynesian weapons are not blunted by the effects of automation there, other countries need have little to fear.

LACK OF DEMAND

When one turns to look at the U.S. economy one must admit that the doubters seem to have a prima facie case. During the first half of the 1950s (and this was a time when the U.S. economy was still benefiting from the stimulus of the Korean War) unemployment averaged 4 per cent – low by pre-war standards, but on the high side compared with most other countries. A decade later, things had worsened: during the first half of the 1960s unemployment averaged nearly 6 per cent. Part of this high rate of unemployment, it is true, stems from the way the U.S. measures unemployment, which tends to give an exaggerated figure compared with other countries. On British definitions the U.S. figure in the 1960s would have been $4\frac{1}{2}$–5 per cent, a point or so lower than as recorded, but still two to three times as high as in Britain.

Over the past ten or fifteen years, then, American unemployment was high and, until recently, getting higher. Is this not evidence that Keynesian techniques do not work in the U.S.? The short answer to this is no. It is not that Keynesian techniques have been tried and failed. Surprising though it may seem in the light of Roosevelt's New Deal policies in the 1930s, until quite recently *they had not really been tried.*

This is not because American economists and civil servants do not understand what Keynes was saying. The degree of economic sophistication in American government departments is probably higher than anywhere else in the world, as is the quantity and quality of the statistical information the forecasters and policy-makers have to work with. The trouble has been the politicians. Congress – and until recently the Administration itself – has tended to view Keynes and all his works as an embodiment of the devil (or the international communist conspiracy), dedicated to the overthrow of all that is best in the American way of life. This is no place for a disquisition on American history or the American consti- tution. Suffice it to say that there are powerful forces in America which insist that it is free enterprise which has made the country great, that any intervention by the federal government is self-evidently bad, and that when such intervention takes the form of a deliberately unbalanced Budget the whole fabric of the nation is threatened; that such forces are strongly and tenaciously represented in Congress; and that if Congress really does not want some- thing the President finds it very difficult to get it. When the President himself is fairly happy with things as they are (as was true throughout most of the 1950s) inertia is complete.

Things began to change under President Kennedy, though it has taken several years for the results to start showing. Kennedy surrounded himself with Keynesian advisers, who insisted that there was a large and increasing gap between what the nation was producing, and what it could produce. The existence of the gap meant that there was unemployment; the fact that the gap was getting larger meant that unemployment was on a steadily rising trend – and that the rate of growth of the U.S. National Income was lagging behind what was attainable. If things were to be put right there must be an expansion of effective demand: there must be more consumption or more investment; more exports or more government expenditure. In short, it was high time that Keynes's twenty-five-year-old medicine was applied to the United States.

Kennedy, after a certain amount of hesitation, operated on all these fronts: government-financed services to exporters were improved; tax credits were given against investment expenditure, and depreciation allowances were liberalized; federal government spending was speeded up; and there was a cut in income tax to boost consumption. Incredibly, it was the tax cut which proved by far the most difficult and controversial change to make. Congress, backed up by much of the nation at large, put up a terrific struggle; until the last moment it was touch-and-go. One may deplore the economic illiteracy of people who resist a tax cut at a time of substantial unemployment, but one must admire their moral fibre. They believed, quite simply, that a tax cut would mean a Budget deficit and that a Budget deficit is coincident at best with inflation, and at worst with nameless evils waiting in the wings to destroy the American way of life. This conviction has survived a monumental amount of evidence showing that such inflation as has occurred in post-war America has not resulted from excessive demand (of which a Budget deficit might be a cause or symptom) but from the operation of the same cost-push factors we discussed in the British context in Chapter 8. Even more remarkable, the conviction that a Budget deficit means inflation has survived the fact that the United States has actually had a Budget deficit* in all but four of the past eighteen years, yet has experienced a smaller degree of inflation than almost any other Western country.

Nevertheless, the tax cut eventually went through – though it is arguable that it did so only because Congress found itself helpless in face of the national mood following the assassination of President Kennedy, and of the long-practised manipulative ability of his successor. Income tax was cut in 1964; indirect taxes in 1965. These tax cuts had exactly the kind of Multiplier-accelerator effects that Keynes had stressed thirty years before: lower taxes led to higher consumption, which in turn stimulated investment; and higher investment raised incomes and led to further increases in consumption. National Income rose rapidly – by $5\frac{1}{2}$–6 per cent in each of the three years 1964, 1965 and 1966 (though the effect of the tax cuts was wearing off by 1966, and much of the growth of National Income in that year reflected a very rapid rise in government expenditure on the war in Vietnam). These big increases in National Income were accompanied by a big fall in unemployment; after hovering around the 6 per cent mark for years, it started to decline during 1964 and by the end of 1965 was down to 4 per cent. In 1966 it averaged 3·8 per cent, and it stayed at much the same level throughout the first half of 1967.

This fall in unemployment was very widespread, in the sense that unemployment fell broadly proportionately in

* That is, on the so-called 'Administrative Budget'. One of the problems facing the policy-makers in recent years has been that the Administrative Budget, which is the one most familiar to Congress, gives a misleading picture of the impact on the economy of government receipts and expenditure. When the Administrative Budget is in balance (the objective of many Congressmen) the impact of government operations on the economy is markedly deflationary. One of the achievements of the Administration in the past few years has been to focus Congressional and public attention increasingly on the more economically relevant 'National Income Accounts' Budget.

most industries, occupational groups and parts of the country. We have already observed this phenomenon in the case of Britain. It is striking evidence for the view that high unemployment in America in recent years has not been the result of structural maladjustments nearly so much as of a shortage of effective demand.

It is too early to say whether American unemployment will come down to European levels. As we saw in Chapter 10, the Americans are acutely conscious of anything which might aggravate their balance of payments difficulties; and they have deep-seated structural problems, to which we shall be returning in a moment. But there is no doubt that as far as the U.S. is concerned Keynesian techniques are now in. The tax cuts have paved the way to a rapid expansion of output and employment, without so far opening a Pandora's box of inflation and other horrors; and even if a low level of unemployment does eventually lead to a somewhat faster rise in prices (as British experience might suggest) there are likely to be increasing numbers of Americans who think that a bit of inflation is a price worth paying for full employment and faster growth.

Perhaps the most striking evidence of American conversion to Keynesianism is to be found in the issue of *Time* magazine for 31 December 1965. The cover picture is a very bad likeness, but it is unmistakable. It is Keynes. Thirty years after the publication of the *General Theory*, and twenty years after his death, Keynes and his views received the accolade of the American Establishment. The prophet is no longer without honour in his cousins' land.

STRUCTURAL PROBLEMS

But although the high level of unemployment in the U.S. in the late fifties and early sixties was mainly due to an inadequate level of demand, we must not lose sight of the kind of structural factors we discussed (in the British context) in Chapter 7. Full employment will not arrive or be maintained in the U.S. without the use of Keynesian techniques, but such techniques will not of themselves bring full employment to everyone. A general expansion of demand can probably bring full employment – indeed rising overtime – to skilled white workers in the modern factories of Detroit and Southern California, but it will not have much effect on ageing miners in West Virginia or Negro youths in Harlem. For America has, writ large, the structural problem we have already seen in Britain: when total demand rises, employers want to take on more people to meet it; but the people they want to take on are not necessarily the ones who are unemployed.

The problem is bigger in America than Britain for a number of reasons. One is the sheer size of the country. An increase in demand in London may well be met by a factory in Scotland (or at any rate by a migration of workers from Scotland), but an increase in demand in New York is less likely to be met by a factory in Oregon, or a migration of workers over a distance of 3,000 miles. The bigger a country is, the more likely it is to have marked discrepancies in employment conditions in different areas.

A more important factor is the traditional antipathy to the activities of the federal government – an antipathy often most marked, ironically enough, in the states which are poorest and suffer the heaviest unemployment. Central government action to increase expenditure in high-unemployment areas, or to re-train workers or help them to move to where job prospects are better, is at a much less developed stage in the U.S. than in most European countries. Because of the limited fiat of the federal government, there are enormous discrepancies from state to state and district to district in the amount and quality of education and training that children receive – and education is increasingly the key to employment.

One of the worst aspects of all is the racial one, which stems partly from the inferior education most Negroes receive, and partly from outright discrimination. Negro unemployment in the U.S. is twice as high as unemployment among whites, and among young Negroes the problem is staggering: between a quarter and a third of Negro teenagers are unemployed, and in the big city slums the proportion can be a half or more. To anyone who has even glanced at the unemployment figures among Negroes in the large cities race riots come as no surprise.

But although for various reasons the structural unemployment problem in the U.S. is probably more intractable than in Britain, the basic causes are essentially the same, as are the remedies required. Keynes saw that general unemployment was possible simply because there was no particular reason why the sum total of investment and consumption decisions should just happen to add up to enough demand to require full employment to meet it. One could adapt this insight and say that even with a high level of demand, with as many vacancies as unemployed, structural unemployment is possible because there is no particular reason why the jobs unfilled should happen to suit the skills and abilities of the people unemployed. Just as a shortage of effective demand requires government intervention, so does a disparity between the skills demanded and the skills of the men available. Even a higher level of effective demand than the U.S. has enjoyed in recent years, and a lower national rate of unemployment, would still leave a large number of unemployed, who would fall overwhelmingly into two categories: either they would have no skill, or they would possess a skill that was no longer in demand.

Both categories are the victims of technological change. As tastes and techniques change, so do the skills that the economy requires. A change from coal fires to oil central heating puts miners out of work; steelworkers suffer from the introduction of increasingly automated steel mills. The steady process of mechanization in manufacturing industry increases the demand for people with professional qualifications and highly developed skills, and cuts down the employment of unskilled workers. Young people who are forced to leave school early find it increasingly difficult to get jobs. 'A boy or girl who drops out of school today without an elementary skill,' the U.S. Secretary of Labor said recently, 'comes awfully close to committing economic suicide; for the number of unskilled jobs is getting smaller and smaller each year.'

In a free economy, in which the decisions on how the bulk of the National Income is spent are taken by millions of individual firms and families, this problem cannot be tackled, except perhaps in a temporary and palliative way, by making demand fit supply: people cannot be made to buy coal because there are unemployed miners, or to employ unskilled labourers because there is no work for them in the farming areas. The problem must be tackled by adapting the supply to fit the demand: people must be provided with the skills which the developing economy needs.

For young people, the answer must lie in ensuring that they do not leave school or training course until they have a skill that somebody is willing to pay for. There are plenty of vacancies for social workers and nurses, electricians and building craftsmen, data processors, laboratory assistants and a whole host of other jobs requiring various degrees of skill and training – but no mechanism for ensuring that enough young people acquire these skills. The educational and training system in the places where the problem is worst – the big city slums and the rural areas – is so bad (particularly for Negroes) that an immense amount needs to be done before the problem is brought under control. But at least the direction of the way ahead is relatively clear.

For the older workers displaced by technological change the difficulties are greater. Usually they do not want to move from where they are, despite the fact that it may be a thoroughly depressed area in which it is difficult to interest new industries. Many of them find it very difficult to learn any but the most elementary new skills. A certain amount has been done in the last few years: the Area Redevelopment Act of 1961 provided for some training of workers in depressed regions to fit them for jobs in new industries being brought in, and the Manpower Development and Training Act, passed in 1962 and somewhat extended since, provides powers and finance for the same kind of thing to be done on a bigger scale. But so far the results have been fairly small beer, and some observers have had an uneasy suspicion that those who have been trained or re-trained through these programmes have been mainly the cream of the unemployed who might have found jobs on their own initiative. According to the President's own economic advisers, experience up to the end of 1966 suggested that 'the typical MDTA trainee was a white male, high school graduate. Only one third of the trainees were from the disadvantaged groups that form the bulk of the hard-core unemployed.'* The problem of dealing with the older workers whose skills have become obsolete is still a long way off solution.

AUTOMATION

One of the factors responsible in recent years for rendering useless the skills of many older workers, and making unskilled jobs more difficult to find, has been something called 'automation'. Journalists have succeeded in a remarkably short space of time in investing this word with the same overtones as words like 'Gestapo' and 'Smersh': the mere mention of it is enough to make one's flesh creep. In fact, looked at through economic spectacles, it turns out to be not the slaver-

* Annual Report of the Council of Economic Advisers, January 1967, page 108.

ing wolf of impressionable people's imagination, but a friendly and helpful St Bernard; though no doubt if mal-treated even a St Bernard can bite.

Engineers and technologists make a great fuss about auto-mation because to them it embodies a new principle quite different from the principle of mechanization. Mechaniza-tion, they point out, consists merely in building into a mach-ine a heightened version of the skill of the human hand and the strength of the human body. Automation, on the other hand, builds into the machine, in a much faster and more accurate form, many of the calculating and controlling capacities of the human brain. A shoe factory that is merely mechanized will do no more than accept sheets of leather, cut them into a particular size, and stitch them together; there is nothing to stop it presenting you with a million defect-ive left boots. A shoe factory that is fully automated, on the other hand, will itself pick out the appropriate kind of leather for particular shoes, examine shoes as they emerge and reject any that are faulty, and indeed automatically change the size, shape or colour of the shoes it is producing in response to market information fed into its computer element on a bit of tape.

To an engineer these two activities are obviously very different; to an economist they are substantially the same. They both represent the substitution of capital for labour, and a reduction in the amount of direct labour required to produce a given output – in other words an increase in pro-ductivity. It is true that the *kind* of labour displaced by the two processes may be somewhat different: mechanization has tended to raise the demand for semi-skilled labour at the expense of skilled workers, whereas automation tends to result in the displacement of particular kinds of skill and low-grade professional qualifications by other kinds of skill and high-grade professional qualifications. These differences obviously have important implications for educational and training policies, but they do not affect the essence of what is taking place. From an economic point of view there is no substantial difference between the displacement by electronic computers of accounting clerks in New York in the 1960s and the displacement by power-looms of the hand-loom weavers in Lancashire in the 1830s.

Quite apart from the economic similarity between present-day automation and the mechanization which has been proceeding for centuries, it must also be stressed that even in the United States automation is by no means the main factor displacing people from existing jobs. The really big labour redundancies in recent years have been the result of much more simple and old-fashioned influences: farm labourers have been put out of work by fertilizers, miners by the cheapness of oil, and railwaymen by better roads.

It is quite wrong, therefore, to think of automation as some monstrous new juggernaut whose arrival threatens the existence of employment in the same way that the arrival of myxomatosis threatened the existence of the rabbit. Automation is one aspect of technological change, which itself is only one of the several changes (changes in tastes, changes in social patterns, changes in organization) which result in certain jobs disappearing and certain skills ceasing to be required. And even in America, which has a level of technology and of output per head much in advance of Britain's, there is no real evidence so far that such changes are proceeding any faster in the present than they have done in the past.

Nevertheless changes in the amount of labour needed to produce a certain output are proceeding fairly rapidly in America – and in other countries – and may proceed more rapidly in future. Indeed *it is one of the main objects of economic policy that they should do so.* For an increase in output per head is what one is really talking about when emphasizing the need to get a faster rate of growth. Neither the United States nor Britain are entirely happy about their rate of growth in recent years. More automation is one of the ways to speed it up. If a country wants a faster growth rate it is because it has unsatisfied wants; and as long as it has unsatisfied wants there is no danger (provided Keynesian theory is understood and applied) of there being a lack of employment opportunities.

No doubt there will come a day when all wants are satisfied by machines, which are produced and serviced by other machines; when jobs for people are few and far between and even those in employment have more leisure than they know what to do with. But such a day is a very long way off, even in America. One calculation has suggested that after allowing for travel-to-work time, etc., the average American has little more leisure time than he had fifty years ago; and millions of Americans are so anxious to have more money to spend that they take second jobs in the evenings and week-ends. Thirty to forty million Americans are officially stated to be living in poverty, with standards of food, housing, clothing and other basic amenities that would horrify the average British suburb-dweller. And leading Americans are quite aware that for every one of their own citizens living in poverty there are fifty people living in very much worse poverty in other parts of the world. There is nothing in all this to suggest any imminent shortage of jobs that need doing.

What is true, as we said earlier, is that people are not going to acquire the skills necessary to do many of these jobs simply by a wave of a magic wand. In America and in other advanced industrial countries people will need to be trained and re-trained to do the new jobs that technological progress is constantly opening up. Some experts calculate that many of the young people now entering the labour force for the first time will have to acquire new skills three or four times in the course of their working lives, because of the pace at which technological change will create new jobs and eliminate old ones. The vast organizational and human problems

involved in this process are only just starting to be thought
about, even in America, where the problem will first become
acute. Tremendous efforts are going to have to be made if
people's lives are not to be blighted by losing the opportunity
to exercise their existing skill and being unable to acquire a
new one. But the fact remains that however successful manpower policy is in training and re-training people in new
skills, it will only make sense against the background of a
Keynesian employment policy; indeed it will only be possible in such a context, since neither business nor unions will
cooperate in re-training programmes if skilled men are already unemployed. It is no good painfully turning a forty-
eight-year-old ex-miner into an electrician if the level of
demand in the economy is too low to employ all the existing
electricians. Mere application of Keynes's theory will not
necessarily get the ex-miner a job; but to ignore Keynes is
certainly to seal his doom.

CHAPTER 12

CONCLUSION

KEYNES's great contribution to economics was to show that the modern economy did not work in the way everyone had supposed, and to provide a new and completely convincing explanation of how it did work. This new explanation has become the foundation of modern economics.

In particular, writing in the middle of the greatest slump in history, he demonstrated that heavy unemployment was not a temporary aberration from the normal state of affairs, but could represent an equilibrium situation which could go on for ever. If the government wanted full employment it was no good doing what orthodox economic theory recommended – sitting back and hoping for the best. It must ensure that there is enough effective demand in the economy to create full employment.

The fact that Western countries have enjoyed virtually full employment throughout the whole of the post-war period is an indication of the extent to which Keynes's ideas have been accepted and applied. Most Western governments practise Keynesianism continuously: they forecast the likely change in the economy's productive capacity, the likely change in demand, and if necessary take steps to bring the two into line. The maintenance of full employment has enabled Western countries to shift their sights on to another economic objective – a faster rate of growth. Once Keynes had shown how existing resources could be fully utilized it was inevitable that attention should shift to the problem of increasing the size of those resources.

However, in spite of the wide acceptance and application of Keynes's theory of employment, unemployment is not entirely a thing of the past. It seems safe to predict that

251

unemployment will never again be more than a fraction of the amount suffered between the wars. But there has been some unemployment during the past twenty-five years, and there is likely to be some in the future. Some unemployment – of a mild and temporary kind – has resulted from errors of forecasting; improved techniques should help to reduce the importance of this. More serious – in Britain – has been the unemployment which has resulted from acts of policy.

One reason for this has been the concern with rising prices. During the century or so before the last war unemployment fluctuated fairly regularly from 2 or 3 per cent up to 8 or 10 per cent. During the boom prices rose; but during the recession they fell. The net result was that over a long period they remained fairly stable. With the advent of full employment prices started to rise fairly continuously; they are now about twice as high as they were twenty years ago. For a long time governments assumed that this was a situation to which Keynes's analysis could be applied in reverse. Keynes had shown that if there were too *little* demand there would be unemployment; the corollary of this was that if there were too *much* demand there would be inflation. To cope with rising prices steps were therefore taken to reduce demand. But the analysis was faulty. Rising prices may be a symptom of too much demand; but they are not necessarily so. Reducing demand, as it turned out, merely reduced the growth of output and increased unemployment; it had little effect on prices. It seemed that the factor making for rising prices was the pushing-up of wages and profits at a faster rate than production – and that this would continue to happen at any level of unemployment short of one so high as to be politically unacceptable. Therefore, gradually, governments came round to accepting the need for an incomes policy – a policy that would prevent wages, profits and other incomes from being pushed up faster than production by operating directly on the decisions which determine increases in wages and prices.

A second reason for deflationary action on the part of successive British governments has been the need to cope with recurrent balance of payments crises. By reducing the level of domestic demand, imports were reduced and – perhaps – some extra stimulus was given to exports. These measures have worked in the short run, but the problem has always reappeared when, usually under political pressure, the government has expanded the economy again. It is to be hoped that the lesson has finally been learned that deflation, by itself, solves nothing.

A shortage of international liquidity – on the way if not already here – has posed a different kind of threat to full employment. If countries have insufficient reserves they are likely to deflate deliberately in the face of balance of payments difficulties which are only temporary. This will create some unemployment, slow down the rate of growth, and hamper the less developed countries in their efforts to get off the ground. Keynes was acutely aware of this problem more than twenty years ago, and proposed remedies which have not yet been adopted. One can have some confidence that some version of them will be adopted in the end; one can only hope that the world will not have to go through an unpleasant period first.

Another threat to full employment – most noticeable at the present time in the United States – comes not from government action but government inaction. In a technologically advanced and fairly rapidly expanding economy new jobs are continuously being created and old ones disappearing. There is no reason to suppose that the workers who lose their jobs, or the young people entering the labour force for the first time, are going to have the right skills to fit them for the jobs that are opening up. Unless the government undertakes the responsibility of training or re-training them many of them will find themselves unemployed at a time when the expanding sectors of the economy are crying out for labour.

But the kind of manpower policy this situation calls for is not a substitute for the application of Keynesian theory; it is an adjunct to it. When the unemployed have been trained the level of demand must be high enough to ensure that there are jobs for them to go to.

Whatever the qualifications, the basic fact is that with the acceptance of the *General Theory*, the days of uncontrollable mass unemployment in advanced industrial countries are over. Other economic problems may threaten; this one, at least, has passed into history.

EXPLANATORY NOTES

I. FULL EMPLOYMENT

'Full employment' is not a term which can be very precisely defined. During the Second World War Lord Beveridge defined it as a rate of unemployment (i.e. those registered as unemployed at any particular time expressed as a proportion of the total number of employees) of no more than 3 per cent. Post-war experience suggests that this definition was too pessimistic: since the end of the war unemployment in Britain has averaged little more than $1\frac{1}{2}$ per cent.

Broadly speaking, one would say that a country enjoys full employment if virtually everybody who wants a job either has one or can get one without much difficulty. In the nature of things this does not mean that there will be no unemployment at all. In Britain millions of people change their jobs every year, usually of their own accord, and many of them are unemployed for a few weeks while they look for another job. At any given time there may be as many as 200,000 people in this position, representing an unemployment rate of something approaching 1 per cent. Taking into account other categories of people for whom it is not always easy to find jobs (for example, people in remote areas, or people with some moderate degree of mental or physical disability) it is clear that it is unrealistic to expect the unemployment rate to be below perhaps $1\frac{1}{4}$ per cent. Indeed, many economists would argue that a rate of unemployment much below $1\frac{1}{2}$ per cent or $1\frac{3}{4}$ per cent is a symptom of too intense a pressure of demand for labour, and there are those who argue that an unemployment rate of 2 per cent or even more is consistent with full employment. (The significance of the rate of unemployment for the country as a whole will, of course, depend on how evenly unemployment is spread over different regions. This question is discussed in Chapter 7, pages 156 to 164.)

Explanatory Notes

2. MACROECONOMICS AND MICROECONOMICS

The distinction between *macroeconomics* and *microeconomics* is based on the Greek words *makros* and *mikros*, meaning big and small respectively. Macroeconomics is the study of the economy as a whole; microeconomics deals with small bits of it. Thus *macroeconomics* asks: what determines the total amount a country produces? What determines the number of people employed in a country at any particular time? What decides the division of the National Income between wages and salaries on the one hand, and profits and rent on the other? Or again (a different break-down), what factors govern the distribution of the National Income between consumption on the one hand, and investment on the other? *Microeconomics*, on the other hand, is concerned with the individual firm, the individual product, the individual worker. It asks: what makes an individual firm produce the amount it does, and no more and no less? What determines the price of the firm's product? What determines the wage or salary a particular individual receives?

This distinction is of fairly recent origin: nineteenth-century economists did not make it. But it was precisely the failure to make this distinction that led nineteenth-century economists (and their twentieth-century successors) into wrong diagnoses and prescriptions for heavy unemployment. They made the mistake of providing what we would now call microeconomic answers to macroeconomic questions – for example in thinking that the theory of price (which, in the way they looked at it, is essentially a microeconomic concept) explained the level of employment (which is a macroeconomic concept). It was Keynes's discovery, that the factors determining the behaviour of the economy as a whole are not merely a multiplied version of the factors determining the behaviour of small bits of it, that brought the distinction between macroeconomics and microeconomics into being.

3. NATIONAL INCOME

The *National Income* is a measure of the value of all the goods and services a country produces. It can be looked at in three different ways: as the sum of all *incomes* in the country as the sum of all *expenditures* in the country; and as the sum of all *output* in the country. These three flows of money are all equal to each other. Suppose, for example, that the economy consists of one factory which makes filing cabinets, and that it produces 100 filing cabinets a year at a price of £10 each. If one measures the value of the *output* of the economy (counting the filing cabinets as they leave the factory, and noting the price) one will find that it is £1,000 a year. Similarly, if one measures all the *incomes* in the economy, one will find that the wages and profits earned are also £1,000 a year – for if the output is worth £1,000 the incomes of those who produce the output must also be £1,000. Finally, if one measures the *expenditure* of the economy (by recording the purchases people make in the shops) one will find that this is also £1,000 a year – for what will be bought will be 100 filing cabinets at £10 each.

The real world is more complicated than this, even in an economy which only produces filing cabinets, because some filing cabinets are not immediately sold to consumers, but stocked, some are exported in exchange for other goods which are imported, and so on. But these are merely complications of the basic picture; the really important thing is that if one adds up all the output in an economy, or all the incomes, or all the expenditure, one will arrive at the same final figure. Whether one talks of 'total output', 'total incomes' or 'total expenditure', one is talking about the same thing. In this book we call this the *National Income* (though in official publications the term *Gross Domestic Product* – G.D.P. – is usually employed, the term 'National Income' having the specialized meaning of G.D.P. plus net income from abroad and minus capital consumption – i.e. the amount available to the economy after setting aside enough to make good wear and tear to the country's stock of capital equipment).

There is one other point to note about the National Income. If one is interested not simply in how big it is in a particular year, but in how fast it is growing, one must know what is happening to prices. To go back to our example: if in the second year the value of the output of filing cabinets (or the incomes of those making them, or the expenditure on them) has risen to £1,100, this does not necessarily mean that output has really grown by 10 per cent.

It is true that if 110 filing cabinets are produced at £10 each, output will have grown by 10 per cent; but if the value of output has only risen to £1,100 because prices have gone up (i.e. production is still 100, but the price of each filing cabinet is now £11) then real output has not increased at all.

In measuring a country's growth rate one is not interested in a rise in the value of National Income (or output or expenditure) that results purely from a rise in prices; one wants to know whether the output of goods and services has risen. In an economy which only produces filing cabinets, this is easy: one merely counts the *number* of filing cabinets produced. But in an economy which produces hundreds of thousands of different goods the problem is more complicated; one has to calculate what the value of output in the second year *would have been* if prices had remained the same as in the first year. In other words one wants to measure the National Income *at constant prices*.

An increase in output at *current* prices, then, is the result either of an increase in the actual volume of goods and services produced, or of an increase in the *price* of these goods and services, or – more probably – a combination of both higher volume and higher price. Over the past ten or fifteen years output at current prices has risen by about 7 per cent a year in Britain. An increase in output at *constant* prices is simply an increase in the *volume* of goods and services produced. In Britain output at constant prices has been rising by only about 3 per cent a year, and this is what is meant by talking about 'a 3 per cent growth rate'.

4. INTEREST RATES AND SECURITY PRICES

The rate of interest is the amount of money a borrower pays a lender for a loan. It is normally expressed as a percentage of the amount lent. Thus if the borrower pays the lender £5 for the loan of a £100 for a year the interest rate is 5 per cent. Government securities are the counterpart of loans made by individuals, or banks or other institutions, to the government. They take the form of pieces of paper which are sold to the public and entitle the owner to a certain sum of money each year. This annual sum is the interest on the loan made to the government.

Interest rates and government security prices move in opposite directions to each other: a rise in interest rates results in a fall in security prices, and vice versa. Suppose that a security entitles the owner to a payment of £5 a year. If interest rates are 5 per cent, then this piece of paper will be worth £100. The reason for this is that one can get £5 by investing £100 in some other way, and will not therefore pay *more* than £100 for the security; but if the price is *less* than £100 one will be able to get a higher return by investing in government securities than in other ways – and the price of the security will be bid up until it is £100.

But if interest rates rise to 6 per cent people will not be willing to pay £100 for an asset that only yields £5 a year – they can get £6 a year elsewhere. The price people are willing to pay for the security will therefore fall (just how far it will fall will depend in practice on all sorts of particular factors we need not bother with here). Similarly, if interest rates fall to 4 per cent, so that people can only get £4 a year by investing £100 elsewhere, an asset which yields £5 a year for a cost of £100 will be such a bargain that people will bid against each other for it, and the price will rise.

5. LESS DEVELOPED COUNTRIES

The less developed countries (broadly speaking the countries which produce primary products – see Explanatory Note 6) suffer from both dire poverty and massive unemployment. In some of them incomes per head are as little as £25 a year – less than a twentieth of what they are in Britain. At the same time unemployment and underemployment are very heavy – mostly among uneducated and unskilled people in the countryside, but also to some extent among people with secondary or even university education in the cities.

This combination of poverty and unemployment cannot be solved by Keynesian policies – as it could have been in Britain in the 1930s. More expenditure by government or consumers would not raise output and employment – it would merely raise prices. For it is not effective demand that is lacking, but factors on the supply side. Men are idle because there are no machines for them to work with, few managers to organize them and few skills or basic educational qualifications to be employed. The whole framework of production is lacking. What is required is not an increase in demand, but an increase in the techniques and equipment needed to raise productivity: education and training, instruction in simple methods of raising agricultural output, investment in plant and machinery, roads and railways, power stations and irrigation systems.

In short, Keynesian employment policies are relevant only when the means of production exist, but goods are not being produced because there is too little effective demand. In the less developed countries the problem is that the means of production do not exist.

6. PRIMARY PRODUCTS

Primary products, as the term implies, are the products which come first in the economic process – the food and raw materials which are grown on the ground or dug out of it. Wheat, rice, coffee and bananas are primary products; so are wool, cotton, jute and rubber; so are copper, lead, zinc and tin. Primary-producing countries are the countries whose output and exports consist to a large extent of primary products; very broadly speaking they are the poorer countries which lie within two or three thousand miles of the equator (though both North America and the Soviet Union are fairly self-sufficient in primary products).

The output of primary products tends to be *inelastic*, which means that it does not change very much in response to changes in price. This is essentially a matter of time-periods. The output of manufactured goods can often be increased quite quickly by putting in new plant and equipment, or simply by working overtime; but it takes a long time to grow more rubber trees or sink a new copper mine. Similarly, the output of manufactured goods can be reduced simply by laying men off; but coffee trees or cotton plants will go on producing regardless. Moreover the demand for primary products fluctuates much more than the demand for manufactured goods, precisely because it is known that a shortage will not result in much extra production, so that people will react to any hint of a shortage by intensive stock-piling; and similarly, when the threat of a shortage disappears, will live off their stocks and thus drastically reduce their demand for what is currently being produced.

This combination of inelastic supply and fluctuating demand leads to very big variations in price. A rise in demand, since it cannot result in much increase in production, will drive prices up very fast. This happened when the Korean War broke out: many countries (particularly the United States), afraid of being caught short of vital raw materials in what might develop into a large-scale war, started massive stock-piling. As a result the prices of many primary products rose by fifty per cent or more in a single year. But once it became clear that the Korean war was going to remain fairly localized, things moved into reverse: within a year or two the prices of some primary products had fallen by as much as a half. Moreover falling prices, particularly for agricultural products, can make things worse: as we saw in the case of America during the Slump, a farmer faced by lower prices for his produce will try to *increase* output, and this will drive prices down even further.

The short-term effects of this on the primary producers can be very bad. They may sometimes gain on the swings, but before long they will lose on the roundabouts. The economic and social effects of big fluctuations in the incomes of the individual producers within the country can be very disruptive; and if the country has planned its development programme on the basis of the imports it could afford when primary product prices were high it is in for an unpleasant shock.

But even in the longer run the dice seem to be loaded against the primary-producing countries, because industrial countries' demand for their products is growing relatively slowly. There are a number of reasons for this. The consumption of many tropical foods and beverages – such as tea, cocoa and sugar – rises fairly slowly, since there is a limit to how much people in the industrialized countries can eat and drink. In any case, agricultural protection policies mean that an increasing proportion of consumption is met by domestic production – this is important, for example, in the case of sugar. Imports of many industrial materials by the industrialized countries also grow rather slowly, partly because modern products often use less materials per unit of output (cf. the trend to lightweight clothing); partly because of shifts in the pattern of consumption towards products which use less imported materials; and partly because of the increasing use of substitutes (e.g. plastics in place of non-ferrous metals, synthetic rubber in place of natural rubber, man-made fibres in place of natural fibres). This rather gloomy outlook for primary products under-lines the urgent need to help the primary-producing countries to industrialize.

BIBLIOGRAPHICAL NOTES

THIS is no more than a very short and subjective list, aimed at giving the general reader the names of one or two works which will enable him to go rather more deeply into the questions discussed in the various chapters.

PART ONE

Chapter 1

R. F. Harrod: *The Life of John Maynard Keynes*, Macmillan, 1951, is the official biography of Keynes; a long, discursive, curiously old-fashioned book, which deals thoroughly with Keynes's life and theories. Much shorter is Austin Robinson: 'John Maynard Keynes', *Economic Journal*, March 1947. An insight into Keynes's character can be got from some of his own non-economic writings, for example *Essays in Biography*, Macmillan, 1933, and *Two Memoirs*, Hart-Davis, 1949. Glimpses of Keynes can be found in the memoirs of various eminent contemporaries; see for example Harold Nicolson: *Diaries and Letters 1930–39* (edited by Nigel Nicolson), Collins, 1966; and the fourth volume of Leonard Woolf's autobiography, *Downhill All the Way*, The Hogarth Press, 1967.

Chapter 2

Sound, in a relentless sort of way, is Eric Roll: *A History of Economic Thought*, Faber (paperback edition), 1961. Much more readable (indeed one of the most entertaining books ever to be written by an economist) is Robert L. Heilbroner: *The Great Economists*, Eyre & Spottiswoode, 1955.

Chapter 3

One of the most recent general histories covering the inter-war period is A. J. P. Taylor: *English History 1914–1945*, Oxford University Press, 1965. Good accounts of the economic history of the period can be found in W. Arthur Lewis: *Economic Survey 1919–1939*, George Allen & Unwin, 1949, and A. J. Youngson: *The British Economy 1920–1957*, George Allen & Unwin, 1960.

Chapters 4 and 5

The basic source book is obviously the great work itself – J. M. Keynes: *The General Theory of Employment, Interest and Money*, Macmillan, 1936, but the book itself is one that even economists approach with some trepidation, and the general reader may find it easier to start with Joan Robinson: *Introduction to the Theory of Employment*, Macmillan, 1937. A more detailed, indeed blow-by-blow account of what Keynes was saying is to be found in Alvin H. Hansen: *A Guide to Keynes*, McGraw-Hill, 1953. Keynesian theory is also treated in any modern textbook – for example Richard G. Lipsey: *An Introduction to Positive Economics*, Weidenfeld & Nicolson, 1963; and is well covered in J. Pen: *Modern Economics*, Penguin Books, 1965.

Chapter 6

The books cited for Chapter 3 are also relevant here; and some of the essays in Seymour Harris (editor): *The New Economics*, Dobson, 1948, may be helpful, particularly Chapters 2 and 3. The Wall Street Crash is entertainingly dissected in J. K. Galbraith: *The Great Crash*, Hamish Hamilton, 1955, Penguin Books, 1961.

PART TWO

The literature on post-war economic problems and policies is so vast that one hardly knows where to begin. A great deal of material is contained in G. D. N. Worswick and P. H. Ady (editors): *The British Economy 1945–50*, Oxford University Press, 1952, and its successor volume *The British Economy in the 1950s*, Oxford University Press, 1962. Much of this is very detailed and technical, but a good deal of it can be read with profit by the general reader. More recent books, to be dipped into rather than swallowed whole, are J. C. R. Dow: *The Management of the British Economy 1945–60*, Cambridge University Press, 1965; and Andrew Shonfield: *Modern Capitalism*, Oxford University Press, 1965. Less forbidding are a number of recent Penguins, such as Michael Shanks: *The Stagnant Society*, 1961; Samuel Brittan: *The Treasury under the Tories*, 1964; and Peter Donaldson: *Guide to the British Economy*, 1965. The most recent conspectus of the domestic economic scene is John and Anne-Marie Hackett: *The British Economy: Problems and Prospects*, George Allen & Unwin, 1967.

Chapter 7

Several of the books just cited are relevant to this chapter, particularly Part I of Shonfield: *Modern Capitalism*. The question of regional unemployment gets thorough coverage in Mrs M. F. W. Hemming: 'The Regional Problem', *National Institute Economic Review*, August 1963.

Chapter 8

A brief but excellent and still entirely relevant treatment of this subject is to be found in the Council on Prices, Productivity and Incomes, *Fourth Report*, H.M.S.O., 1961. A more detailed assessment is contained in the Organization for European Economic Cooperation: *The Problem of Rising Prices*, 1961.

Chapter 9

PEP (Political and Economic Planning) has published a lot of useful work in this field; see for example *Growth in the British Economy*, George Allen & Unwin, 1960, and three broadsheets on planning: *Planning for Growth* (March 1965), *The National Plan* (November 1965) and *Inquest on Planning in Britain* (January 1967). For a strong statement of one viewpoint, see Fred Hirsch: *The Pound Sterling: a polemic*, Victor Gollancz, 1965.

Chapter 10

The subject of international liquidity is now one that is dealt with frequently and competently in the financial pages of the serious newspapers. The problem is covered briefly in Christopher McMahon: *Sterling in the Sixties*, Oxford University Press for the Royal Institute of International Affairs, 1964, and more technically in Fritz Machlup: *Plans for the Reform of the International Monetary System*, Princeton University, revised edition, 1964. The urgency of the problem is powerfully argued in Sir Roy Harrod: *Reforming the World's Money*, Macmillan, 1965.

Chapter 11

A wide range of views can be found in Arthur M. Ross (editor): *Unemployment and the American Economy*, John Wiley, 1964, and a good conspectus of the problem is provided in Robert H. Ferguson: *Unemployment: its Scope, Measurement and Effect on Poverty*, Cornell University, 1965. Michael Harrington: *The Other America*, Macmillan, New York, 1962, Penguin Books, 1963, is a devastating indictment of poverty in contemporary America. For a detailed account of how Keynes became accepted in America, see Robert Lekachman: *The Age of Keynes*, Random House, 1966, The Penguin Press, 1967.

INDEX

Accelerator principle, 40–44, 133n., 137, 241

Automation, 246–50

Balance of payments,
current account, 189–90;
British pre-war, 48–56;
British post-war, 171–3, 189–201, 205–6, 208;
and deflation, 195–9;
and devaluation, 192–4;
and physical controls, 194–5;
and rising prices, 171–3, 190, 205–6;
U.S., 213–15, 225–8, 233, 235;
see also Exports, Imports, Exchange rates

'Bancor', 217–18, 221

Bank, Central, 50–52, 81–2, 84, 86

Beveridge, Lord, and Report, 19, 151–2, 255

Bretton Woods agreement, 19, 221–3

Budget,
British pre-war, 61–4, 131–2, 135, 145–6;
British post-war, 154–6, 161, 166–8;
in Germany, 145;
in Keynesian theory, 88, 103;
in U.S., 143, 239–41

Capital goods, 39–40, 74;
in classical theory, 24–9;
in trade cycle, 40–46;
U.S. output of, 58;
utilization of, 80, 85–6, 141, 144, 147–8

Chamberlain, Neville, 69, 146

Change, technological, *see* Innovation

Chicago School, 120

Consumer goods, 39–42, 74

Consumption,
determinants of, 74–7;
and effective demand, 73–4, 86–105;
marginal propensity to consume, 77–8, 93–101, 105, 147–8;
Marx's views, 28–9;
and New Deal, 142–3;
and tax cuts, 142;
underconsumption, 147;
in U.S., 241;
and 'wealth effect', 120–21;
in 1920s, 131–2;
see also Saving

Credit Anstalt, 63

Credit squeeze, 51, 120n., 196, 204

Deflation, 54, 195–201, 204–5, 208–9, 215–17, 232–4, 252–3

Demand,
effective, 72–4, 78, 119–21, 128–9, 130–36, 140, 146–8, 151–6, 166–7, 207, 238–42, 249–54;
excess, 153–4, 166–7, 171–6, 184–6, 198, 252

Devaluation, 49, 53, 64–5, 192–4, 201, 212, 217, 226, 233

Diminishing Returns, Law of, 32–4, 46, 56, 115–16, 122–3

Employment, Full employment, Unemployment,
and automation, 247–50;

Employment, etc. – *contd*
British pre-war, 9, 48–9, 54–6, 61, 64–7, 128–30, 133–6, 146–8;
British post-war, 9–10, 151–70, 179–83, 185–7, 197–200, 206–7, 251–3;
cyclical, 35–47, 164–70;
'full employment' defined, 255;
and international liquidity, 208–9, 215, 217, 220, 231, 236, 253;
in less developed countries, 123n., 259–60;
regional, 156–64;
theory of, pre-Keynesian, 22–8, 33–4, 44–7, 65–9, 107–11, 115–23;
theory of, Keynesian, 66, 71–4, 86–8, 91, 101–5, 111–23, 147–8, 251;
in U.S., 56–8, 136–8, 140, 142–4, 238–50
Equilibrium, as a concept, 88–9
Exchange rates, 49, 50, 53, 65, 133–5, 190, 206, 225, 226, 235
see also Devaluation
Expectations, 80
Exports, export prices,
British pre-war, 48–9, 54–6, 65, 130, 133–5, 140, 146;
and deflation, 196–7;
and devaluation, 192–4;
encouragement of, 194;
and effective demand, 129;
and gold standard, 50–52;
and rising prices, 171, 190, 206;
unpredictability of, 165–6, 169
see also Balance of Payments

Forecasting, economic, 155, 165–9, 176, 252

Gold,
hoarding, 213, 215, 230;
outflow, 61, 64, 227;
price, 230, 233n.;
reserves, 212–15, 226–8, 235;
standard, 18, 50–55, 60, 63–5;
supply, 212–13, 215
Government expenditure, 62–70, 102, 105, 126–7, 129–31, 135, 142–7, 152, 155–6, 167–8, 240
Growth, economic, 202–7, 209, 248–9, 251, 257–8

Imports, import prices,
British pre-war, 55, 65, 130;
and deflation, 195–9;
and devaluation, 193–4;
and excess demand, 156, 159, 166–7, 171–2;
and gold standard, 51–2;
and less developed countries, 231–3, 260–62;
restrictions, 139–40, 194, 216–7;
and rising prices, 190;
in U.S., 58, 138–40;
see also Balance of payments
Incomes policy, 134, 147, 186–7, 206, 252
see also Prices
Inflation,
and Budget deficit, 240;
'cost-push', 176–84, 186–7, 198;
'demand-pull', 176–7, 184–6, 198;
and excess demand, 87, 102n., 153–6, 166, 252;
and international liquidity, 224–5, 233–4;
uncontrollable, 53, 153
see also Prices
Innovation, 38, 147–8, 163, 170, 244–50
Interest rates,
classical theory, 109–11;
Keynesian theory, 78–9, 81–6, 111–14, 141;
and policy, 135, 141, 155, 176, 204;

and security prices, 258–9;
and the Trade Cycle, 37–9, 43–6
see also Money
International Monetary Fund, 19,
221–3, 226–31, 235
see also Liquidity, international
Investment,
and accelerator, 40–42;
between the wars, Britain, 48,
132–3, 135–6;
between the wars, U.S., 58,
136–8, 141–4;
and deflation, 195–6, 203–5;
government attitude since war,
155–6;
grants, 169;
overseas, 59–61, 190, 226–8;
public, 66, 69–70, 102, 122,
126–7, 135–6, 154–5, 162, 168,
196;
theories of: classical, 22–9,
44–5, 107–11; Keynesian,
73–4, 78–92, 95–105, 111–14,
125;
unpredictability, 165–7;
U.S. since the war, 240–41
see also Saving

Jevons, W. S., 36

Kahn, R. F., 94n.
Kennedy, President, 239–41
Keynes, John Maynard,
biography of, 13–20, 242;
works by: *Economic Consequences
of Mr Churchill, The*, 18;
*Economic Consequences of the
Peace, The*, 17; *General Theory
of Employment, Interest and
Money*, 9, 18–19, 21, 70–106,
115, 118, 123, 126, 127, 153,
171, 173–4, 180, 187, 242,
254; *How to Pay for the War*,
19, 174; *Indian Currency and
Finance*, 15; *Tract on Monetary
Reform, A*, 18; *Treatise on
Money, A*, 18; *Treatise on
Probability, A*, 15
See also Bibliographical Notes,
page 263

Less developed countries, 123n.,
190, 228, 230–33, 253, 259–
62
see also Primary products
Liquidity, international, 208–35;
Anglo-Saxon and Continental
views on, 224–8;
and International Monetary
Fund, 221–3;
Keynes's proposals, 216–8;
and less developed countries,
230–33, 236;
and price of gold, 230, 233n.;
rate of growth of, 210–11, 223;
summary of problem, 209,
234–6, 253;
see also Balance of payments,
International Monetary Fund,
Reserve currencies
Liquidity preference, 82–5, 113–14,
141
Lloyd George, David, 16, 18

Macdonald, Ramsay, 64
Macmillan Committee on Finance
and Industry, 18–19
Macroeconomics, 26, 256
Malthus, Thomas, 22–6, 28, 32,
110
Marginal Productivity, Theory of,
32–4, 46–7, 49, 56, 115–16,
122–3
Marshall aid, 16, 222
Marshall, Alfred, 14, 30
Marx, Karl, 13, 26–9, 36
Mature society, stagnation in,
146–8
May Committee Report, 63–4
Microeconomics, 26, 29, 256
Mill, J. S., 108n.
Money, demand and supply, 31,
37–8, 81–6, 120n.

Money – *contd*
see also Interest rates
Monopoly, 177, 179–82
Multiplier theory, 93–102, 112,
119–20, 132, 133n., 137,
138, 143, 209, 241

National debt, 62, 131–2, 143, 189
National income,
consumption, investment and
saving, 73–8, 86–92, 103–5,
111, 141, 256–8;
definition of, 73n., 256–8;
distribution of, 22, 75–6, 119,
123, 131–2, 147, 188, 256;
and employment, 71, 101–2,
105, 113;
and Great Slump, 58, 137–9;
growth of, 188, 201–7, 257–8;
and the Multiplier, 93–101,
111–13, 137;
share of exports in, 130
see also Consumption, Investment, Saving
National Insurance Fund, 61, 63
New York Stock Exchange, see
Wall Street Crash
Norman, Montagu, 53n.

Pigou, Prof., 14, 68, 106, 115, 118,
120
Prices,
and balance of payments,
189–90, 197–200, 205–7;
behaviour between wars, 48–9,
54–7, 67, 134, 138–9, 142;
behaviour since the war, 156,
171–6;
controls, 153, 175n.;
and cost inflation, 176–83,
186–7, 205–7;
and demand inflation, 172–7,
184–6;
and incomes policy, 186–7;
and interest rates, 81, 83–5,
110, 114, 258–9;

primary product, 59, 138–9,
231–2, 260–62;
of shares, 57;
theory of, 29–31;
and trade cycle, 35, 38–9, 44–7;
and wages, 117–23, 178–85
see also Exchange rates, Exports,
Imports, Incomes policy,
Inflation
Primary products, 57–9, 138–9,
232, 260–62
Productive potential, 129–30, 135,
141, 155, 188, 201–7
Profits,
in classical theory, 22, 107–8,
108n., 110;
and exports, 49;
and Great Slump, 61;
and investment, 22, 80, 107–8;
and Marx's theory, 27–9;
and prices, 181–3, 186, 198–9;
and saving, 25, 76, 107–8, 108n;
and share of National Income,
22, 76, 119, 123;
and trade cycle, 35, 38–9;
in the U.S., 56–7
see also Prices, Wages
Public Works, see Government
expenditure

Rationing, 153–4, 175n.
Reddaway, W. B., 60n.
Reserve currencies, 191–4, 211–15,
226–9, 234–6
see also Liquidity, international
Restrictive practices, 56, 180n.,
204–5, 209
Ricardo, David, 22–6, 28, 29, 42,
44, 71, 107, 109n.
Robbins, Lionel, 68–9, 115
Robertson, D. H., 66, 136
Russell, Bertrand, 14, 15

Saving,
capitalists', 22, 25, 107–8;
compulsory, 174–5;

and investment, 66, 75–7, 88–92, 95–101, 104–5, 107–14, 141–2, 146–8;
marginal propensity to save, 93–4;
as a vice, 124–6
see also Consumption, Investment
Say's Law, 24–5, 44–5
Smith, Adam, 13, 21–2, 26, 29
Snowden, Philip, 63
Stamp plan, 230–31
Stop-go policy, 195–8, 201–7, 253
Strike, General, 54–5, 134, 135

Taxation,
allowances, 163;
and effective demand, 102, 122, 131–5, 155–6, 167–8, 174, 175n., 195–6, 240–41;
and government expenditure, 61–4, 131–5, 145–6, 155–6;
in New Deal, 142–3;
and size of Multiplier, 95n.
Thorneycroft, Peter, 199
Trade cycle, 26–7, 35–47, 48, 49, 65, 68, 71–2, 76–7, 79–80, 108n., 154, 164, 167

Trade unions, 47, 54–6, 68, 115, 178–80, 181–7, 198
Treasury, 15–17, 19, 66, 144
Triffin plan, 230

Unemployment, *see* Employment

Wages,
behaviour between wars, 47, 48, 54–6, 134;
in classical theory, 23–4, 27–8, 31–4, 46–7, 65, 68–9, 115–23, 134;
and 'cost-push' inflation, 177, 180–83, 186–7, 205–6, 252;
cuts, 49, 53–6, 64, 65, 67–9, 134–5;
drift, 184–6;
in Keynesian theory, 115–23, 134;
real and money, 116–23, 134;
in Trade cycle, 35, 38–9, 45–6;
traditional differentials, 183–4;
see also Incomes policy, Inflation, Prices
Wall Street Crash, 56–9
Whateley, Archbishop, 29
Whitehead, Alfred, 14

MODERN ECONOMICS

J. PEN

In 1936 Keynes published his famous *General Theory of Employment, Interest and Money,* and the science of economics has never been the same since. Gone is the comfortable 'classical' belief in a self-adjusting balance between supply and demand: moreover, allied to Keynesian theory, the growth of exact quantitative economics has tended to produce a distinct 'modern economics'. A silent revolution has occurred.

It is widely held that Keynesian theories can only be comprehended by the expert, and this in itself delays the application of modern ideas, since every citizen, when he shops, works, or votes, is a practising economist. Professor Pen, the well-known Dutch economist, challenges this assumption in this Pelican, in which he sets out to explain to the non-expert the meaning of Keynes's ideas and the finding of modern statistical methods.

His book provides a clear (and frequently humorous and hard-hitting) introduction to modern theories regarding international trade, national budgets, the function of money inflation and deflation, wages, economic growth, and many other economic topics in daily discussion.